Dancing on One Foot

Growing Up In Nazi Germany

A Memoir

PRAISE FOR
Dancing On One Foot

"I'm drawn by the mystery here, the child's perspective contrasted with the realities of war, just out of reach. Fantastic establishing of time, place in a unique, believable fashion."

—Jon Sternfeld, editor at Jane Goodman Literary Agency

"*Dancing On One Foot* is an ambitious, brave, passionate memoir. Shanti can evoke places, people, and hard-to-name emotional states with care, candor, and energy. She created a structure that can bear the weight of no less than a life story.

"Shanti's mother, Isolde, and to a lesser extent her grandmother, are at the center of the book; but *Dancing On One Foot* also examines the more enigmatic figures of the writer's father and grandfather, among others. Intelligently placed uncaptioned family photographs and illustrations are an integral part of the narrative.

"Supporting her meditations with some historical research and allusions to work by Böll and others, Shanti begins to examine what it means to be 'a perpetrator and a victim.' She also draws on her wisdom and experience as a seasoned therapist to reflect on the 'art' of grief and forgiveness.

"Hers is a gleaming 'new' voice from a wise soul."

—Jocelyn Lieu, author of *Potential Weapons, A Novella and Stories* and *What Isn't There: Inside a Season of Change*

"Beautiful, gorgeous writing. You are an amazing writer with great talent."

—Dina McQueen, editor, author of *Finding Aster*

"Shanti, bravo. You have written an incredible book, and it made me cry.

Dancing On One Foot is a very moving book, in equal parts sad, brave, and lovely in its imagery. A book which seeks, in many ways, to remember a lost mother and a childhood of war in World War II Germany. Bravo, excellent work.

"[This is an] incredibly honest appraisal and adoration of the mother, of sex, of female power in its 'isness' — of life. The musings feel so grounded, and they are tender and raw and honest. I love the homage to women — specific and strong.

"Restraint in language is often — I think — how to write war and suffering — like a stone dropping into water: simple clean quietly loud.

"I am in the grip of the story completely, Shanti — Bravo."

— Micheline Aharonian Marcom, Author of *The Mirror in the Well, The Daydreaming Boy, Draining the Sea* and *Three Apples Fell From Heaven*

"Your book has the value of being real, of being the story of someone who actually lived through the events of one of the most tumultuous times in the Twentieth Century, and as a child. Many books have been written by soldiers about those times, and many have been written by Jewish people who survived the Holocaust, but I don't know of a book (in the United States, at least) that recounts the true experiences of a German child growing up in wartime Germany. I believe it is a unique viewpoint among memoirs, and your book contains many interesting things that I had no idea about.

The story you tell has an emotional impact, as people read it, they will empathize with the child caught in a world not of her making, as she tries to make sense of all the things going on around her. I believe your book is a powerful one, and that it will reveal to Americans a side of history that they probably never considered. The viewpoint of a child is a unique one; even though you look back now as an adult, we see most of the events through the eyes of a child."

— Tony Burton, *Honey Locust Press*

"In lush and vital language, Shanti Bannwart gives us a rare vision of one of the central stories of the 20th century. She reveals the deep wound those who enacted genocide inflicted upon their children, leaving many of her generation at war with their families, and within their own hearts. That others suffered more is without question; that Bannwart has engaged in a wrenching, lifelong process to face the guilt she had never earned, is a story that on every page whispers and sings of what is at stake, what is worthy in our lives; and will challenge and nourish each reader."

— Anya Achtenberg, author of *The Stories of Devil-Girl, Blue Earth* and others.

Dancing on One Foot

Growing Up In Nazi Germany

A Memoir

Shanti Elke Bannwart

SANTA FE

Sunstone books may be purchased for educational, business, or sales promotional use.
For information please write: Special Markets Department, Sunstone Press,
P.O. Box 2321, Santa Fe, New Mexico 87504-2321.

Book and Cover design › Vicki Ahl
Body typeface › Book Antiqua
Printed on acid-free paper
∞

Library of Congress Cataloging-in-Publication Data

Bannwart, Shanti Elke, 1938-
  Dancing on one foot : growing up in Nazi Germany : a memoir / by Shanti Elke Bannwart.
  p. cm.
  ISBN 978-0-86534-856-1 (softcover : alk. paper)
  1. Bannwart, Shanti Elke, 1938---Childhood and youth. 2. Children--Germany--
Biography. 3. Germany--History--1933-1945--Biography.
  4. World War, 1939-1945--Germany. I. Title.
  DD247.B317A3 2012
  943.086092--dc23
  [B]
                            2011050611

WWW.SUNSTONEPRESS.COM
SUNSTONE PRESS / POST OFFICE BOX 2321 / SANTA FE, NM 87504-2321 /USA
(505) 988-4418 / ORDERS ONLY (800) 243-5644 / FAX (505) 988-1025

This book is dedicated to the creativity, enduring spirit and strength of women and children facing war and loss.

CONTENTS

ACKNOWLEDGMENTS

Special and heartfelt thanks for their encouragement, patience and inspiration go to:

My dear partner Claude Phipps, my writing coach Eugenia Kim, my advisors at Goddard College: Victoria Nelson, Aimee E. Liu, Jocelyn Lieu and Micheline Aharonian Marcom. Also to my teachers Anya Achtenberg and Meredith Hall; my friends Denys Cope, Dr. Theo Capaldo, Irenka Taurek, Betty Kronsky, Dominique Mazeau, Catherine Jones, Charlotte Hansen, Suzi King Wit; my children Eric Bannwart, Alex Bannwart and Esther Bannwart-Cohen; and my publisher, editor and consultant at Sunstone Press James Clois Smith Jr.

Excerpts from this book in slightly edited form have been published in the following anthologies and magazines:

The Chalk Circle: Intercultural Prizewinning Essays
Muse and Stone Literary Magazine
The Sun Magazine
Pitkin Literary On-line Magazine
Aquila Literary Magazine
Pitkin Literary Magazine
The Tokyo Advocate
Sacred Fire Magazine
Sculptural Pursuit

And those who were seen dancing were thought to
be insane by those who could not hear the music.
— Nietzsche

The Child Elke, Dancing. Photograph by Hans Roessner

1

ROOTS AND RIVER

The day I would see her again, I departed Hamburg Central Station at six thirty in the morning. The train headed north towards the Baltic Sea. It jerked and rumbled, shaking me in the seat when crossing other tracks. Pigeons in irregular rows gathered on wires along the train track, arranging themselves like notes in a children's song. Dusty light of dawn powdered the city's roofs and towers. After leaving the suburbs, the train sped through blooming flax and sand-colored wheat fields. Windmills marked the tops of hills, resembling giant grasshoppers waving their wings above farmhouses with thatched roofs.

I stood and leaned my forehead against the window. "That's my land, that's my home," I whispered. My throat ached with tears in recognition of longing. We passed country roads leading into

I don't believe in age.

All old people
Carry
In their eyes
A child,
And children
At times
Observe us with the
Eyes of wise ancients.
— Pablo Neruda, *Ode To Age*
University of California Press

purple fields of blooming heather. Children on bikes stopped and waved towards the passing train and I returned their greetings. Yes, I remembered these country roads; they snaked through my visions of childhood and awakened memories of warm summer days. My sister, Helga, and I used to gather armfuls of blooming heather for our mother, and once we found a lazy bee tumbling inside, intoxicated by sweet pollen.

Yes, my life was rooted in these forests and fields blanketed by deep sailing clouds, as well as in the beloved city of Hamburg. This is where I ran with kites and climbed trees, where I found fox holes and gathered tadpoles, where I mothered dolls and hid in bomb shelters during air raids.

Crooked pine trees fanned their branches across sandy marshes, shaken by a stiff wind from the Sea. The train headed towards *Timmendorfer Strand* at the Baltic Sea, where my grandmother had settled after my grandfather's death. It was 1982 and I was on my way to visit and also to say goodbye to her, two weeks before my move to the United States. At forty-four years of age, I had enrolled in Lesley University in Cambridge, Massachusetts, to study psychology, eager to understand the workings of the human mind. Born in a country that had imprinted deep traces of shame into my heart, I was wounded by the darkness of my own culture. As I grew older, I felt an urge to uproot my German identity, unable to reconcile with this country's past. But before I would leave the continent, I traveled alone, without my husband and grown children, to see my beloved grandmother, possibly for the last time. After thirty-five years of absence, I had returned to visit my *Oma* and my city, to assemble the pieces of my memory into a whole picture, like a puzzle that needed completion.

My heartbeat attuned to the monotonous rhythm of the train's wheels and carried me back to the events of the past. All through WWII, when I was a child, we lived on the outskirts of Hamburg and I bonded with the town as if it were a member of my family. At the hand of my grandmother I discovered this city's glory and secrets, her dark alleys and open spaces, her land and water. Oh, she triggered all my senses and encouraged childish dreams of sailing the oceans of the world. Like a living body she exuded fragrances and sounds that marked specific areas and quarters. St. Pauli and the *Reeperbahn* were scented with the vanilla from Turkish honey and whiffs from trashcans in damp alleys, where red lamps marked the street corners and shriveled balloons from last night trembled in the morning air. The stench of fresh caught halibut and flounders crawled along cobble-stoned streets of the *Altona* fish market. Pounding boots of fishermen punctured the screeching of cranes. And when Grandma and I rested on wooden chairs in the park of *Planten 'n Blomen*, we watched how downy duck babies bounced on the surface of dark ponds.

Marionette Player Near Alster Pavillon. Photograph by Claude Phipps.

After much gawking and walking, my short legs were tired and we settled on the benches near the Binnen-Alster, the inner city lake, watching white steamers and boats with puffed sails, while eating our homemade liverwurst sandwiches. A marionette player leaned against the railing, his hands dancing above the puppet, infusing the little man with life. Currents of air stroked and ruffled the open water in the heart of town, carrying along the unmistakable perfume of Linden trees in bloom. We marveled at the chic hotels bordering the lake and at the women who climbed the stairs to their portals on high heels. The seams of their silk stockings marked a straight black line upwards from their calves to the rim of their swinging dress. And finally, sitting on the deck of the renowned *Alster Pavillion, Oma* and I drank lemonade out of tall glasses with a tiny colored paper umbrella stuck in the straw. I stared, enchanted by the beauty of women who had their legs crossed, while their hair played across their pencil-thin eyebrows, tousled by the wind. This wind, this Hamburg wind, always blowing and restless, tossing the seagulls around and scattering their cries. Life here seemed arrested in pleasure and the sound of war was a faint drumming.

I begged Grandma "take me to watch the boats and cranes," and she nodded. We would always end up at Hamburg's harbor to observe the ocean-going ships unmoor and sail down the Elbe River, heading towards far away exotic countries. The ship's ropes, as thick as my arm, squeaked when stretched by the ships' rocking and leaning. The dark Elbe River, waxing and waning with the tides, breathed in the rhythm of oceans. Salty tasting winds rippled the murky water and whipped the funnel smoke above the ships, a revolving crowd of boats, small or gigantic, always moving, arriving or leaving, barnacle crusted, expelling steam and blasting sounds from big chimneys or small pipes. And often there was fog like wet veils above the river and around the swarm of moving ships and cranes, and all was rocked in the lap of the ancient river goddess and her mother and her grandmother and their fish-finned daughters.

I longed to sail away on one of those rusty freighters or fly like a seagull behind the moon where, as Grandmother told me, the wind slumbered.

On Sundays my sister and I used to swim near *Blankenese*, along the shallow shore of the enormous Elbe River, which provided a generous link from Hamburg to the North Sea and the rest of the world. After its long passage through the eastern regions of Europe, it moved unhurriedly now, like an old woman. Little did we know that years later, on May 8, 1945, along this very river the Soviet and American forces would meet to declare the end of World War II. From that day on, this mighty river carried the burden of marking a hostile border between the Russian and the Allied troops that occupied Germany after the war, dividing the country into Eastern and Western Zones.

The train stopped in Lübeck. *The town of Marzipan*, I remembered, and then it continued with high speed towards *Timmendorferstrand*, where Grandmother was awaiting me. My childhood was encapsulated in her existence like a small fly or plant in translucent amber. I envisioned her mighty back. It was round like a mountain weathered by the climate and the history of the land, by rain and storms. She carried herself with a towering presence, nonetheless. *What an artist she is*, I thought, *an artist of life*. She knew how to deal with catastrophes, like the war, in straightforward ways. But she also knew how to lift ordinary events to the level of celebration.

Sitting in this rattling train, I remembered such an event when I was about six years old and we travelled to town together. The Hamburger *Stadtbahn* jangled and jerked from left to right; I leaned backwards against Grandma's belly, pressing her hand toward my chest. The train's wheels pounded and screeched. We had no seat. People around us stood crowded, their heads stooped over. Nobody talked. In the field of my vision was a poster showing a woman smiling and stretching a box of laundry detergent toward me. *Persil wäscht weisser als weiss,* the woman stated, 'Persil washes whiter than white,' the words bubbling out of her open mouth. The edges of the poster were curled upward as if somebody had chewed on them. A dull stench wafted from the coats of the passengers and sifted down to the floor, where I stood, so short that I had to look at bulging crotches and frayed knee patches and torn shoes without laces.

We rolled through the suburbs of Hamburg towards the center. Smoke swirled upwards from some areas where the fires from the previous night's bombing still smoldered.

We left the train at *Bremertor* station; it was now called a subway because its tracks ran underground. These tunnels meandered through the guts of town and offered escape routes for people during air raids. We had to climb many steps to reach daylight. The edges of the granite stairs were worn by the boots of travelers hurrying up and down. I wondered at how jam-packed it always was here. If people died every night in this town, I thought, there should be fewer and fewer of them. Where did the new and alive ones come from, all those who now congested the station?

Trümmerfauen, **Rubble-Women Searching for Goods. Photograph from The Fire by Joerg Friedrich, courtesy of Columbia University Press.**

I held onto Grandma's thumb as she steered in the direction of *Bremerstrasse*. She was quiet and observed the pavement to avoid stepping on blackened bricks and rubble that spread into the streets from the fallen houses. *Trümmerfrauen*, women scouring the rubble, scarves around their tired faces, scavenged the ruins for whatever seemed usable. Grandma negotiated the obstructions along the way like a big ship with me in tow.

People stood in clumps together, bartering, exchanging goods with whispering voices. A man took position at the corner, trying to hide a living chicken under his coat. The chicken hung upside down and struggled frantically.

"Oma," I turned to her.

"Hmmm."

"What do people eat? People who don't have a garden or rabbits, like we do?"

"We are lucky, *min Deern*," 'my little girl,' she said, using a term of endearment grandmothers frequently apply here in the north. "Hunger's the thing. Everybody's hungry. It's the first worry in your mind in the morning and the last thought in the evening. Our garden helps to get some peas, and potatoes and see, we're still alive."

I remembered our rabbits. We ate one or two every month, with red cabbage from our garden, and later my mother made gloves out of their fur. My sister and I fed them dandelions to fatten them, but we didn't make friends with the rabbits, because you can't eat your friends. Hunger was our steady companion, familiar and almost dear because it was such a delight when you finally ate something and filled the gaping black hole inside your guts.

When we turned the next corner I detected the pink and blue sign of Herr Ackermann's store. "Ice Cream Salon," my grandma spelled out loud. Those letters pretended to melt into sugary drops made from glass that wiggled along the lower rim of the sign. Herr Ackerman's store was still intact, and he stood behind the counter, growing a pleasant smile on his face when he saw us. He nodded while polishing silver spoons and goblets by pushing them under the purple colored stump of his left arm and rubbing them with the cloth in his right hand.

We climbed two marble steps into the shop and Herr Ackermann shook Grandma's hand. He wore a white jacket and a matching cap with blue rim. He was the captain of his store in town, but his home was in our neighborhood and his daughter Uschi was my sister Helga's best friend. Grandma and Herr Ackermann talked about the garden and about his wounded brother and how he had repaired his bike, fixing a new wheel into the old frame. "Ya know, my dear Frau Henschke," he said, "when a family has a bike that works, they are like kings and queens. That's how I feel." He always said 'my dear,' to everybody.

Herr Ackermann offered eight different flavors in his parlor, displayed behind glass in eight metal barrels slightly tilted towards the customers. Each of them had a name clipped to the edge, written in the colors of the ice cream in the barrel. I couldn't decipher the letters yet, so I looked at the color and texture, making my choice by imagination. All the surfaces of the various ice creams showed smooth spiral indentations on the top, because Herr Ackermann knew the art of scratching his scoop along the upper layer in a way that left it decorated with the pattern of a snail house.

I chose the greenish cream that tasted like peppermint and left a cool feeling in my mouth, even half an hour after it had dissolved. My grandma stepped behind me and placed her hand on my shoulder. She said, as if following a sudden impulse, "You know, Elke, today you can taste all of the eight flavors. All of them! Yeah, all of them." Her voice sounded raspy and, for a moment, she seemed to me like a strange, enormous fairy.

We sat down at one of the small round tables topped with cold marble. The edges were rounded so that they didn't leave imprints on the underside of my arm when I leaned against them. Herr Ackermann carved into each barrel with his scoop and dipped it into a glass of hot water in between the flavors. All eight balls were artfully arranged when he walked around the corner of the counter and placed the silver goblet in front of me with the peppermint flavored ball slowly sliding over the rim. Water drops formed on the outside of the metal bowl and zigzagged down, leaving shiny trails in the foggy surface.

I ate without haste. My tongue compared flavors and mixed them, judging each for its distinct character and texture. I fed my grandmother spoonfuls and we selected our favorites. My whole body filled with a melting, engrossing pleasure. It expanded, and seeped through my skin and into the space around us and out through the door where it stretched into the sky and lingered, a quivering silver and pink cloud above the town and beyond the black smoke.

My grandmother put her hand on my head and then she let it slowly slide down over my shoulders and towards my fingers that held the spoon. She licked the last drop, and we two were very quiet. She leaned back and rested her hands on her belly. Her golden wedding ring made a deep indentation around her swollen finger. I was so satiated with delight that I arrived at the boundary of *enough*. I had not known *enough* for years. It was calm and serene at that border and there was no more hunger or even desire. I encountered the end of wanting, surprised by the stillness of this amazing place. Time stopped breathing.

We stayed a while before rising and saying goodbye to Herr Ackermann. As my grandmother and I walked towards the Altona fish market, we stepped over rubble and a blackened tin bucket with holes in the bottom and a single baby shoe inside. The sole was burned away and one could see the rusty bottom of the bucket through the opening in the shoe. I gripped my grandmother's hand and we exchanged a hasty glance.

Born in 1938, I had lived through WWII with the attitude of a child. My innocence was a protective shield; it allowed me to interpret reality with curiosity instead of judgment. I had no comparison and was not familiar with a life without war. The surrounding events of total destruction seemed like a normal backdrop to my childhood. There was always a sense of play and a strand of light braided into the darkness of those days. I delighted in being alive and vibrated inside with a sonorous hum of happiness. Throughout my life I have preserved a sense of naiveté, committed to joy—like a child or a sage. The presence of war did not reduce my love of life. An intrinsic delight buffered the harsh reality of my young years.

Living in a society of women, I trusted the strength and ingenuity of my mother, grandmother, aunt and sister. The men were at "the front," absent and estranged from their families. It was the women who sustained life at home in all their straight and crooked ways. Surrounded by those women, I felt safe in the midst of chaos.

The men had gathered somewhere in the mysterious place where the war happened. That's where they loaded the airplanes with bombs and where they shot at each other. My father was probably one of them, and I wondered what he really did in this war. The "front" was an uncanny and puzzling location where the war turned into something real, where people died and got wounded.

Face of War, relief by Alex Bannwart.

In the Hamburg subway, when I was still very little, I observed a man in uniform who had lost one whole side of his face; it had disappeared as if fallen out of his head. There was only brown and red rough skin with scars all over and nothing was left that looked like a human face. My stomach clenched tight and my throat hurt from the pressure of not crying out loud. I noticed that most people looked away and I tried as well, but my eyes always turned back to the face that was no longer there. My heart ached and I was surprised how one person could feel so much the pain of another, even if he was a stranger.

So, that's what happens at the front I thought. *Why would anybody go there to leave half of his body behind? Were the parts of his face still there on the ground, for other soldiers to step on? Would dogs eat the nose or chin? Would flowers grow through this man's severed ear? What happened to this man's torn-off face, somewhere far away?*

Later on, I observed Hamburg as it fell apart during the fire bombings of 1943 to 1945. The heartache I experienced about Hamburg's destruction occupied a dark corner of my brain, locked away from recognition. I needed distance from the haunting images of rubble and lonely walls that stood like rotting teeth, monuments to people's destroyed lives. As a child, I had felt helpless observing her ruin, like sitting at a dying person's bed, emptied of words. I had to grow to adulthood before I could face the grief and open the door to scattered recollections. A renewed encounter with the past was the purpose of the trip I had now embarked upon.

The train slowed with screeching brakes, huffing and puffing white steam. I caught my meandering mind and came back to this moment of reunion. Leaning out of the window I saw my grandmother waiting for me at the station platform. She appeared hunched and a bit shorter than I remembered; her hair was hidden under a scarf, a habit from times of war. She stood with feet apart, like a captain on deck of a ship. I jumped down the stairs of the still moving train and into her arms, laughing and sobbing. "Oh, *min Deern*," she cried, "*min Deern*." I had come home into the fold of my own childhood. Every cell of my body remembered *Oma*'s comforting touch and the smell of her skin.

The following morning I woke from a dreamless sleep. The first thing I noticed upon opening my eyes was my Grandma's red high-backed armchair squatting in front of the window. In the dim light, it seemed like a sleeping elephant dominating the room. To the right of it stood the dresser with a mirror that reflected the memorabilia she had neatly arranged in front of it. There were pictures of her grown children and grandchildren and a much loved photograph of my young mother, Isolde, taken a year or two before she died. *How I missed seeing her growing old. How I wished I could unravel with her the chaotic family stories of war and peace,* I thought Next to her smiled her sister, my aunt Margarete. My grandfather once told me that he gave his daughters these dramatic names, like Isolde and Margarete, because he loved opera. As for my mother, she was really called 'Dolly' by all who loved her. Yesterday I had brought yellow roses, and they extended an umbrella of colored light over that gathering of familiar faces. The assembly of people leaned towards each other like plants in orderly rows in my grandmother's carefully tended garden. She was old now and all these relations grew and arranged themselves according to their own rules; she just watched and mused, but she was not involved through actions or opinions. She was living her life with the hard-earned detachment of old age, filled with quiet contentment.

A warm down duvet nestled around my body. There was no cover in the world that provided such a feeling of safety and comfort like a German *Federbett*. My grandmother, too, had been a comforter for me as a child. She had embraced, given warmth and shielded me from the harsh and fierce reality of war.

I heard my *Oma* move around in her tiny kitchen, and then she opened the door and entered the room, a broad smile on her face. Her features were not imprinted by wrinkles, but arranged in soft folds. She didn't wear her dentures because "they hurt my gums," she had explained. "I only put them in for your welcome yesterday; now I can be comfortable again and leave them in the bathroom. You see, my dear, teeth or no teeth, I'm a crusty old beauty," she grinned and showed her gums with glee.

Grandmother and Elke in 1982. Photograph by Shanti Elke Bannwart.

She stacked the pillow behind my back as if I were a small child, then placed a cup of tea in my hands. It was elegantly shaped with blue flower patterns on the surface. "Delft," she said, "I love those colors. See how the flowers dance. It's like music. I admire it every day and imagine it's made for me."

She pulled a chair towards my bed and sat down, folding her fingers and resting them gently on her belly, such a familiar gesture. Brown blotches and blue veins marked her skin, as if gnarly roots crawled along the surface of her hands. "Oh, *Oma*, I'm so glad to be with you for the whole week, there's so much to talk about. I believe you know stories and secrets which you didn't tell Helga and me, when we were children."

She nodded, bending towards me like an intimate woman friend.

"Secrets are the ghost in our family," I said. "We didn't talk about things; so many questions scramble around in my head. I want to hear your stories, Oma, the real ones and those you made up, too."

I slid down a bit until the rim of the comforter covered my chin.

"I'm happy, *min Deern*," that you haven't forgotten your old *Oma*. You've come all the way here to visit. I can't believe you're going to America, but that's what young people do today; your children grow-up and the mother flies out of the nest. Being independent. I remember, when you were little and we watched the big ocean steamers in Hamburg Harbor, you always had those wild ideas of going far away across the big waters."

She looked at me with her straight and firm gaze. The deep folds beside her mouth spoke of a long life full of grief and laughter. They darkened in the dim light of this morning and reminded me that I had inherited those lines from her. I stroked along the contours of her strong fingers and across the creases in her palms. I lifted her hands toward my face and leaned my forehead into the gnarly shape. *Oh, this Oma of mine, how I loved her.*

This down-to-earth woman had at old age fulfilled a dream that she kept alive and sheltered in her heart: to live and die near the Baltic Sea. It unfolded late in her life, like a neglected plant at the outer edge of a garden, finally receiving nourishment. After my grandfather's death she settled into a small apartment close to the water, where seagulls sailed overhead and called out into the wind, where feathery clouds stroked along the edge of the horizon and the air rubbed the taste of salt on her lips. She took long walks along the shore and was free of any responsibility for others. She enjoyed every moment.

"Tell me about the time when you were young, *Oma*, I know so little about that," I asked.

"Oh, *min Deern*, I was so naïve and there were so many things I had no idea about. We were eight kids and we all worked hard and my parents were tired at the end of the day, there was not much talking between us. When I married your Grandfather Otto, I was seventeen and I didn't know 'bout men. Your grandfather was my first. So when our doctor told me that I was pregnant, I was perplexed and asked him where the baby would come out. He washed his hands at the sink and then he turned around slowly, looked at me with big eyes and mumbled, 'Good woman', he said, 'where it came in, that's where it'll come out, too.' That was the whole instruction."

We looked at each other and burst into laughter.

"After we had those two girls, your mother and aunt Margarete, I'd gotten an idea about sex and that it was sweet like honey in my whole body, from the top down to my toes. I thought it was one of the best things in life. Yeah! But your grandfather was so much older than I, and one day he just said: 'That's it! Sex isn't necessary. One does it to make children; we have two girls and so we can stop it now.'

"I wouldn't believe him! I begged and cried. But you know your grandfather and his stubborn ways, when he made a decision, not even God could change his mind. So that was the end of sex in my marriage. I believe that's why I got those horrible migraines."

Yes, I remembered her in the bedroom during the migraine attacks. The curtains were pulled, her face was red and my mother placed wet towels across her sweaty forehead. During those days she was eerie; a ghost that groaned and sighed in the dark like a sick animal.

"Oh my God, *Oma*, you didn't have sex in all those years? Did you still love Grandpa?"

"You know, *min Deern*, that's the last question we'd ask in those years. We women folk did our duty and had our daily chores to deal with. Every woman was worrying and sweating to keep her children and family fed and alive during the war and after. But if we had a minute in between the worries, we women had some fun and laughter and slapped our thighs and got a slice of sweet life wherever we could steal it. Your Mom was so good at having fun and she just had a natural gift for enjoying herself, even when life was rough. She always pulled us up when we sank into a dark place. She baked some cookies, or somebody had a rare cigarette to share, she grabbed me and twirled around in the kitchen or slapped my behind. What a women she was! She could turn tears into giggles."

Grandma rubbed my hand between hers.

"Remember our trips to hunt for food?" she said grinning, exposing her gums.

Yes, I remembered how we went out to visit the farmers, and she had a big backpack strapped to her shoulders. She looked like a knight going into battle.

"You knew how to crack jokes with those farmers and how to barter," I said. "We exchanged our china and mother's jewelry for butter and eggs and ham and I walked beside you for hours. And sometimes it rained and our shoes were so full of mud that we couldn't see them anymore. We had to cut the dirt off with a knife."

She sighed, "You know, my dear, we women had our ways to survive. The men were out there killing and bombing, we saw them so rarely. But we women at home made new babies and kept them alive using our womanly tricks. The bread we ate was earned with our bodies, like with the baker at the corner. He met me in the forest between the bushes and trees."

I looked at her, stunned. *Herr Finkelman*, I thought, *that smeary guy with black fingernails and hair on the back of his hands? He touched my beloved grandmother? He groped with those hands underneath her dress, on her belly and her breasts, in the forest where I played hide-and-seek?*

"How'd you stand that?" I whispered.

"That didn't matter much. I would lift my skirt standing up against a tree. I would close my eyes and he'd be done soon and then I'd go home, happy, with loaves of bread rolled into my apron.

"Come, *min Deern*, put on your boots and warm stuff and let's walk a bit along the water. You see, I don't regret anything, no, I don't. Finally, in my life, I have all I always wanted: my little cozy apartment, my warm bed with down comforter, a big old grandmother chair with red velvet and lace, and china with blue flowers on it from Delft. And the best, you know, the best is the sea and the seagulls and the wind with salt in it."

"I don't even put my dentures in," she grinned, "I am so happy! So happy!"

Along the Baltic Sea. Photograph by Alicia Otis.

Nobody in our family had known that grandfather was rich. My grandma had been so accustomed to living a frugal life, constrained by war and her upbringing. As the couple grew old together, even after the war had ended, she still habitually scratched the butter into a thin layer on every piece of bread. My grandfather was secretive. He was a stranger wrapped in his own myth. When his will was read to my grandmother, after his death in the 1960s, she was informed, to her and the family's great surprise, that he had secured one half a million German marks in stocks for her, stocks with the most desired companies, like Mercedes Benz and Deutsche Bank. My grandmother, this practical and hardworking woman, was suddenly showered with options she never had known. A door opened to all her humble dreams of comfort and beauty. She began to create some glorious years of old age for herself, providing her with deep satisfaction. My Grandpa Otto, whose early life was as crippled as his crooked leg and forged by poverty and tenaciousness, had secretly created a soft pillow for his companion, this women who was a foot taller than he and stood by his side throughout all those years of war and hunger and finally through his struggle with colon cancer, leading into death.

When we stepped into the street, a blustery gust came from the Baltic Sea, and the scent of salt and seaweed spiced the air. We walked towards the beach where my sister and I had played during our family vacations. Red brick houses with thatched or tile roofs lined the sidewalks. Climbing roses arched over the entrance to tidy gardens. The windows were small to keep the weather out and framed with lace-rimmed curtains. My grandmother and I leaned towards the wind and towards each other, holding on tightly.

The door of the church along our way was open. I followed my grandmother into the dimly lit oval space. "I often sit here on that bench and look back at my life," she pointed to a corner. "I remember my Dolly, your Mother, and I hurt when I think how young she was when she died and that we still don't know how it really happened, because your father never talked about it, especially not to me."

We sat down beside a burning candle and she turned her head towards me. "Just before all of you left Hamburg in 1947 and moved to Munich, your mother mentioned to me, 'My period is late.' I asked her, 'Is it his baby, is it your husband's?' and she nodded. She was sure about that, and your mother never lied.

"So, I wonder," my grandmother sighed, "I wonder if she was tired of her marriage and didn't want another child with your father. It might have been an abortion that killed your mother. But women don't have to die from an abortion any more." Although a grown woman now, it was still painful for me to talk about the darkest time in my childhood, the bitter cold winter, when my beloved mother suddenly died. My grandmother's thoughts unfolded, and I shared her struggle to unearth the truth. I had not seen her for many years and we rarely talked about my mother's unexpected death. It was a shameful family secret, and we all colluded in that silence. And now we carry the unfinished story, like a ghost that cannot rest.

"I need to finally find peace and know what happened, *Oma*," I said, "I'm going to visit my father before I leave for America, and I will dare to ask THE forbidden question. Yes, I'm scared, but I'll do it, I have to!"

Sitting beside her, in this place of family history, allowed us to linger in a safe enough space where monsters could unveil their faces and angels might step forward unexpectedly. I had no answer about this mystery, either. Secrets are burdens and they keep us stuck in the past; we carry them like an iron trap around our ankles. They are neither dead nor alive, but make us bleed from time to time. Secrets don't sink to the bottom of memory to be washed away by the outgoing tides.

"I'm old now," she said. "I let those questions rest in God's hands. He knows why my Dolly was taken so early, and maybe one day he'll let me know, too. It's so hard for a mother to survive her own daughter, it never heals, the scar stays." We sat beside each other for a long time, without words; the murmur of waves along the nearby beach stitched sounds into the web of silence.

Leaving the church, we followed the trail to the shore of the Baltic Sea. Our shoes sank into the white sand and the sharp dune grass scratched our legs.

"Time and again I walk to the shore and look at the water," my grandmother mused. " I love — I just love — how it moves and sings and whispers its tales to me. The ocean's stories are forever; ours are so short.

"I know all the trails. I stroll here alone but I'm never lonesome. I have my whole long life to think about and, after more than eighty years, there's so much still to find out. I look at my life like the big ol' Elbe River as it rolls along, and I'm sad and happy and all is right just how it is. All is right."

She held my hand firmly in hers.

"Life is like dancing on one foot," she said. "One foot is on the ground and the other is up in the air. You hobble and jump and sometimes you fall, and the dance jiggles your belly. But there is music inside you, humming and singing, always music."

The talks and silences between us, during this day after my arrival, were rich and warm. The presence of my grandmother elicited vivid memories of the past. Sometimes, during this visit, I wished that I were not so encapsulated in my love for her. I felt myself falling back into childish needs, wanting to be tucked in and protected. At times she got on my nerves with her never-ending caring and concerns that I would eat well and dress warmly, and both of us got so overly entangled in our closeness that it seemed sticky, like spiders' webs.

But when I stepped back and watched her walk or stand quietly, I was amazed how clear she was. Her womanly authority was simple and straightforward, resembling a big old tree planted into the earth hundreds of years ago. She was the one who stood firmly at the center of my childhood. Her female lineage reached backwards and into the future. She had given birth to my mother, Isolde, who gave birth to me, who gave birth to my daughter, Esther, who gave birth to my grandchild, Sophia—a long and winding river of woman-power that reaches into the next generations and beyond my granddaughter who already carries the tiny eggs for her own children warmly packed inside her body.

My grandmother and I arrived at the Baltic Sea and stopped. "Look here, *min Deern*," she pointed, "look at this long *Timmendorfer Strand* landing bridge. It's here where your father saw your mother for the first time, almost fifty years ago. She jumped from the highest point of the bridge with an elegant dive into the water. She was so beautiful and strong and wild, my Dolly, and Hans fell in love with her just there and then. When she climbed back up the ladder, he talked to her and that's how it all started. That's the beginning of your story.

"And you see, *min Deern,* mine's going to end here at the Baltic Sea. All is well! All is well!"

Birthing: Elke and Daughter Esther. Photograph by Keni Cohen.

I imagined my mother standing there at the very end of the white bridge, a young and vivacious woman who fell spontaneously in love with my father at exactly that spot. And I saw her also on the beach as Mother, teaching me how to swim, her hair yanked and twisted by the wind caressing her face. I trusted my mother and would dare to move into the deep water where I could not reach the ground underneath my feet. From my mother's arms, I would observe the ripples of light that the sun sprinkled onto the bottom of the sea, a net made of sunshine pulled along to catch shells and sea creatures and mermaids and children who could breathe under water.

Mother Isolde in *Timmendorf*. Photograph by Hans Roessner.

I thought about the many summers spent here with my parents, my sister, and I. When our grandparents joined us, they kept their city clothing on and sat like queen and king in our *Strandkorb*, watching us children play.

After all that talking, my grandmother and I fell into a delightful silence. Time moved slowly. She turned and looked at me. "My dear, I want you to know something. After I die, I want to be burned and want my ashes to be gathered in a small brass urn. And then I wish that our Pastor will carry the urn out on a boat into the open sea and put it into the water with a blessing and let it sink down to the bottom. I imagine how it sits there between the sea weeds—fishes swimming nearby and the sun moving in golden sparkles all around it."

"Yes, *Oma*, my dear!" I said. "How I love your idea. And you know, it makes me so glad to imagine that you'll be a part of this big water which reaches from here to America."

We stood in silence. I put my arm around her shoulders and felt the deep hum of joy vibrating in both of us, like the purring of big old cats.

Nobody knows what makes the Soul so happy!
Maybe a dawn breeze
has blown the veil
from the face
of God.

—Rumi

The wind softened. Seagulls gathered in one straight row along the railing of the bridge. They cleaned their feathers and readied themselves to sleep, hiding their heads underneath their wings. The setting sun left faint streaks of pink on the crest of the clouds. The imprints of our shoes were still visible in the sand along the lacy edges of the waves, but they, too, would soon disappear.

The next day I took a long walk along the water. Childhood memories flickered around me like light on the waves, eliciting sadness and joy. Soon, I would be leaving this continent. My life was shifting like tectonic plates in an earthquake. But this place pulled me back into the past; I needed to untangle the strings before I could go forward.

Grandparents. Photograph by Hans Roessner.

2

TRIBES AND TREASURES

I was five years old in 1943, the year when my story really begins. We lived in Hamburg on *Volksdorferdamm* #154. A giant beech tree stood in front of our home, stretching higher than the roof of the two-story brick house. The tree hugged the corners and bent down to the window of my sister Helga's and my bedroom, the branches knocking and scratching when the wind made them sway. Those branches were crooked, as if somebody had broken the limbs. There were elbows and knees that stuck out and offered places for a child to sit and hide. "Mama Beech, bony beech, lift me up as far as you can reach!" I hummed. I climbed into her arms every day and knew the rough and cool touch of her bark against my thighs when I perched high up in her green folds like a bird. I understood the language of her raspy rustling and windy whispers. She made happiness vibrate inside

...the immensity of the tenderness, the dark and terrible depths of the flesh.
— Marguerite Duras,
The Lover

me, made it hum with a sound that had its source in my own body. The beech tree wove her limbs carefully around me, but I was also aware of the empty spaces that lurked in between the leaves.

Mama Beech. Drawing by Kappy Wells.

From this perch I gazed toward the center of Hamburg, where a fiery glow bulged upwards into an orange and yellow sky. Purple patches of color, like the cosmos flowers in our garden, floated in between. And sometimes a hot red streak would stretch and devour the purple. A black cloud hung above the glow, a floating pillow that kept the heat and smoke down near the earth, *so that*, I imagined, *God wouldn't get disturbed by all the turmoil*. My grandmother often said, in winter, when the sky was colored like that, "The angels are baking for Christmas," and I wondered who was cooking and baking now, in summer, and was it heaven or hell?

They called it war, but this name explained nothing to me. I observed war as I would notice a thunderstorm rolling across the northern landscape or this ladybug climbing diagonally from my fingers to my elbow. Four black dots on its wings meant she was four years old, one year younger than me. Lifting her toward my mouth, I blew warm breath across her orange body. She raised her upper, hard wings and spread the silky, thin ones underneath until they reached outward like the edges of a kite, and the wind and my familiar children's rhyme carried her away.

> *Maykaefer flieg,*
> *Dein Vater ist im Krieg,*
> *Deine Mutter ist in Pommerland,*
> *Pommerland ist abgebrannt,*
> *Maykaefer flieg.*

> *Lady bug soar,*
> *your father is at war,*
> *your Mama is in Pomern-town,*
> *Pommern-town is all burnt down,*
> *Ladybug soar.*

To get into the tree, I climbed a small birch first. It leaned towards the big beech and allowed me access if I clung to the lowest branch of the beech and pulled myself up and toward its trunk, right hand, left hand, right, swinging like a pendulum. I invented this trick, since the beech stood tall without branches in my reach. The boys of the neighborhood wondered how I scaled this mighty tree.

This evening I settled down on the side that pointed towards town to watch the red and orange blaze. There was urgency in the upward force of the heat, as if the fires were punching the belly of the sky. I put one arm around the trunk and pressed my knees into the branch in front of me for firm hold. Mama Beech trembled in the wind that ruffled my hair. The leaves rustled and fanned out around me in the shape of a wide coat. I wished rather to be a tree, than a five year-old girl.

Underneath, three neighbors huddled together on the path. Their foreheads were furrowed and their shoulders bent towards each other, one of them stretched her arm and pointed at the blazing horizon. They were all women. Most men fought at the front and rarely came home, like my own father. I didn't know what "at the front" meant, but I knew it was treacherous and far away.

"My brother's family was bombed out last night," said Frau Heidegger, "They all fled the city and knocked at our door this morning, half-dead with tiredness and fear. We moved them into our bedroom. We're crowded now, but so glad that they're alive. We'll make do."

I thought about my father and wondered if he might be in danger of being burned or shot. He never wore a uniform, like our neighbors and other soldiers, but only a long black leather coat and brimmed hat. He had a bony jaw with sharp edges and green eyes that turned dark when he was angry with me. Sometimes he stayed with us and even joined us on vacation to the North Sea or Baltic Sea. At the beach he would swing my sister and me around in a circle, holding both hands, or one hand and one foot, lifting us up and playing "airplane." The speed squeezed the stomach and took my breath away, especially when he let me rise and fall so that my nose almost scraped along the sand and the wind pressed the hair into my eyes. It felt heavy in my chest when I remembered my father and how he was never with us for a long time.

The daylight faded and I climbed down from the tree. I didn't use the smaller birch as a ladder, but jumped from the lowest branch. It was a long stretch and my groin tickled from the fall and my shoes dug into the wet ground. I scratched the mud off the heels with my fingers.

My mother was working in the kitchen, leaning over the baking board when I walked in. Her hands were white from flour. I sat beside her at the corner of the table in front of the window, where I always observed what happened outside in the garden or inside the house.

"*Mutti*," I asked, "what if...what if the orange fire burns our grandma and grandpa? They live in town where the fires are. What if their home crumbles and the bricks pile on top of them? Frau Heidegger's family got bombed out. They all live together now. In their small house."

Father Hans Roessner swinging Elke. Photograph by Isolde Roessner.

My mother rested her white hands at the rim of the flour pot and took a slow breath that made a whistling sound. She let her eyes wander outside, over the young apple tree in our garden and the peas, which had grown so much in the rain that they reached above my head and I could hide inside that green chamber.

The skin on my mother's elbow made a fold. I put the tip of my finger there and held it in this small cave. I knew the touch and smell of her skin like I knew the bark of the tree.

"I believe that your *Oma* and *Opa* are well," she said. "Next Sunday we'll take the *Stadtbahn* and visit them and you can see for yourself."

I wanted to ask more questions but my mother turned towards

the hot stove, opened the door and shoved the loaves of bread into it. The kitchen was the place where we talked, but I rarely asked about the bombs or when my father would come home. I had understood that those questions were not to be stirred up, yet they hung like cobwebs in the corners. I turned my head and observed a gray cloud moving slowly from one side of the window to the other, while the aroma of warm dough spread from the oven.

The airplanes with bellies full of bombs flew over our house during the dark of night. When the eerie howl of the air raid sirens penetrated my dreams, my mother woke my sister and me with great haste and pulled warm sweaters over our sleep-heavy bodies. She put on our little hand knit hats and socks, and wrapped us in woolen blankets. She could do this really fast, even in the dark. Then she carried us down the winding wooden staircase into the cellar, our eyes still full of the dreams of night. Our neighbors had already gathered. They huddled together quietly, locked into silence. Their eyes closed, they held hands with each other or had their arms folded across their chest.

The bomb shelter had a weighty concrete door hung on rusty iron hinges that groaned as it closed, sealing everybody inside. There were usually about twelve or fifteen people hiding in it during the air raids, because our neighbors from across the small walkway had no shelter and they would rush through the opening in the hedge to join us.

Frau Gnade, from the apartment above ours, sat in "The Royal Chair." At her side, like a guardian, was her grown son, Jürgen, he was shot through his shoulder and allowed to stay home, the only man in our house of four apartments. Our neighbors from across the path were lumped together in the other corner. They had the strangest name: *Pförtner-von-der-Hölle*, that means 'Guardians-of-the-Hell.' There was an odd collection of furniture in this room: discarded chairs from kitchens or gardens, bunk beds for the children and an old lamp with a heavy metal shade that looked like a warrior's helmet. Mother lifted Helga and me onto one of the bulky mattresses of a bunk bed, which smelled moldy, and we fell asleep again, hearing in our dreams the faint explosions, far away...

During the day, the bomb attacks of the nights disappeared into the cracks of memory and seemed like fairytales or bad dreams. The nightly sirens provided an eerie backdrop to my life. There was one reality for the night and one for the day; they fluctuated, like exhaling and inhaling. I didn't really care about the war, because I didn't understand its effect and reason. Yes, I heard frightening stories when I listened to the grown-ups and their whispered talks, sensing their worries. But I posed my own world, my own experiences and fantasies, as a bulwark against their sorrow. In my world I would make up my own stories. Oh, there was the potato field with yellowish slugs between the plants, or the rustling trees in the forest and there were black-and-white swallows that raised their babies in our garage. I closely watched their nest on top of the water pipe in the corner, and I saw the mother feed her children spiders or butterflies so big that they stuck sideways out of her beak and she had to really stuff them into her babies' yellow beaks. And there was an orange snake that lived under a rock at the edge of the wheat field. For hours, my friend, Dieter, and I waited for it to come out. We stretched out in the grass, lying on our bellies, and we argued whether the snake was real or part of a story in our books.

"Maybe, Dieter, the war's just a made-up fairytale. Maybe it's over tomorrow, and your and my dads' come home. Maybe, next Sunday, our parents will tell us the real story and we can sleep again without sirens in the night, they sound so scary and sad, like howling animals or wind that hurts inside. When the sound goes down, at the end, it feels like running out of breath and drowning."

Dieter nodded and tied a loose shoestring.

"I always sweat in my pajamas, when the sirens howl. And sometimes I pee in my bed," he said.

"But, you know Dieter," I responded, "and don't tell anybody, I'm excited when I watch the fire in the sky. How it hangs above the town and changes from red to purple and orange and yellow. I think it's really beautiful and mighty and big."

Early in the mornings, Dieter knocked at my door and I jumped off the chair in the kitchen and ran to open, knowing already what he would say.

"Elke, will you come out and play with me?" He clapped his hands. Always the same sentence and gesture, like a magic rhyme that opened a gate and bonded us inside the same story.

And I would say, "Yes, in a few minutes." That's how every day started, a ritual that confirmed for me that the world was safe and that a tomorrow would follow this day. Dieter had a round face and the hair on his head stood straight up like dry sea grass in the dunes. He always wore short pants, even in winter. I was a year older and he accepted me as the leader in our plays and adventures. I believed that I knew more about things, and if I didn't, I made it up. Dieter always followed my suggestions.

He came into the kitchen and watched as my Mother braided my hair and fixed colorful ribbons at the end. He sat quietly and pressed his fingertips against the crumbs on my plate, when they stuck he put them in his mouth. Dieter lived in the neighboring house on the ground floor.

We were best friends and the same size. When we walked or ran we held hands, or we would put our arms around each other's shoulders so that they crossed in the back. Together we explored the forest, the fields and the hidden places in our homes, for example, the garden entrance to the cellar where the bomb shelter was concealed.

"Let's go to the dark stairs and watch the spiders," I suggested that morning, and he nodded and clapped his hands.

We slipped down the narrow staircase. It was built out of cement blocks but they were softly covered with moss because it was always damp there and no sunrays reached this place. The stairs led down to a wooden door with a small window. It was so dirty that only some dim light shone through. In every corner of every step there were clusters of spiders huddling together, Daddy-long-legs in all sizes.

We sat on the musty steps and poked into the spider clusters with little sticks to wake up the lazy critters, so they would leave their mossy corners and dart around. Spiders revolted me and the hair on my arms stood up. They scrambled up my naked legs and I imagined them wiggling underneath my bottom. A surge of disgust cramped my belly but I wanted to learn fearlessness.

"You see," I said to Dieter, "I wasn't afraid. And now you need to let them climb up your legs, too, and into your trousers!"

And he did. We put our faces close together to observe the construction of those fragile spider-running-machines. A round body like a coffee bean was suspended between all those long legs, and the joints were bent in several places, like a twisted drinking straw. They could make their coffee-bean-bodies move up and down as if pushed by a spring, and they did this yo-yo thing when standing still or while running forward at high speed.

Dieter closed his mouth tightly because his face was hanging just above them.

"Look," he whispered, "they never get their long legs entangled when they climb over or under each other; I wonder if they ever tie knots in those stringy limbs and get into fights. I wouldn't want to live so close on top of each other." Dieter was an only child.

I had an older sister, Helga, and I asked her and the grow-ups many questions about everything, except the war. I wanted to know things. Once I had asked my father why this and why that and then I said, "*Vati*, why do I always ask why?" He laughed and said that this was finally too much, and I should stop my questions now. I knew that he didn't really mean it. He wanted me to be smart and was proud of my curiosity. My father didn't laugh much. His face was so square that the half-round shape of a smile didn't seem to fit into it.

When I understood things, they were not scary anymore. I wasn't afraid of dogs or horses or dark forests because they were familiar. I loved the word *familiar*; it meant that something was part of your family. "I'm so glad that you play with me, Dieter. When you are with me it feels so *familiar*." I liked to say "familiar." Every week I had a new word that I tried out and loved more than others because it wasn't used up yet. And there were words that sounded fantastic, like *Kakadu*, that was never used up.

That day we found the door to the basement unlocked and we sneaked inside to explore the dimly lit cellar like Jonah in the belly of the whale. We peeked into two booths full of food. They had lath doors with spaces in between and a hanging lock; we could see everything.

"This one is ours," I pointed through the laths, " and that one is Frau Gnade's."

"Do you know," Dieter poked his finger in my chest, "why her name is Frau *Gnade*? My mother says that her name describes who she is, she is graceful and brings grace to the neighborhood. Everybody loves her."

"Yes," I said. "She is the most beautiful old woman I know. I wish to be like her, when I am old, and wear the same golden watch with a snap lock on the wrist and white stockings with flowers woven into them. But I still believe that my grandmother is even more wonderful. Her name is Louise and that's a good name, too. If you say it with closed lips, then it sounds like the wind blowing through grass. Try to say it: Louuuiiissssse." Dieter poked his lips out and looked funny, and we laughed and sang "Louisssse, Louisssse."

My mother stored all the marvelous things that grew in the garden in our cellar. There were potatoes with dry dirt still on them, carefully layered in a wooden crate. During a long weekend, my father had nailed and screwed the crate together out of used boards. He was rarely with us, but when he came home, he usually did something practical that made our life easier. I always helped my father with those projects. I picked out the nails or held the hammer and I was the one sawing the small triangular pieces of wood with my own handsaw. He needed them to strengthen the corners of the potato crate. I loved to do manly things and knew well how to handle tools. My father explained the work to me by making drawings on paper scraps, and I always understood.

"Do you see, Dieter, all those long wooden shelves with beans and peas, peaches and gooseberries in glasses? My mother preserved them. Look at those green, red, yellow and orange colors. One can see what's inside through the glass and it looks almost like candy." Dieter put his nose between the wooden laths and we both just stood there for some time and heard each other breathe.

Then we tiptoed down the dimly lit hallway were the door to the bomb shelter was open, all the rotten furniture inside. But there was one single chair in the right corner that looked like somebody had brought it from a king's castle. It had a high back support, wide armrests and a red pillow on the seat, imprinted with flower patterns and framed with lace. I knelt in front of the Royal Chair and touched the slick fabric with both palms of my hands.

"This is Frau Gnade's chair," I whispered. "Only she is allowed to sit in it during the air raids.

"I always watch how she walks," I said and imitated her, nodding my head slowly. "She moves so gracefully, as if she's rolling on wheels, and she sits slowly down in this chair like a queen on a throne. Then she leans back, her arms tired and hanging down over the carved arm rests. I can see the skin on the back of her old hands, they look like crumbly peaks and deep valleys, and I can smell her perfume, lavender and cinnamon."

Dieter didn't listen. "I want to sit in it and lean back and be a king." He said.

"No. Wait, there's something more exciting. I'll tell you a secret about this throne. I've never shown this to anybody. Not even my sister Helga knows about it. You are my best friend, so you're the only one to know."

Dieter leaned forward and I saw in the dim light that his eyes were wide open. I loved secrets; they were like birds caught in a small cage, hopping around and wanting to fly. They made me feel important, but the most exciting part of secrets was the tickle in the belly when one released them by telling somebody. I felt giddy and nervous. We listened if somebody was approaching, but it was uncannily quiet in this room. I wondered for a moment why we huddled together underneath the feet of the house, playing in the bomb shelter and bringing night and day together, easing the spell of the dark.

"Look here, I can take that pillow off the seat and then lift the whole lid — what do you see? A wonderful chamber pot is underneath! Can you imagine, something beautiful like this? Our soup bowl on the table isn't as precious!"

I slowly rubbed Dieter's fingertips over the fine patterns of blue flowers and spirals all around the curves of this miracle chalice. And then I took his hand and let him touch the golden rim that was ice cold and slick and sparkled with a dim glow. " The holy grail of King Arthur's Court shines like this in candlelight."

"Wow," whispered Dieter, and then he reached for the handle that was curved and long, like a swan's neck.

"No, No, you cannot take it out! It's a magic charm.

"I'd wish so much to sit on it and try it" I whispered, "but if you break it, you would have to die or turn into a toad. This isn't made to be used. This is only here to be beautiful and make this bomb shelter special. It's a secret protection for all who hide here."

Before we left, we put the hinged lid and the pillow back into their places. We clutched each other's hands as we stumbled along the passage and out into the light of the day. *How good it is to have a friend to share important things*, I thought, *because sometimes it is so lonesome and frightening to be a child.*

We climbed up into Mama Beech and leaned against her trunk. Adventures are like food, like bread or apples, they made me feel round and satiated.

"You know, Elke," said Dieter, "when the sirens howl and we crawl into the shelter, we are like the moles in our garden. They live in dark holes, too. They don't even have eyes, don't need them because it's dark in their burrows."

"But, we are people and we've magic and we have real eyes. The treasure inside the chair, it's magic and it keeps us protected," I insisted.

Dieter nodded, "And my father, too. He says he keeps us protected. He has a big gun. And he knows how to use it; he's smart. I think that works, too."

Dieter rubbed some leaves between his fingers and then he blew air in between to make them whistle.

"I wished my grandparents were here with us," I said. "They live in town, in *Altona* near the harbor with the big ships. That's were the red and orange fire glows; I'm afraid that the fire will eat them up one day."

Dieter put his arm around my shoulder and we sat quietly together, as if we had stepped into the river of sorrow, holding our breath under water. And then Dieter's mother called him to come home for lunch; her voice penetrated our cocoon. We scrambled out of the tree, startled like birds.

I want to talk about my father now and how he met my mother, because that's the other place where my story really begins. My father had an extra tooth, one more than people normally have. It stood out on the left side in front of the other teeth and made a little bump under his lip. That intensified the square look of his face, making it appear to be carved in wood. My father was proud of this extra tooth. When he grinned, the tip of it peeked out over the edge of his lower lip.

The tooth pronounced the curves of his jaw and gave an impression of fierceness, and so he was. When he sank his teeth into a task or challenge, he would not yield until there was a solution. He did all his work devotedly, no matter who was the master he served, and that would earn him recognition and rewards in the later years of his life.

My father was born 1902 as Hans Roessner, and grew up in *Aussig*. This area was called *Sudetenland* and belonged at that time to the Emperor of Austria. Hans studied in Dresden to become an engineer. He lived there when the town had not yet been bombed and the castles, churches and stately houses stood in full splendor. Dresden was so beautiful, he said, that it was called the Venice of the North. When my father told my sister and me about his life as a student in Dresden, his gaze would get teary and go far away. I thought he might have some special memories, because I had rarely seen tears in his eyes.

When he was thirty years old, he worked for the *Motorenwerke* in Hamburg, and on the weekends he drove his Opel car to *Timmendorfer Strand*. Many people from Hamburg and *Lübeck* regularly visited this attractive Baltic Sea resort to enjoy the clear water and white sand. There were heavy beach chairs made from straw with roofs that sheltered against the wind. Two to four people could sit inside on the upholstered bench; some chairs had armrests that turned into tables to put drinks and food. Fathers and their children built walls out of sand around their chairs with an indentation as an entrance. Some also wrote their names by placing shells like letters. They wanted to let others know that this was their territory. After the walls were shaped and sprinkled with water to make them firm, they built dragons, towers and sand castles. Sometimes they dug deep holes where the fathers lay flat as in a grave. Their children covered them with sand until only their heads stuck out of the ground as if they had grown there, like cabbages.

An elegant white bridge stretched about 1000 feet from the beach into the blue-green water of the Baltic Sea. Men in white pants and straw hats, their shirtsleeves rolled up, walked leisurely back and forth and greeted the women whose hair and colorful skirts were lifted and tousled by the wind. Their skin was tanned and full of tiny sand crystals that made it shine like gold. Ships moored at the end of the bridge and took on passengers for Sunday trips to one of the other resorts or to watch the shoreline with its stately white houses and red tile roofs. Wind from the east blew scattered tunes of dance music from the ships towards the shore.

My father was an athlete and an excellent swimmer. He climbed upon one of the posts at the end of the bridge, fifty feet above the water. He posed for a moment to attract attention and then he performed a head jump with great style. He arched his back and hovered for a second in midair like a seagull against the wind, his arms stretched wide like wings, his fingertips elegantly aligned. In just that moment, his body seemed weightless and arrested in time and space. Then he bent forward and directed his dive in a smooth curve downward, entering the water like a seal, without a splash. Onlookers applauded as he dove up again. He smiled and climbed all the rungs of the rusty metal ladder to the top and repeated his performance.

Hans, the Athlete, Performing. Photograph by Isolde Roessner.

One Sunday afternoon, a young woman stood at the bridge and watched the dashing young man. She, too, was a superb swimmer and diver. "Are there stinging-jellyfish down there?" she asked when he was back up on the bridge. And these were the very first words my mother, Isolde, spoke to Hans. He shook his head and watched her as she jumped with great elegance from the same spot he had used before.

In later years my mother would draw pictures of this encounter in her funny cartoon-like style and show them to her two daughters. She was twenty years old when they met and she had just enrolled at the Academy of Fine Arts in Hamburg. She was gifted and passionate about her career as an artist. Her joyful brown eyes sparkled with life. Her forehead was high, like a moon ascending. She wore her hair in the boyish style of the thirties, the arch of her eyebrows shaped like Greta Garbo's. When she laughed, she would push her chin forward and her whole body trembled. Her amusement was contagious, and her joy of life electrified my father. He invited Isolde and her sister Margarete that same evening for a date— and the next day, just Isolde.

First Date. Drawing by Isolde Roessner.

Falling in love, Hans and Isolde Roessner. Photograph by Margarete Henschke.

The Accident. Drawing by Isolde Roessner.

Some weeks after they had started to see each other, my father drove alone in his convertible Opel car, heading home after a long trip. He realized that he was very tired and he said to himself, 'I really need to sleep a bit. I'll drive to the side of the road to rest, just after this next curve.'

But he fell asleep right that moment and drove out of the curve and directly into a tree that separated the road from the field. He was catapulted out of his seat, thrown straight upwards into the air and he woke up when landing back onto the seat. His face was bleeding. He had lost his nose, or most of it. The edge of the car's metal roof frame had shaved it off, and it was hanging loosely from his face.

He was transported to the hospital by an ambulance, and had to undergo several surgical procedures. Doctors skillfully reconstructed his nose with an artificial bone to give it shape. This wide nose looked a bit like a boxer's, and my sister and I would later believe that's how his face had always been. But he showed us pictures of his profile in earlier years to make us understand what he had lost. His original nose was fine, long and elegantly shaped.

The Apple in Paradise. Drawing by Isolde Roessner.

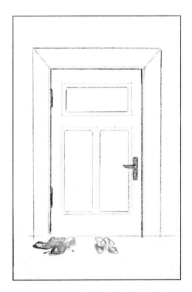

Seduction. Drawing by Isolde Roessner.

My mother went to the hospital every day and took care of him. She baked cookies with chocolate frosting and gathered apples and cherries from the market. Once she brought him a glass bottle full of salty water from *Timmendorferstrand* with some sand, seaweed and shells in it. A tiny crab scrambled along the bottom.

She drew cartoons of him with bandages on and they laughed about his strange looks, like a mummy with only the mouth and eyes as openings on his bandaged head. She later showed those drawings to us children, when she told us this story. Never in his life had Hans received so much caring love and attention because, in his family, he assumed second place to his older brother, Ernst, who was the 'good' son and prince. The bond between my parents was forged at his sickbed during his recovery. They fell passionately in love.

Isolde embodied what Hans longed for. She was fire, but he was frozen. She was yielding, but he was rigid. She was humming with joy, and he was rather serious and introverted. And she found in him what she admired; his sharp intelligence and skillful ability to tackle whatever needed solution or action. He was mature and grounded and ten years older, and she was like a young wild bird that had just learned to fly.

"Will you marry me, Isolde?" he asked her shortly after he had recovered from his injuries.

"Yes," she said, "yes, Hans, yes Hans, yes," she said it four times, this *yes*. She wanted this man with all her wild and passionate heart. That's how she became a wife and dropped her plan to study at the renowned Arts Academy of Hamburg.

Our young family lived in a home at the fringes of Hamburg. We were four: my parents, my older sister Helga, and I. The house had four apartments, two on each side. The elderly Frau Gnade and her son, Juergen, above us, were like family members. Their home had the same shape as ours, but a very different feel. When I was invited inside, I would take my shoes off and didn't dare to touch any of the wonderful porcelain figurines or velvet pillows with red tassels, but I admired them up close and observed how my breath clouded the silver candleholders. In contrast, our home was more simply furnished and we children could run and play there with our friends. My mother held the center in it. She sang and moved around with vivid gestures and her fast hands put everything in order. I was like a kite, pulled outwards by the wind of the world, but securely tied to her presence. In the morning, after my father had left for work, while my sister played with her friends, I knocked at the door of my parents' bedroom and opened it.

"*Mutti*, can I come in, please?"

My mother nodded and I scrambled up on the unmade bed where my parents had slept, to settle quietly on a crumpled pillow. I put my spindly arms around my knees, rested my chin on my wrist and observed her. The bed smelled sweet from human bodies, like moss after a summer rain.

My mother had opened the windows to exercise and had taken off all her clothes, twisting and turning her naked body in the cool air of the early day. As she bent over to touch the ground with her fingers, her breasts swung back and forth like church bells on Sunday morning. Her round hips rolled and her skin shone red and gold with the soft radiance of apples in the garden.

I leaned my head into the bow of my arm and watched. My mother's breath streamed rhythmically, like the ocean waves at the edge of our northern country.

I inhaled deeply and said, "*Mutti*, when I'm grown up, I want to be a woman like you!" She lifted her head and stretched her arms, smiling at me as if listening to music singing inside her body.

Later I played with my friend, Dieter, in the sand box and from there I watched Mother as she walked into the garden and picked green beans for lunch. After that, she dug potatoes out of their muddy beds. With bare hands she stroked and caressed the dirt off the brown lumps. Stepping carefully around the salad plants, she stopped in front of her flowerbed.

Mother had one garden bed reserved for herself. She planted it full of flowers, when all the neighbors only cared for what was edible. She lined the edges along her flowerbed with bleeding hearts and small blue grape hyacinth that looked like frozen teardrops. The sturdy dahlias had blossoms bigger than my head; they were lined with red and white stripes and stood tall in the middle of the bed. Short sunflowers leaned against them and wrangled for space. In spring, the tulips were the first to poke through the ground, announcing that all plant creatures would now wake up from their winter sleep. Their stems and leaves felt sturdy and cool; bugs and bees lived inside their blossoms. The light shone through the colored petals, and one could see where they crossed over each other because the color was darker in those places. When my mother asked me to pick tulips for a bouquet I cut their stems with a knife and squeezed them gently together until they made a crunchy sound.

I heard her talk to the flowers before she broke them. She had kept this moment for the end of her garden stroll. Finally, she picked one and fixed the blossom in her hair. She leaned her head back and towards the sun. My hands in my lap, I held still, as if watching a swallow in flight, or a rainbow at the horizon.

She opened her eyes, turned to the house and strode very carefully along the garden path, holding the bowl with beans and potatoes under her arm. The blossom at the side of her head swung in the rhythm of her steps. And that is how — for me — she still walks through eternal gardens, somewhere above all memories, radiant and luscious, wearing a flower knotted into her hair. The poet Pablo Neruda might have met her there, when he wrote the *"Ode To A Woman Gardening"*

> *Everything*
> *grew from you,*
> *penetrating*
> *the earth,*
> *immediately*
> *becoming*
> *green light,*
> *foliage and strength.*
>
> *You touch*
> *my chest*
> *while I sleep*
> *and trees bud*
> *from my dream.*

Sometimes I had nightmares. I woke up and cried and mother came in the dark and lifted me out of bed so that I would not wake my sister Helga. She closed the door quietly and carried me to the kitchen where she sat me on the table with a soft blanket around my shoulders. Then she dissolved sugar in warm water or milk and filled it into the small white cup with purple stripes and grooves around its middle. She sat me in her lap and let me slowly sip the warm sugar water.

I leaned my head against her chest right into the valley where the two breasts met and inhaled the familiar scent of her sleep-warm body. With one finger, I followed the edge of her nightgown around her neck. My finger crawled slowly. When I reached her neck, I traced a half circle and pressed my fingernail ever so slightly into the crease in her skin. At the place where my own hair mingled with hers, I turned around and walked my fingers all the way back again. Then I slipped my hand into the fold under her left breast where I felt her heartbeat like a gentle, rhythmic pressure against my palm.

One night I had a dream that was different from any I had ever dreamt before. It seemed as if it had really happened, and it emanated a vicious dark power that was stronger than my mother's arms and warm sugar water. It imprinted itself in my memory and made my hair stand up at the nape.

I stood in a landscape devoid of any plants or trees. Soft sandy hills stretched into vast distances. A feeling of numbing loneliness lingered above the space like invisible smoke. Total silence saturated everything. A body of water sat nearby, lifeless and unmoved by air. Maybe there was no air at all.

I felt that I did not belong here. I was painfully forlorn, at the end of the world or beyond. But suddenly I saw my mother standing at the edge of the water.

"*Mutti!*"

I shouted her name and stumbled as fast as I could towards her, but when I came close, I saw that she was as hollow as a dead tree. Only her empty skin was standing there and there was no life inside this strangely twisted form with a human face. She was absent, and there was no substance to inhabit that empty shape. I woke with a scream that stuck in my throat like hot ashes.

The next morning, Mother was in the kitchen preparing yeast dough. She tossed it around with a big wooden spoon and it made a *pflofff, pflofff, pfuuuff* sound because the bubbles of air got caught inside the sticky mass. Mother formed round loafs with hands full of flour and settled them on the baking tray. They looked like the backs of turtles. Then she covered the loaves with a white towel and put the tray near the oven so that the dough would rise.

"*Mutti,*" I felt shy and my chest was tight. "I have been thinking how much I love you."

She wiped the flour off her hands and sat down at the table for a moment of rest. I reached to hold her hand, tracing with my fingertips the edges of her nails, and rubbing the skin that covered the strong joints of her fingers.

"Yes, my little one. I love you, too, very much."

"*Mutti*, I don't want to live when you are not here," I said.

My mother listened quietly and nodded. "I'm here for you, all the time."

After a pause I said, "If one of us dies before the other, we could decide to do it together, the dying. When you die, you'll tell me and I will sit beside you and we will hold hands. I'll die with you, at the same time, I mean. We'll both die a little bit more and more and always say to each other, 'I'm a bit more dead already, are you, too?' So, we'll know that we're both going together and neither of us will leave the other behind."

I don't remember how she responded, but I knew that for me this was a firm commitment. I was five years old.

Mother Isolde and Elke. Photograph by Hans Roessner.

My sister, Helga, was two and a half years older than I. We shared the bedroom at the end of our hallway, and in the evening, we would often climb into each other's bed.

"Helga, tell me a story, please!" I would insist and cuddle close to her. She liked to be important and to receive my devoted attention. Her straight brown hair feathered out across the pillow. Helga had her eyes closed, but I watched how the lashes shivered, indicating that she was still awake.

She skillfully invented her stories in the very moment when she told them, but I thought she had read or heard them somewhere. I was eager to hear her stories and impatient to find out how the problems would be solved, and how people escaped the quandaries they got themselves into. It would always start with a promising and harmless beginning that turned miserable by blunder or innocence. After some hemming and hawing, an ordinary person would rise to great strength or courage and rescue or repair what seemed lost and damaged. When that happened and all problems found a good solution, I would cry tears of happiness.

"There were three men in the dark woods," my sister began. "No moon was shining, and the men were a bit scared, and it was cold. They found a hollow tree and thought they might sleep inside so no wild wolves or bears would eat them or drag them into their caves to feed their young ones. The men didn't want to be food for those bear children, so the travelers stretched their hands inside the hollow tree to see if anybody else was already inside. And as they did that, lots of bats flew out and one of them got caught in one man's hair and held on tight and didn't let go. It screeched and wiggled and bit the man. So they got out a knife and cut a bushel of the man's hair off and threw the bat with the hair into the hole of the tree." My sister's eyes were closed and she spoke more and more slowly, and little spit pearls rolled down her chin, because she fell asleep. I shook her awake and she went on: "The three men realized that the bat fell down and was gone. They searched and found a long ladder that led downwards into the hollow tree. They lit a piece of wood to see in the dark and decided they would climb downward and find out where this was going. The most courageous one, the one with the cut off hair, went first...." Helga got tired, her well of imagination went dry and she drifted off into sleep.

But I was wired up. I shook her and pulled her arm, "What happened after they climbed into that tree, Helga, what happened?"

To my dismay, her stories often ended in the middle. I still remember those tales that never found a conclusion. Stories needed endings and completion, I believed, like days and nights or the seasons of winter and summer or like a dessert after a well-cooked meal, all the tension and suffering should be rewarded at the end. Otherwise, the stories and their listeners could not live in peace. The unfinished tales would float around somewhere and whine and groan like a person without legs or arms. I was frustrated that she left me hanging without a solution. Her tales seemed like a movie reel that had got stuck—and so, the story could not live or die. I was convinced that if I made up the endings myself, the story was not really true. I imagined that stories and the creatures in them were real beings and they were this way or that way and one should not change them randomly by freely inventing something. Otherwise the stories would be mad and take revenge on whoever told them without truth and made up the wrong ending.

The following weekend we took the *Stadtbahn* and subway to visit my grandparents, my mother's father and mother, in downtown Hamburg. As we climbed up the five stories to their home, the stairway smelled from the typical German Sunday meal: sauerbraten with red cabbage and mashed potatoes. Helga was tall enough to reach the brass bell. Grandma opened the door and grandpa hobbled from his chair near the window, swinging his cane naturally in small half circles, as if it were part of his body.

I hugged them and hurried out through the kitchen door onto the little balcony that clung like a swallow's nest to the outer wall of the apartment. This was my favorite place in their home. Deep down on the street, under my grandparent's balcony, people and streetcars crawled along. They looked small from my place, from where I saw them with the eyes of a bird on wings.

I put both hands on the railing and felt the cold metal, careful not to disturb the pots where my grandmother had planted parsley, dill and chives to season her meals. She was a great cook, and what I liked best was her potato-salad with golden baked flounder and fresh herbs on top.

After stepping back inside, I sat on one of the elegant chairs, covered with red velvet and doilies in the place where the head would lean against the precious fabric. My short legs stuck out straight in front of me. Grandma loved these chairs but seldom sat in them, because she wanted to keep them beautiful. She was a practical and down-to-earth woman who grew up without luxury. I had never met her mother or seen her childhood home. I think she was embarrassed to show us where she came from. She collected a few precious things, like china and crystal glass, just for the delight of looking at them and stroking them along their contours and surfaces with her big, strong hands.

"Grandpa, will you wind up the clock?" I pulled on his hand, his skin felt dry and sandy, like tissue paper.

We stood in front of his cherished clock. Dark carved wood panels covered each side, and a glass door with brass knob protected the front. He stuck an ornate key into the hole on its face and stopped the long brass pendulum with one finger. Then he turned the key to wind up the machinery inside, and that created a harsh, crackling sound. When completed, he gently pushed the pendulum into movement. The clock itself had a small window on the front and that window could be opened.

"Look, grandpa, watch all those tiny golden wheels inside and how they move and hold onto each other. I can see everything through this window, how it works and spins. The big wheel in the back goes slower than the small ones. Those tiny edges are sharp like cat's teeth. I wish next year I'll be tall enough to wind up the clock. Can I?"

The following year there was no more clock, and no key to start and stop time or possibly even turn time backwards. Our lives would be marked by loss and destruction. My grandparents stood like guardians between a collapsing world and me, though we didn't know it then.

Summers in Hamburg were splendid, with sun and rain in balance. Bad weather never lasted longer than a day or two, or maybe a week. Summer opened the doors and windows of our house and we spread our plays into forests and fields. About five miles from our home at the outskirts of town was a pond with sand at the banks and an old wooden waterslide with a copper cover. It jolted children, flapping like grasshoppers, five feet out into the water. On days when the sun was shining, my mother packed a picnic lunch in her blue bag. She layered the hardboiled eggs inside the towels and between our bathing suits; sandwiches with tomatoes and parsley sat separately. Then she loaded my sister on the back seat of her bike and me in front where the basket with the food was also hanging. I sat in between her arms on the small leather seat that my father had fixed for us children on both of their bikes so that we could go on outings, all four of us together. My mother laughed as she pushed the bike with its heavy load and then she jumped on the wobbling seat, trying to find balance. We drove through meadows blanketed with loads of white marguerites and blue cornflowers. Larks sang so high up in the sky that one could only see a jiggling dot against the blue. There were bike stands in front of the weathered entrance gate to the pond, and a kiosk with lemonade and *Penguin* ice cream in two flavors, chocolate and vanilla. My mother locked the bike and we spread our towels on the lawn. My sister immediately left in search of friends.

Mother and I walked slowly into the pond and we splashed water on each other to cool down. The shock of cold on my hot body electrified me and made me jump and shriek. Then she let herself into the water and I put my arms around her neck, intertwining my fingers beneath her chin. I felt safe in deep water with her. She began to swim and I floated above her back, moving my feet in rhythm with her strokes. We glided all the way to the other side of the pond, where dragonflies sat on top of each other and tadpoles scurried below the overhanging grasses.

We dried in the sun and then we turned around, because my sister was waving to us from the other side of the pond. When we swam back, I looked down into the deep dark of the water and remembered that I could not swim. But the touch of my skin on my mother's back and the support of her shoulders underneath my arms assured me. She was breathing rhythmically. The push of her arms and legs created swirls around us on the surface of the water where they spread away from us like the shivering wings of a butterfly.

I leaned my forehead against her neck and the water reached my chin. Observed from the side, the water striders looked like monsters. Then I closed my mouth and eyes and sank my whole face into the water as long as I could hold my breath. The streaming water splashed into my ears and pulled my hair. I was either in the light or in the dark, either under water or above, shifting from being a fish into a bird and back into fish. I was able to live in two elements, and my mother's back was the central place where both met and mingled.

3

BIRDS AND BEASTS

Grandpa's silvery gray hair stood out thick and wild in every direction around his head like the feathers of a bird-of-paradise. I imagined that he was born with white hair because his eyebrows were silver-colored, too, striving upwards in the shape of wings. My grandma thought his face was so noble that it should be carved in marble. Although he was only about five feet tall, his erect stature and the curved walking stick in his right hand made him look like the commander of a ship. This commander didn't lean on a wooden peg, but on a crooked leg; it poked out sideways at the knee joint like a half opened pocketknife.

My grandfather's name was Otto Henschke and since I was born on Otto's birthday, the fourth of September, I was given the middle name Ottilie, to honor him. It was an odd name, so I avoided telling anybody about it.

There was a time when
  meadow, grove and stream,
the earth, and every common
  sight,
to me did seem apparrell'd in
  celestial light,
the glory and the freshness of
a dream.
— William Wordsworth,
Intimation of Immortality

Grandfather Otto grew up as a child in a poor family near the border of Germany and Poland, in an area called *Pommern*. This land is situated in the North of Europe near the Baltic Sea where the winters carry loads of snow; the seasons to grow food are short and provisions scarce.

Otto was one of six siblings. They had to share beds and never knew the calming feeling of a full stomach. When Otto and one of his younger sisters were about twelve years old, their parents planned to ease the burden of the family and to give the two oldest ones a better chance at life than what could be expected in their dismal situation. They came to the conclusion to send them to the Czar's court in St. Petersburg, where children were hired for minor tasks. This mild form of slavery was called *Verdingkinder*. The evening before they would leave the family, his parents told Otto and his sister, "Imagine, you'll live near the king of Russia! You'll have a better life there, than with us at home."

The next morning, the neighbor came with a horse carriage to Otto's family cottage to pick Otto and his sister up. Great Grandfather loaded the bundle with their possessions and then he waited to lift them onto the back of the vehicle. The two children stood outside. Otto had turned his back to the horse carriage and watched his mother stumbling around inside the house, her eyes red and swollen. He stared at the holes in her blue sweater, holes that had always been there as long as he remembered. Her bony elbows poked out. He wished to be back in bed where he had restlessly tossed during the night beside his two brothers, who could not sleep, either, holding their breath as he sobbed quietly into his fist. His siblings gathered behind the scratched windows to watch the departure. One of them cried, while the others' faces were pale gray.

His mother stepped outside and took the two departing children into her arms. Otto could feel the bony ribs under her sweater. She shivered from the cold wind and stepped backwards when the horses moved and the cart drove slowly away. Otto turned around and caught a last glimpse of his parents, of the house and the fading faces of his brothers and sisters behind the windowpanes. Then he felt a snap inside, like the sound of metal shutters being closed. They never were to be opened again, and he would get accustomed to the darkness and loneliness inside.

So it happened that Otto and his sister grew up at Czar Alexander's court in St. Petersburg, far away from parents and siblings. They slept in a damp room with other quiet children, did their daily work in the gardens or barns, and tried to forget the cabin and the window that framed the faces of their siblings. They had enough to eat now and each was in possession of their own blanket.

One day, when Otto crossed an open space in the Czar's court, a horse carriage approached. Suddenly, the horses reared and the driver lost control. Startled, Otto jumped and fell on the bulky cobblestones. The carriage ran over him. The wheel drove across his leg exactly at his knee joint. Too shy to call for a doctor's help, he left his leg to heal by itself. Ever since that accident, his limb was oddly bent sideways. And from that time on, Otto walked with a cane and with the slow and awkward sway of a swan out of water.

Under Czar Alexander the III, in the second half of the nineteenth century, there were great upheavals around the court. This Czar reversed the liberal Alexander II's politics of freedom for the poor serfs. Being treated like slaves under the new Czar, they revolted against their living conditions and the guards shot at them ruthlessly. My grandfather heard their screams. He remembered his own family and how they scrambled to live off the land, hunger churning inside their guts. The same night, Otto and his sister packed a small bundle of belongings and left the court as the fog of the early morning lay on the fields. They fled all the way from Russia to Germany on foot. Hiding during the day, they walked in the dark through the Tundra and the endless sandy pinion forests of Poland, Pommern and the Baltic Land. They were hungry and tired, like Hansel and Gretel in the fairy tale, but this story was real. They clung to each other and sought their way for weeks and months until they reached Hamburg.

That's the story my grandmother told me when I visited her in 1982 for the very last time. She had carried it in her heart and it had fermented there like an old wine: through time it had gained body and scent and a deep red color that allowed the light to reflect in it and throw a colorful shadow.

As I listened to her, the old and sad children's rhyme hummed in my mind; it was so much a part of my German childhood, uncanny and mysterious in its origin:

> *Ladybug soar*
> *your Dad is in the war,*
> *your Mother lives in Pommern-town*
> *Pommern-town is all burned down,*
> *Ladybug soar.*

My grandfather obscured the memory of his home, his siblings and parents. He loosened the knots of his connection to the past, like ropes of big ships get untied from the shore. And that might be the reason why, in later life, my Grandpa never spoke to my sister and me about his childhood or the sister who had shared his journey. In my family, we avoided talking about painful events.

We saw our father very sporadically. When he was in Hamburg, he had the habit of creating for himself a ritualistic entrance into the home, after work. He stood at the open kitchen door and leaned his right hand against the oven pipe that stuck out like an elbow. From this place he pontificated, telling us what happened that day and how his colleagues had messed up and caused problems, but he was the one who resolved them and straightened everything out. He always portrayed himself as being right and others wrong. I sat on the chair in a corner, swung my legs and ate bread with strawberry preserve. Observing quietly, I noticed that the women simply continued their cooking and cleaning in the kitchen, almost as if he were not there. He came from a different, manly work "culture" and tried awkwardly to find a way in at home, but he was subtly ignored. His critical remarks passed by and there was no response from the audience, not even a nodding of the head. I asked myself if he would tell others, too, when I messed up, because in many of our interactions he gave me the feeling that I made bad mistakes and he had good reasons to punish me. I felt shy and crooked in his presence, as if I could not unfurl and stretch into my own shape because there was something wrong about me. When he was angry, his eyes changed color; the gray turned green and he stared into mine as if I was a stranger. I felt paralyzed and couldn't breathe.

When my father was home during air-raid alarms, we didn't always retreat into the bomb-shelter, but we all stayed together in my parents' bed where it was warm and safe. I would curl underneath my mother's armpit, and Helga would bury her face into my father's hand; he held still and put his other hand on her back. He was loving and tender with her, because she was his favorite. And that was fair with me, since I was my mother's darling. In those rare moments, I felt how love wove gentle strings around all four of us, as if we were made from the same fabric. Outside, a sense of danger and dread surrounded us, but inside this cocoon of family, everything was calm as if storms and sounds had gone to sleep.

Sometimes my father said during breakfast, 'Today I'll come flying over our house with my airplane. Look out for me. I'll spin some circles and wave at you!'

After that promise, we children were giddy and wouldn't stay inside. We rushed into the garden and looked up to the sky, as if we were expecting a fiery dragon to appear. We told our friends, and usually nine or ten children gathered, all with their necks craned backwards and their noses up in the air. They wiggled and pushed each other as we stood on top of the bench near the sand box to be a bit taller and closer to the approaching plane, because it was a friendly plane, and nobody had to fear bullets or bombs.

Suddenly, there was the familiar hum in the air! A dot appeared between the clouds and it grew as it advanced. The red plane had a black nose and white stripes at each wing. Only one propeller sat in the middle where the black nose protruded, so that it looked like a face.

We children stretched and waved with shawls and pillowcases to be more visible to my father in the sky. The plane flew three spirals around us in the air and, in those moments, I thought that my father was the most magical man and I was very proud of him.

After he had disappeared into the clouds, I walked back into the kitchen and stood for some time beside my mother who stirred starch and vanilla beans into milk to make a pudding. I watched how the mass inside the pan got thicker and firmer and the spoon left traces in the shape of a spiral. Every turn of the spoon made a new path, and then it was crossed by the next one.

"Why am I sometimes afraid of *Vati*?" I asked my mother.

She turned and looked at me with surprise but did not respond. So, I thought it might be my own fault if I feared a father who could fly circles in the sky in a red airplane. He was powerful, a mysterious and hidden man who wouldn't say sweet words; but sometimes I would recognize his love for us in his actions. The creation of my toolbox was one of those actions, and also the construction of our hand-made skis.

When I was five years old, he built me a toolbox for my birthday. That day, I saw him walk home from the train. He carried a big case in his two arms all the way from the train station to our house. I jumped in circles around him until he set it down on the table where other gifts were already placed. Finally, my mother rang a glass bell, and only then was I allowed to unpack and touch the toolbox. It looked like a small cupboard sealed with a door that was held in place by brass hinges. And there was a lock that I could close by knotting two leather strips together, so nobody could open it without my permission.

I untied the red leather strings and opened the door gingerly.

"Look *Mutti*, look Helga, look what I got from *Vati*. There's a real hammer and pliers and here is a tiny box with nails and screws," I exclaimed, breathless with joy, tears of happiness smudging my cheeks. "And here is a plane to smooth wood and two screwdrivers with blue handles, a small one and a really strong one."

I took each tool out of its silver holder, as I showed them to everybody and let them touch the cool metal. Before I handled the next one, I put the prior one carefully back. The wood was slick and smelled like turpentine and fresh paint.

"Watch that! The holders are fixed on the back of the cupboard and," I turned and faced my father with amazement, "there is blue felt behind all of them; feel how soft it is! It's more gorgeous than our doll-house."

My father helped me carry the box, as we retreated into the garage searching for a board to work on. He demonstrated how to hold the hammer at the end of the handle to drive some of the nails into the planks. I also tried the plane on a gnarly part of the shelf, little pieces of white curled wood fell to the floor as I pushed the tool back and forth with sweaty hot hands.

"Let's pull the nails out, *Vati.* I want to use them again and always have them in the little container in my tool box."

On the evening of this birthday, my father and I carried the box into my room and placed it at the side of the bed. I gave him a long hug and wiped a strand of hair out of his forehead. Lying down, I hung my left leg out from underneath the comforter so that the sole of my foot rested on the door with the leather band that my father had tied to the edges. After the tools had been introduced to my family and to me, their new owner, they rested snug in their holders. I wondered where he had found all those magical pieces, and was eager to use them and help him with his projects.

I always assumed that my father was very disappointed when I was born as a second daughter. I thought that he desired very much to have a son, teach him all his technical skills and play father-son games with him. So he treated me like a boy, taught me how to use tools, and he even bought me Lederhosen. During weekends, when he and I solved practical problems together and built useful things for the women's household, we connected and I wasn't afraid of him.

Grandmother stood at the stove and brewed a cup of fake coffee made from roasted and ground wheat. Real coffee was rare. But when my mother was lucky to barter some from a mysterious source, she would invite her friends over, and all the women had a feast together in the kitchen. They laughed and told stories, and then they called mother's friend Aunt Kate, whispering 'we have real coffee, come and hurry!' She traveled all the way with the *Stadtbahn* from town to celebrate the aromatic brew and enjoy the chats and warmth of the women's circle. They would keep the windows closed, because the definitive coffee smell made any passerby suspicious, wondering how the women were able to find the treasured beans that everybody desired. The women sat around the kitchen table and put their elbows on the table-top and their chins in their hands. Sometimes, one of them brought a cigarette and would share it with all the others. We children sneaked in and found a choice of laps to sit on and various breasts into which to lean our heads. Grandmother performed a jig. She lifted her skirt so that her underwear showed, pretending to be a young, flirtatious girl. She told jokes, using the northern dialect called *Plattdütsch,* and the women laughed and slapped their thighs. Streaks of sunshine fell onto the hair of the women and into the curly steam from coffee cups. Happiness hummed in the air, weaving shiny patterns out of the laughter and gossip.

But this morning, our *Oma* was very quiet and thoughtful. I sat beside Helga in the kitchen and we ate our breakfast. There was one precious slice of bread for each of us, carefully metered out every day. Bread was the foundation of our meals; bread was essential, bread was a living being and it was the first thought when imagining food. We spread fake honey or strawberry preserve on it and Helga and I had the habit of pushing the sweet load with our front teeth ahead of our bite, like a snowplow. So, at the very end, when the pile almost fell over the edge, we would anticipate the full and burgeoning pleasure of a mound of sweet. And all the way up to this moment of final delight, the smell, taste and texture of strawberry or honey was just in front of our nose and tongue. We even competed for who could wait longer to swallow the last bit before we burst into a frenzy of giggles.

74

I understood that some pleasures were outstanding, and others rather ordinary. Coffee was one of the big ones, and so was butter. My grandmother never just called it butter, but always *"gute Butter,"* good butter, and she endearingly called it by that name until she reached old age. She always said to the storekeeper 'I want a quarter pound of *Gute Butter* please,' and she would hold it in her cupped hands as if it were a kitten or bird.

Grandmother slurped her fake coffee slowly, and when she put the blue cup down, she rolled little beads out of the breadcrumbs on the table. She gathered them in her hands and looked at them.

"Your grandfather is powerful, like an emperor, and people look up to him with admiration." She paused and we knew that she would tell us more as she was spinning one of her homemade stories born at the border between myth and reality.

"He settled in Hamburg when he was a young man. He was a child of poverty and hardship and he decided, with an iron will, that he would get rich and never ever again would he live in grim and humbling circumstances. So he applied for an apprenticeship in a firm called: 'Export/ Import Of Chickens and Eggs' and worked his way up, steadily and with determination. And now, you see, he has a really important position. He's the boss. He makes the big decisions and his colleagues listen to him. He is short in his body, but in stature he is grand. I've always admired that about your grandfather."

She sat up straight and whispered with a soft voice, "You know that your grandfather has the most beautiful office in town? He overlooks the whole harbor from his windows and watches the ships come in from the ocean, long clouds of steam dangling out of their chimney. Little yellow pilot boats hurry around them and show them the way. The ships carry the chickens and eggs that your grandfather buys in other countries. From his window in the tenth floor he oversees when the workers carefully unload them in crates and boxes, and then he decides who will get the brown chickens and who will get the white eggs." She stroked the small cup with her big hands and took another sip, her gaze now sparkling and excited.

Fine lines radiated from the corners of her eyes outwards towards the gray hair at her temples.

"Your grandfather is the boss. That's something like a king. So he doesn't sit on a normal chair when he works in his office. No, he sits on a throne! A throne made out of eggs. He takes his seat carefully, so as not to break their shells. His secretaries stand beside him, one at each side, to hold his walking stick and take his orders. One of the secretaries is a fine, fat, big chicken with white, glossy feathers named Betty, and the other's name is Miranda and her feathers are gold, brown and black with green edges. Those feathers hang over her sturdy claws and cover them like bedroom slippers."

My sister and I had stopped eating and listened to every word, our hands sticky with honey, our mouths open with anticipation.

"Wow, *Oma*," I sighed, "I want to see his office. I knew it all along, I always thought that grandpa looked like a king."

That same day I told my friends about the throne made out of eggs white as snow, and I described the chicken secretaries with their gold, brown and green feathered dresses and feathers hanging over their chicken feet. My friends envied me and competed by telling scary stories about their fathers and grandfathers and how they fought in the war and resisted bullets and fire. One girl said her father had lost a leg and it was probably still lying around somewhere in a forest in Russia, or in a hospital where they made soap out of people's limbs. But I was not impressed. I thought sitting on a throne made of eggs was far superior to being a hero in an attack with guns or airplanes. My grandfather's throne was more fantastic than anything a child could dream of.

One day, my *Oma* and I went to town. Such a trip was always full of surprises, like getting a scoop of green or purple ice cream with a red cherry on top, or boat rides or fish and chips in a paper bag at a greasy store window where the smoke from the stove swirled out of the window and along the sidewalk.

"Can we please visit Grandpa? I want to see the big ships in the harbor from his window, and the throne made out of snow-white eggs and the chicken secretaries with feathery shoes." My grandmother nodded and we both smiled, bound together in the web of our imagination.

We arrived at a tall building ten stories high. There were black and white marble tiles on the floor arranged in zigzag patterns, and built into one wall was a continuously moving lift. "That's called a *Paternoster*," said my grandmother."

We had to be attentive and wait for the right moment to jump into one of the open boxes that went continuously up and down and all around to transport people from the lower levels to higher ones and back down, so they did not have to climb stairs and could do their important work faster. One had to know how to use a *Paternoster*. So I stood with my Oma for some time and observed how others hopped into the moving boxes that looked like small rooms with only three walls. The front was open to step in and out. The other three walls were decorated with golden mirrors and little lamps and brass handles to hold onto.

When a totally empty cabin came by we stepped quickly into it and I held on to a brass handle until my grandmother said "Give me your hand, the next floor is number ten. That's ours." We grabbed each other's hands firmly and leaped out of the moving room. We were a tiny bit afraid and I observed that the other people smiled about us. I didn't like when my *Oma* was lacking confidence, and I was a bit ashamed about our clumsiness.

My grandmother said "Good Morning" to the receptionist—a heavy woman in a red dress She knew my *Oma* and had enormous breasts that she leaned on the top of the counter. Grandmother asked her "How's your new baby girl?" and the two women talked women's talk, chatted and laughed with each other. Whenever my *Oma* liked somebody, she was very warm and relaxed, but when she didn't, she could be highly opinionated and rigid. She had a good instinct about others. I walked slowly around and touched with light hands the wood panels that had pictures on them of men with serious faces and big mustaches. Dark and yellow wood cut into curly shapes decorated the walls. Brass signs on heavy doors had names on them telling who worked in that room, serving my grandfather. I discovered red knobs behind glass, with fire signs on them that one would pull in case the building burned down, and there were red arrows that pointed to exits.

Then I arrived at a door that was marked with bold, golden letters: "Grandfather Otto." I could read a little bit and knew the shape of the two Os. Although the door was closed, I imagined how my *Opa* was inside making important decisions. I envisioned him, sitting on a white throne built from fresh eggs. He was the leader of his emporium and overlooked the whole harbor from his window. His silver-white hair stuck out into every direction as if his thoughts had wings. I thought he would be busy ordering hundreds of chickens from other countries in the world to be shipped to Hamburg so that all the hungry people here could be fed.

I stood quietly and was aware of the fine and feathery curtain between my grandmother's story about him and this real world of business, and I decided not to lift this curtain and not to disturb its texture. I turned around on tiptoes and grabbed my *Oma*'s hand. After we came home, I told my sister everything and a bit more, like how the *Paternoster* stood on its head when coming to the top and turning back down, or at least that's what I imagined.

A year later, when my grandparents lost their home during the firebombing, all the ten floors of this office building got destroyed and crumbled into one enormous pile. Grandfather couldn't visit his emporium anymore. The fire alarms in his office had yelled, but the exits were clogged with broken windows and blackened bricks. The *Paternoster* had stopped going in circles and lay somewhere in the rubble like a beast on its back or a centipede, still humming, and twisting the brass handles in the air resembling broken legs. Grandfather's office was ruined and the throne was smashed into thousands of pieces, while the chickens drowned in the harbor. People all around us had so little to eat, I thought, because my *Opa* could not buy and deliver the eggs and chickens any more.

My father didn't sit on a throne, but he, too, was a king. He was an athlete and had won prizes. He told his two daughters often about his skiing adventures. As a young man he had climbed the *Zugspitze,* one of the highest mountains of the Bavarian Alps, on skis. He was born in the year 1902, so these adventures happened around 1922, when skiing was rough and dangerous. He had a whole collection of first, and second, and third prizes, won in national competitions. They looked really important and had printed seals on them and four or five signatures underneath.

He described to us how he tied strips of fur underneath his skis so that they would not slip backwards when he scaled a mountain. "After hours of climbing, when I arrived at the top, I would look around all over those peaks, in every direction, and it was very, very beautiful." He rarely talked about the beauty and wonder of things. But this moment his eyes were gentle, and his edged cheekbones round and soft. I wished to touch his face with my hand, but we were not used to those gestures.

"And the best thing about this climb was that one had achieved it all through one's own effort. That felt so good. At that time there were no ski lifts or alpine trains. One had to conquer the mountain with muscles and sweat and afterwards the whole trip down was pure pleasure. Only those who made it up could enjoy the downhill skiing. It was fantastic!"

"Once a year," he said, "I participated in the national competition for ski jumping. I jumped distances of more than one hundred meters."

I imagined my dad standing on the top of a big mountain, looking like a god, surrounded by sunlight and blue sky. And when he glided downhill he grew wings so he would not fall or slide over an edge. And in the picture here, he still has his unbroken and elegant real nose.

So, when I was five and my sister Helga was seven, my father decided to teach us how to ski. Around Hamburg there are only small hills to glide down, we lived in flat country and I had never seen mountains, but the winters carried loads of snow from the cold north to our area.

My father ordered somebody to cut four long, slim pieces of wood; and then, with a knife, he sharpened the edges at one end into points. My sister Helga and I sanded the corners. He placed them on the worktable with the tips bent upwards, held in that position by clamps. He made the wood wet and let it dry, repeating this procedure until it kept this rounded shape. Then he polished and varnished those boards and put them in pairs down on the floor. My sister's skis were a bit longer because she was taller. All three of us were in the garage and the room smelled like a pharmacy.

Hans on Top of the Zugspitze, Bavaria. Photographer unknown.

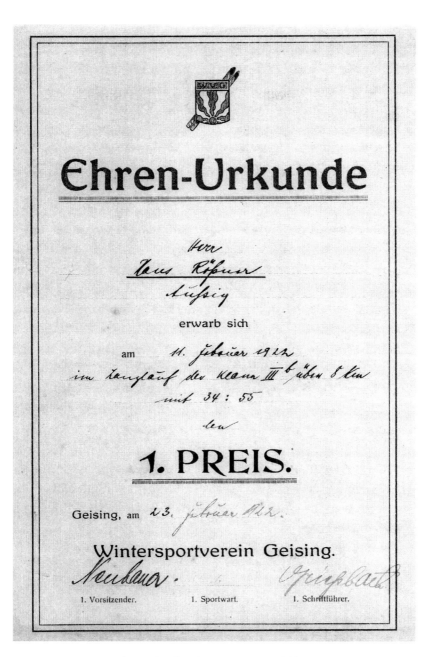

Ehren-Urkunde

Herr

Hans Rößner

Aussig

erwarb sich

am *11. Februar 1922*

im Langlauf der Klasse III b über 8 km

mit 34 : 55

den

1. PREIS.

Geising, am *23. Februar 1922.*

Wintersportverein Geising.

Neubauer.   *Griesbach*

1. Vorsitzender.   1. Sportwart.   1. Schriftführer.

First Prize for Cross Country Skiing.

"Now, you two stand very still and I will mark where the bindings go."

He moved us back and forth until he decided that front and back were in the right proportion. Then he marked with a pen around our feet and it tickled as he followed the edges of the toes. We laughed and it was hard to stay still without wiggling.

"Now, watch. I'm using the rubber of an old tire to create the soles where your shoes will be fixed but stay flexible, nailing one end of them on the ski. And these leather strips with clasps will tie it all together."

We stood closely by his side and watched his every move. When he worked on something, he was alert and serious. He wiped his hair from his forehead and puckered his lips. He had the habit of whistling when he knew he was being admired and watched. It satisfied him to create something from scratch, something that had not at all existed before, but took shape as he created it with his hands. He was very competent at building functional items, and I admired him for this skill. He thought me those abilities, too, and it helped me to develop technical cleverness.

The glue between the bindings and the skis had to dry and sit for one more night, and the next morning our father and we two girls got out of bed early. We dressed in gloves and boots and woolen hats and then we rushed outside.

We stood on the skis as my father tied the leather straps around our boots. Then he positioned himself on his own skis in front of us, and we followed him like ducks in one row, scrambling and falling and getting up and sweating and puffing with joy. This day shines as one of the best ever spent with our father.

4

WINDS OF WAR

One morning, after another night disrupted by sirens and sleep in the bomb-shelter, the doorbell rang. I slid off my chair to respond. The warm kitchen was filled with scent of beans and potatoes cooking. I could smell that there was a slice of bacon in the pot, adding flavor and spice. My mother wiped her wet and greasy hands on her apron, but I got ahead of her, skipping through the hallway. *That's my friend, Dieter, I thought, and today it's raining, so we'll play inside with his train and build mountains and bridges, which the train has to cross. And then we run the trains off the tracks and…*

I opened the door to find my grandparents standing in front of me, their shape fuzzy against a cloud-covered sky. They appear like ghosts. Grandmother's face is gray, carved out of granite, the lines on both sides of her mouth dark valleys and the light in her radiant eyes gone dim. Grandfather

Last night's
storm
ripped out its silvery
roots,
left them twisted
like tangled hair, a tortured
mane
unmoving in the wind.
—Pablo Neruda, from
Ode to a Dead Carob Tree.
University of California Press

is bent over his cane. The two beloved people are stranded like tangled driftwood at our doorstep. The tree behind them in the neighbor's garden twists and groans in the wind. *Ooogh* and *aaagh,* and *ooogh* and *ohhh!* A dog howls in distance: *Ooouu, aaauu,* and *ooouu.* I'm frozen, don't breathe.

A dull, leaden silence hovers around us.

I want to rush into my Grandmother's arms — but cannot move.

A dung beetle crawls slowly across the red rug. It falls off the edge and scrambles for a foothold, legs twisting in the air.

Grandma and grandpa both wear their nightgowns, hanging like dirty flags from poles. Ashen feet in house slippers, burnt at the edges. Dusty coats slip from their bent and sagging shoulders. The rims of their garments are singed and black.

My mother scuffles from the kitchen; she hurries to the door and stops. Her breath sounds like wailing wind. Grandmother and grandfather stumble forward into her arms, sobbing. They drag themselves to the kitchen. Mother warms tea and soup simmers on the fire. The three huddle and talk, their voices thin and rusty. I hide in a corner and listen but can't hear them. The wind of war sifts into our home. It wraps long, thin fingers around our ankles and pokes them into our rooms, beds and pots. Scratching through the skin they thrust icy fear into my body.

My grandparents had escaped their burning home and city, had climbed over smoldering corpses and stumbled down into the subway tunnels. They walked all through the night to arrive at our home outside town at dawn. They had left everything behind, and it was lost. They owned nothing but their worn-out bodies.

This morning, the swinging gate between the protected world of my childhood and the reality of war outside was pushed open and stayed agape. Until that day, the war had not seeped through the walls of our home. But now, it had broken the door.

How were my grandparents able to reach the subway opening

as they struggled through streets with houses burning on both sides, roasting people in the middle? How could they stumble along for miles, in dark tunnels? What about the other people with them? I imagined there were thousands? Years later, when I was a grown woman, I asked my grandmother many questions about her life, but never about their escape from the fire-bombed city.

Driftwood of War. Photograph by Shanti Elke Bannwart.

In eyewitness reports, I read later, that the heat of the firebombs melted the pavements and charred the fragile bodies of humans instantly as they panicked to escape the inferno. People shrank to the size of dogs, unrecognizable. Women and children got stuck in the molten and burning asphalt. At the height of the bombings, forty-two-thousand people were killed in this town during one night, mostly women and children.

Hans Erich Nossack describes in his book, *The End,* how groups of humans were huddled together against the heat, in the center of bomb shelters, and they all burned into one big clump of dead bodies.

The heat created its own climate; high winds blew through the burning town, ripping the clothes off victims and pulling them upwards into the air like fall leaves. It sucked the oxygen from shelters and suffocated those who were still breathing. The heat and storm raced through the streets and created a howling sound that had never been heard before: a wailing firestorm.

The attacks were well designed. The combined bomber planes of the Royal British Air Force and the US Air Force conducted Operation Gomorrah in July of 1943 based on the plans of British Marshall Arthur Harris, whom they called "Bomber Harris." The air raids over Hamburg took mostly civilian lives. The bombings were the first in human history to have such an excruciatingly devastating effect. It was later called the "Hiroshima of Germany." Harris boasted, "No air raid ever known before had been so terrible as that which Hamburg had endured. The second largest city in Germany, with a population of two million, had been wiped out in three nights." But in a post-war account, Harris stated that the area bombing of German cities was "comparatively humane."

The story of my grandparents' escape was one of those puzzles in my life that I did not dare touch or turn over when I was young. There are spoken and unspoken events in the books of families. This one was mysteriously never talked about again. I don't know why, but I believe that the horror was so immense that collective memories got erased by shock. Friedrich Reck describes in his *Tagebuch eines Verzweifelten* his encounters with survivors. *...the severely confused state of mind of these refugees from Hamburg...their amnesia, the way they wander around clad only in pajamas, just as they were when they fled from their collapsing homes.*

And W.G. Sebald assumes that *Obviously, in the shock of what these people had experienced, their ability to remember was partly suspended.* To avoid talking had become a way of survival, and not asking questions helped let the monsters sleep.

My grandparents moved in with us that morning. My mother and father gave up their bedroom and slept on the couch in the living room. My aunt Gretel, my mother's sister, joined us later and lived in the attic. With all the people I loved now surrounding me, I felt like a bird in a warm nest.

The women worked together to sustain us. They stole firewood and bartered food. My mother made two winter coats, for my sister and me, out of one army blanket. She made them look beautiful, with cuffs and collars in different hues of brown. She grew food in our garden and preserved it for the winter. My grandma bartered and carried heavy backpacks with food for miles. My aunt baked and cooked. And we children made *survival* one of our games.

In our family, the presence of war sat with us quietly at the dinner table like a ghost. Amidst the delight of potatoes with herring and green parsley hovered a gray shadow of avoidance. I got the message and I understood the unwritten rule that this ghost was to be ignored, but I sensed how the silence kept it alive. The ghost filled the pauses between our conversations and knotted dark meaning between glimpses of eyes. I assumed that, if one called horror by name, it would stand up, step forward and devour my mother and father, grandparents and aunt and uncle, and my sister and me. Ignorance was a shield and silence was protection.

My father was rarely at home and I didn't really miss him. That made me sad and filled me with shame for having such unloving thoughts. He was like a stranger to me. I longed for him and I feared him and that waged a war inside my own heart. I believed that a child was supposed to love her father; in this I failed.

Then there was my grandpa. He would sit every day on the left side of the kitchen table in front of the window and read the newspaper. He underlined every row with his pencil as he read, and that drove my dad crazy when he got the paper after him. My *Opa* didn't care for general rules in our home. He was an outsider, but for me he was a quiet center in our crowded space. He taught me how to play with poker cards in a game called "Sixty-Six" and I was so proud when I sat beside him and played like a grown-up. I thought that he was the only one who engaged me in something serious. All the others treated me like a small child, but I was five or almost six years old.

Grandma prepared her wonderful meals now in our home. Every Friday the fish man rang his cracked bell when he stopped his horse-drawn wagon at the corner of *Volksdorferdamm* and *Grenzweg*. As if the pied-piper had played his flute, the women hurried outdoors, shawls slung around their hair and bags in their hands. They gathered in a long line, gossiping and shouting, eager to buy whatever fresh fish had come in this night from the North Sea. The usual catch was herring or flounder. The fish was stacked on ice in the back of an open carriage and the fish-man would grab the ones the women pointed to. He'd throw them on a scale and wrap them in old newspaper. Beside all the scarcity around us, the fish man was the only reliable source of food.

It smelled sour, like a muddy pond, around this carriage.

"Look," I whispered to grandmother, "he has eels today. They look like snakes and maybe they're still alive." They made me shiver with disgust. But my *Oma* delighted in smoked eel. She peeled the white meat out of the greasy, brown skin and ate it with her fingers. She rolled her eyes with pleasure as she swallowed. I stood in front of her and giggled, trying to roll my eyes, too.

Friday was the day when my grandma made her famous potato-salad with golden baked flounder or herring. Friday was better than Sunday. Flounders on Friday set a weekly marker that made life seem dependable and safe.

We were now seven people living at home and all of us had to share one small bathroom with one sink and a bathtub. My sister and I noticed that my grandfather used it every morning for half an hour, all by himself. That seemed acceptable by everybody, because he had an air of royalty to his demeanor and was allowed special ways of being in our crammed-full home. Helga and I heard the rumor that grandfather bathed in cold water, even in winter. He believed in the purifying effect of the bath, and the added torture of the cold was a sign of courage and health. Germans believe in such things: 'What does not kill you, makes you stronger,' he quoted and grinned.

Sometimes I huddled in the corner near the door and listened during his mysterious and secretive baths. I rarely saw my grandfather without his shirt, tie and suit and to imagine him naked was embarrassing. He never exposed his right leg without pants covering the distorted knee. He was a proud man. The sounds in the bathroom unfolded like an immutable piece of music. He had the habit, I concluded, of splashing the water around, scooping it with his hands and throwing it against his body. I heard those splashing, spattering, spraying sounds and I imagined the shape of his body as the only firm object in the middle of all the moving water that he kept flying through the air, against the outline of a naked grandfather-body, like a rock in the river. Every so often, the water sounds were punctuated by a faint squeak or scratch that came from shifting knees or haunches. I knew the sounds because my sister and I usually shared the bathtub during our once-a-week Saturday bath, when we wrangled and fought and had a lot of fun. But my grandpa was silent, as if he was not physically in the room—only the gurgling water told a tale. *What if he was secretly a fish or sea lion,* I imagined, *and once a day, in the bathtub, he returned home into his natural element?*

At the end there was the 'pop!' when he opened the drain and then one could hear the gurgling sound of water as it left the tub. It climbed up the scale until the song ended with a high-pitched whistling sigh. A bit later, grandfather would appear, clean and shaven and in his usual shirt and tie. I walked out to tell my friend Dieter, thinking about the adults and how they had so many things going on behind closed doors, that left much to my imagination.

The following year my uncle Albin joined Grandfather with special bathroom privileges. Uncle Albin was the husband of my mother's sister, our aunt Margarete. They got married during his short home-leave from the front. We celebrated the wedding on a Sunday and then he was gone Monday morning, back to the war, wearing his uniform and boots. Shortly after, he came home from the front with a fresh wound—a bullet had entered his stomach in the front of his body and left through his back. He had two holes and, in the middle, the colon was punctured. It had been sewn together by a doctor who was greatly in a hurry, because, so said uncle Albin, the roof of the hospital was already burning during the surgery. The colon had not healed right and worked very slowly, 'like a garden hose with a sharp bend in it,' said uncle Albin. He needed almost an hour to finish his business in the bathroom. He read the daily paper sitting on the toilet, and everybody respected that he was not to be disturbed. For the grown-ups, the bathroom seemed to be the only place for some privacy.

My aunt told me in later years that she abhorred the wounds and could never get used to the damage to his body. 'The man who came home from the war was damaged. He was different from the healthy one who left after the wedding,' she sighed and distorted her face.

Uncle Albin was funny and made us laugh. He even made jokes about things that we children didn't dare to talk about, like the stories about the man who hid in the forest and appeared naked in front of women to scare them. We all called him *"Naktsteher,"* the-man-who-stands-up-naked. Uncle Albin decided to scare him back. He put on lipstick and my mother's coat and hat, pretending to be a woman. He wanted to catch the man and beat him up, so he would not come back. We had a lot of fun watching my uncle stagger away on high heels, and we were all disappointed when the man didn't show up to get his beating. This was another story without a satisfying ending.

In this extended family, my grandfather was the oldest and I was the youngest. My grandfather lived at the fringes of our daily life with a quiet presence. He ate his meals without talking, and went for long solitary strolls with his walking stick, his hat pulled deep across his forehead. He was given the privilege of age and rarely participated in any of the women's endeavors to keep all of us fed and alive. But sometimes, my Grandpa would say, 'Elke, put your boots on and let's go out into the forest to collect wild mushrooms.' He took his stick and a basket and I grabbed a short knife from the kitchen drawer. I knew where we were heading and followed him on the slim trail towards the nearby forest. I watched him closely and noticed that his coat hung down on the right side, where the shorter leg collapsed his body. The fabric was thin and fragile. Walking behind him, I imitated the rolling rhythm of his gait to try on his personality. He leaned on his walking stick towards the right side, supporting his crippled leg. Then he pushed himself to the opposite side to take the weight off and he grew a bit taller. Then he swung back to the right onto the stick and the bent leg, shrinking a bit. He proceeded in that rolling movement, like waves in the ocean as they hit shore and receded again. If he was in a good mood, he swung the tip of the stick high up like the conductor of a band, before he'd set it down. That needed skill and balance and looked like a mysterious dance. I observed him and swayed in the same rhythm as I followed his steps.

I felt very competent hunting mushrooms. My grandpa said I had 'mushroom-eyes' because I sensed their hiding places and observed the small indications of their presence. I spotted the places where they pushed their slithery heads through the wet and fertile ground. The brown mushrooms gently lifted the grass that grew as a dense carpet in those northern forests. The thrust from underneath created bumps on top that looked like the backs of small turtles.

When I discovered those bumps, I knelt beside them and cautiously moved the grass aside until the round, shiny brown head of the mushroom would appear. Sometimes the streaky pattern of the grass was imprinted in the glistening skin of their tops. The mushrooms liked to huddle in families, like people, and I would usually find clusters of them. I talked to them gently as I cut only three or four at once. I took only the biggest ones, because the small mushrooms were not grown up enough to die. I left the little white stumps of their feet in the ground so that new ones would emerge from them.

My grandpa carried a round basket and I would put the fat, crunchy mushrooms inside it, stacking them like shingles on a roof to leave their pretty faces unharmed. My grandpa watched me and held the basket patiently, and there were soft lines around his stern eyes.

When we walked home, we carried the full basket together. I matched the rhythm of my steps to those of my grandpa. *He is here with me,* I thought, *because his home is destroyed and burned down. We need each other in this family. I have my grandpa close, because the war has made him homeless. That's a story with a bad and a good ending.* Leaning my head back, I looked up into the arch of the tree branches and sensed how the giants observed us two small people from above. Then I turned my gaze towards grandpa and thought that he himself was like a crooked tree that was hit by lightning and had lost all its leaves.

My sister and I were on our way home from *Bergsted,* a little village about two miles away. We scurried along the bramble bushes and blackberries that lined the wheat fields. The tart fruits made our tongues and teeth blue. We talked about the angels in the church and the farmer's pigs and the weeping birches beside the graves in the cemetery. Time trickled slowly, and things were touched by the warm, soft hands of summer. But suddenly, the first warplane came into sight and everything changed. The plane flew very close to the road, heading towards us with screeching engines and terrifying speed.

But. Long ago. Before that attack, my sister and I had spent a leisurely afternoon visiting farmers' houses and watching the cows in their barns. They had dirt on their behinds and smeared it with their tails into big black blotches. Green flies buzzed around them and tickled my skin when they landed on my arms. Pigs dug their snouts into kitchen debris of carrots, potato peels and salad leaves. Ducks and geese wobbled along the paths and made scary noises when we leaned against their fence. They stretched their long necks and hard beaks towards us, and we stepped back to be out of reach. Their big feet, flat like pancakes, made funny sucking sounds in the mud.

Village Church. Photograph by Shanti Elke Bannwart.

"Look, Helga, how awkwardly they walk. They lean from the one side to the other, and just when you think they'd topple over they swing back to the other side, like our grandfather."

"I think you shouldn't say that," Helga responded.

"Look, there's the big bull with red eyes," I said. "I'm glad he's locked behind a barbwire fence, because he's really dangerous. I'm not afraid of cows, but of him."

"Yes, I remember when we couldn't go home after school," she said, "because he had escaped from the fields and blocked our way. We kids stopped, all clumped together, and we were afraid."

"Oh, yes, that was the time when a man had hanged himself in the forest and you said that you saw his feet in the air in between branches. I didn't want to walk that way ever again," I said and thought that I had never seen a dead person, only the beached dolphin at *Timmerndorfer Strand*. He had green foam come out of his eyes and mouth when I poked into the openings with a stick. We kids whispered about the hanged man for long time, making up stories about him and fantasizing why the man didn't want to live any more and why he would kill himself along the path where people walked home from the subway. Did he want to scare them on purpose?

Helga and I ambled around, stopped by the pond with the tadpoles and finally arrived at the village church. The heavy door opened with a sigh. It was cool and quiet inside. A fly rattled around in erratic patterns and hit the glass of the windows. The wooden benches were painted in a light-blue, like the sky, and there were statues of Jesus and angels.

"This angel has two fingers broken off." I pointed. "Dieter says that he might have stolen something and God punished him by cutting off the fingers. That's what people do here on earth, too."

Jesus was nailed against a wooden cross and had always the same expression on his face. I thought he might get tired of hanging there, but he looked calm, his eyes rolled upwards, blood dripped from his hands. On each side of Jesus was a vase with blue cornflowers and white marguerites; they covered the surrounding fields during the summer, mirroring the sky on the ground.

On our way home we came by the cemetery at the end of the village. It was a very old one, and the trees stood high with branches reaching far into the space where the swallows flew swiftly. Stone plates and statues marked the graves. Some figures were neatly chiseled, like the angel with lilies in her hands and stars braided into her hair. I touched her and followed the contours of her face with my fingers. The stone, warm from the sun, was like a living body.

"I think it is beautiful here, Helga. When I'm dead I want to be buried in such a park, too. Our *Oma* already has a space reserved in this cemetery. She has ordered a stonemason to carve and place a bench, so we can sit and rest when we visit the people in our family's grave. And she bought a white headstone, were one would carve the names of those who would sleep here forever."

I did not understand what 'forever' meant, but assumed it was a very long time, if one needed stone benches and angels with stars. My grandma had planted a weeping birch tree on each side of the little square of earth. *How would we all fit in there? It might just be as crowded in the gravesite as in our small flat*, I thought, and enjoyed imagining the cuddly closeness. Helga and I sat on the bench and watched the long branches of the birch trees sway in the wind. Tiny birds rested on their thin arms. Those two trees were as young as we were. We didn't know, as we sat there during that morning, that the first name carved into this sandstone would be our mother's.

"Let's go home. I am hungry," said my sister, and I followed her quietly as we ambled along the fields. Suddenly we heard the roaring of an approaching plane and stopped in the middle of the road. Fear yanked our heads around. A small fighter-plane raced toward us. Appearing from nowhere in bright daylight, it followed the curves of the road.

Gunshots explode from its belly, smacking around us into the asphalt of the street.

We freeze for a second and then, with one big leap, we throw ourselves into the wild plum bushes. Thorns pierce my arms and face. I clutch Helga's hand. Panic makes her eyes bulge as if they would pop.

A second airplane follows the first one immediately. It flies close to the ground. I catch sight of the head of the man sitting inside the round glass at the top. He wears a brown leather cap. And glasses. Fish-eyed. The bullets bang into the ground and ricochet into the fields, like grasshoppers, dirt explodes into the air.

Am I dead, am I dead already? Mama, am I dead? Mama, I want to live for you. Mama, not now, not that! Mama, my heart bangs inside like men's boots on stairs in the night. Mama, I can see only one eye of Helga, it is planted in the dirt, between the bushes with thorns that press into her skin. A snake of blood crawls along my arm and drips into the earth. Mama, you are as far as the clouds, everything shatters into pieces.

Stones fall apart and die. I am a stone. And I am dead.

"Helga, Elke, Helga, Elke!" My mother's voice pierces and shoots into my head, an arrow in the skull. I pull my limbs from the thorns and my sister's head from the ground. We scramble out of the bushes and run towards our mother. Her hair tangles around her face. She moves swiftly, as though on skates. The apron around her neck twists in the wind, left and right, like broken wings. She flies towards us.

"Mama!" we scream, the sound squeezes through our throats. It screeches like the squeaking of the pigs we had heard today, so long ago, in a different time.

"Mutti!" We race and stumble into her arms. She holds us tight. We kneel and we sob, all three of us, our faces pale, tears mingling, sticky blood and dirt. My heart skips inside, *it's so close to the surface, just under the skin, anything can pierce and destroy it. Every being with a skin can break.*

We sit on the ground, a triangle of arms and heads and hair. *I wish my father were here. I taste terror on my tongue, it is bitter, rusty, and it hurts like barbwire in my mouth and nails in my flesh.*

Later, my grandfather told us, that those small planes were called "Mosquitoes," fast day-bombers used to scout the city with photoreconnaissance. They were swift and manned only by one pilot, like the one I saw in the cockpit. What made him pull the trigger and shoot at two children walking home from the village?

Every person has a river or landscape and familiar weather that belong to their childhood. My river was the wide and majestic Elbe. Like a turtle, slow and old with wrinkles at its edges, its brackish banks resembled ancient skin. It changed shape with the tides that pressed the water upwards from the North Sea towards Hamburg or pulled it back into its wide expanse. The river seemed to flow in two directions, depending on time and tides. Rain-heavy clouds lined its path and raked the fields and skies with soft giant's fingers.

In the north of Hamburg, where the town thinned out and fields wove in between villages and suburbs, the river provided pleasure; children played and splashed in the water and lovers rowed their boats along the tree-covered embankments. Gulls flew with the currents and snatched fish during flight. Ducks raised their babies and taught them to rip and eat the fine green stems of plants just underneath the surface. Blue dragonflies paired up in twos and flew in tandem to find a place for their eggs.

But in the heart of town, the river was serious and hardworking. It sustained the enormous harbor. Day and night the cranes moved with long giraffe-necks and gutted out the wares from the hollow bodies of the ships. They moved up and down and to the sides or all around. They lifted bulging containers and boxes from trains to ships and from trucks to flat-beds. Metal chains clanked and blinked in the glare of floodlights. During daylight workmen with rough hands in orange overalls waved and yelled, shouting orders into chaos.

The more elegant parts of the harbor was called *Lombards-Brücken* and served to board people. It was a place where big oceangoing ships left to reach foreign places. Those destinations lay at the edges of mysterious countries along the oceans of the world. The ships were so tall that I had to lean my head back to see the railings where the passengers crowded together and waved to their loved ones down on the pier; that's where I stood, too, holding my grandmother's hand.

Strong sailors in blue uniforms with white caps over one ear would untie the ropes from their moorings, ropes as big as my arm. And then the ship's engines would roar and spit foaming water against the walls of the harbor. The behemoths moved slowly away and increased speed. They would toot their horns by blowing steam through a whistle like a dragon out of his nostrils. The ground on which we stood trembled from all the stirred up water. *What a mighty captain,* I thought, *who could tame such a majestic machine!*

The passengers had lined up high above us at the railings. They appeared small, like heads of matches. They stretched their arms and waved with handkerchiefs and the people beside me on the quay waved back and wiped their tears. Some sobbed and their bodies trembled and they held on to each other, others remained quiet and pale. *Ships seemed always to be departing without the promise of return. Water was so wobbly, and one does not know if one can trust it.*

"Where are those people going?" I asked my grandmother "And why are they crying?"

Grandmother had those dark lines beside her mouth, "They go to countries on the other side of the world," She said, "Very far away. And people here are crying because they don't know if they will ever see each other again." I observed the sorrow in their faces and thought that something forced them to go, something more devastating than the loss of their home and family.

When the wagons were loaded and the bundles secured,
the small children jumped up and down with delight,
thinking that this thing called exile would be a great adventure.
—Micheline Aharonian Marcom, *Three Apples Fell From Heaven*

In July of 1944, the air raids intensified and rolled across the town day and night. The RAF from England bombed during the day and the USAF continued in the night. There was an order issued by the Hamburg

City Authority, urging the people who had survived the ravaging fires to leave their homes immediately and find shelter outside the boundaries of town to avoid the deadly attacks. We lived at the fringes of Hamburg but we, too, were in danger and were ordered to evacuate. One day a black, dust-covered truck stopped in front of our house and we were told to pack and get in. I don't remember a discussion about this move but all of us were ready to leave. The truck in front of our house was originally meant for baking goods. It was as high as my bedroom, closed all around with no windows, but it had two big doors in the back to load and unload. I held my doll Susan in my arm after I had gathered her belongings into her tiny blue suitcase: a sweater and socks and a little pair of pants and the small brush because I loved to braid her hair and fix ribbons and flowers in it, like my mother did with mine. I didn't care for other things and was unconcerned about leaving the house. I thought we were going for an outing in the country.

When we climbed into the truck, it was already packed with people. We squeezed in between them. Two young men lifted my grandfather up. They handed him his cane and he looked like a shepherd in the crowd. He was very uncomfortable as he sat down on the floor in his suit, his crooked leg poking into somebody else's back. I cuddled into my mother's lap, my doll Susan in my arms, and watched how the men tied a wire around the handles of the two back doors and left a gap that allowed air and some light to blend with the dark. My sister leaned on my grandmother. We drove for a long time through an unfamiliar landscape that was partly visible through the crack between the doors. We entered and left strange villages, fields and forests. *As long as we are all together in our family, nothing could be too bad*, I thought. The travelers in our truck were quiet, their faces covered with a thin gray veil of shadows.

The truck stopped. The two men unwound the wire from the door and light flooded in. The children and my grandfather were lifted out and set on the ground. We stood in front of a farmhouse. Chickens walked around with dirt-crusted legs and picked here and there, ignoring our presence. Cows mooed and two Shepherd dogs came running, kicking up the pebbles behind them. They barked and tried to bite our calves, spit dripped out between their yellow teeth. My mom put our suitcase as barrier against the dogs to protect us from their fury.

Our group of strangers stood silently when the truck left with the others to drive to a different farmhouse. We waited motionless like a pile of wet leaves, randomly raked together in fall. Any wind could blow us apart across the muddy road and swish us into ditches.

Our family got one room for all of us. There were my *Oma* and *Opa* in the corner bed, my aunt Margarete on a couch and my mom with Helga and me in another bed that screeched when we sat down. We disturbed the lives of the farmers and intruded into the web of their days. We were strangers to them and they had no choice to accept us in their home or not. This war changed all the rules of everyday life and everybody pretended that it was normal. All the pretending seemed like a thin thread that held things together, but it could break at any moment.

Helga and I tried to be as invisible as possible. We sneaked through a backdoor into the barn to watch the farmhand milk the cows. He pulled with his hairy fingers on those long pink tits and the milk made "swoosh" as it hit the inside of the metal can. "Swoosh!" When he was done he turned around and grabbed a metal cup, dipped it into the milk and handed it to Helga and me. We felt in our palms how the body warmth of the cow was still stored in this magical, thick fluid. Too shy to drink it in front of him, we hunkered down in the straw and slurped without a word. I blushed when I brought the cup back to the man. He had a fierce face, closed like the barn door, but through the cracks I could see the light inside.

The toilet was an outhouse in some distance to the main building. It leaned to one side against an old truck without engine. Blackberries and stinging nettles grew through its window frames. I was so afraid of falling into the dark hole, where one put one's behind that I never went there without Helga. We held on to each other's hands as we bent forward to keep balance above the opening that was big enough for children to fall through. Swarms of iridescent green flies hummed inside the hole and crawled over all the private parts of my body. We would find them everywhere. They came with the war, an invasion of a new breed of hostile insects. Some people told us that the green flies lived and multiplied in the flesh of corpses that decayed in barricaded cellars and under piles of rubble in town.

I remember the time we spent in this farmhouse as if it were a bleached out black-and-white photograph. We hid there for weeks, or months, or longer? Nothing was sharp and clear, only one single night's memory stood out like a gigantic nightmare.

After a hot day, thunderclouds had gathered all afternoon above Hamburg and the country around us. Darkness fell and we closed the curtains as usual, not only to follow the order of blackout but also because of the storm that rolled in above us. Lightning bolts smashed down so close that one could feel the electricity like a gush of wind hitting the body.

The bursts of thunder and lightning increased with ferocity. Everybody in the house gathered, huddling in groups in the living room. Like animals, we sought each other's closeness. *This is bigger than my mother's power and my grandmother's protection,* I feared. *The whole sky is angry, the stars tumble down and the wind has claws and bangs his fists against the walls.*

The den was crowded with people, their eyes staring or half closed. Nobody speaks. Only one candle quivers and spreads a faint light like a fragile circle. The surrounding walls retreat into darkness.

Thunder and lightning blast through every opening in the house. I grab my sister's hand: "Come and sit with me, Helga. I am afraid. Is this how the world ends?"

I crouch on the floor beside my sister near the candle that lights one corner of the sofa. This corner is a buoy that sticks out of the stormy sea of darkness. The lightning bolts and thunders now follow each other so rapidly that there is no break in between them; the clashes happen at the same time as the flash. Furious flares hit the windows and roll over us in waves. The house seems to burn. Nobody talks. Sweat and fear stick to our clustered bodies like an oily blanket.

The flashes and explosions punch into my brain. My mind walks towards the candle and into the fire and leaves my body behind like an empty shell. Terror tastes like ashes inside my mouth, dry and bitter and poisonous.

And then, suddenly, silence. The thunderstorm skids away, rumbling and mumbling.

Some days later, I sat in the farmer's kitchen when a man walked through the open door. He wore a gray felt hat pulled deep into his forehead. A curved pipe stuck in one corner of his mouth and made his face look crooked; the pipe wiggled when he spoke and his steady grin showed teeth with black stains. He sat down, put his elbows on the table and then he talked to the farmer's wife and to the assembled refugees about the events of that night during the thunderstorm.

"That's what happened," he said and paused, "the Allied Forces had planned to do the city in. They tried to blast a last and total death stroke at Hamburg" he scratched his forehead. "They'd loaded their warplanes with fire-bombs up to the gills. The English, the *Tommies,* flew over the Canal like a huge flock of vulture birds." It was very quiet in the kitchen. "When they came close to Hamburg, the planes were headed directly into the middle of the thunderstorm. That storm! " He scratched again, "I've never seen some *godverdammten* storm like that, as long as I've lived. My God, that was like being in hell, in living hell!

"The *Tommies* flew directly into that hell. And they got their pants full of fear, real shit fear. They must've thought God Almighty himself was throwing those bolts of lightning. Or maybe the devil, ha, ha! Yes, the devil" he roared. "The *Tommies* got the order to drop the bombs before they reached Hamburg, and forget about bombing the city. They'd rather turn around right then and save their asses."

He sucked on his pipe and shifted the old hat to the back, grinning and bearing his teeth, delighted about the attention he got.

"So, and that's what they did, saving their asses and our city. Or whatever's left of it and that's not very much anyway."

Everybody in the kitchen took a deep breath; water dripped from the fosset. I stepped outside to sit underneath the Linden tree at the corner of the field. *Things are not what they appear to be*, I thought. *The horrifying thunder and lightning had not damaged us, but they actually saved our lives.*

The next week the air raids slowed down and we were allowed to go back home.

The night of the thunderstorm was so much like a dream that I thought sometimes it had been just that. But my sister, too, remembered it with horror and confirmed it to me. In later years I found a report by David Lippman in a World War II Magazine, published in July 1998, that described the event: *The last Hamburg strike was August 2, 1943, with seven-hundred-thirty-seven bombers that ran smack into a massive thunderstorm, the worst many pilots had ever encountered. Four hundred bombers plowed through lightning to hit the city, but there was no order in the attack. Bombs rained down on all kind of different areas, damaging a vegetable oil factory and the opera house. The auditorium was burned out, but the stage, loaded with bread, was undamaged. The RAF lost thirty-three bombers.*

5

FOOD AND FIRE

In our world there was no balance. We yielded to necessities, and our day-to-day life was ruled by the basic needs of our bodies. But the women knew how to soften the bite of hunger by weaving it into the warm web of bonding in the kitchen. They created delight out of raw stuff that we had to pull from the earth. And I embroidered with my childhood fantasies the efforts that were related to survival and hunger. Especially hunger. It was a living companion, familiar and almost friendly, balancing the pain of need with the joy of satiation. And somehow, the satisfaction of eating was even sweeter if the hunger was strong, like a lover who longs to be filled with the presence of the beloved and delights in ravenous yearning. Satiation melted into stark want, like honey into bitter medicine. Pain clasped to pleasure like brother to sister.

Struggle for life, indeed!
The curse of battle and toil
leads man back to the boar,
to the grunting beast's
crazy obsession with
the search for food.
—Vladimir Nabokov,
Speak Memory.

Helga appeared in the frame of the bedroom door, wearing boots and a raincoat. Her brown hair was stuffed under a hand-knit cap. How thin Helga is, I thought and forgot that I, too, had edgy elbows and sharp corners around my shoulder blades.

"Elke, hurry up! Take this bag and help me find potatoes. Put your old shoes on; it's muddy in the field. The farmers have just finished and left, our neighbors are already digging to gather what's left."

We children were assigned very specific tasks to help with the food supply. Scanning a harvested field was one of those. I liked it, because it combined hunt and play with something useful. Our household was built on a hierarchy of significant activities. Sleeping, eating, cooking and cutting wood for warmth stood in the first line. Meeting friends, playing and dreaming or talking to trees and animals were second or third.

Just across the street from our red brick home was a large potato field. I walked behind my sister and held the dusty bag slung over my shoulder. Hunting potatoes required skill. I ruminated that only the smart potatoes had not been found by the farmers, because they knew how to play hide-and-seek and how to be quiet without wiggling. Familiar with their tricks, I would discover them anyway. In the end, I believed, the potatoes wanted to be found and eaten instead of rotting in the field during wintertime. They used the sunlight to grow fat and so to be enjoyed, to be cooked, looked-at and craved. How exciting for potatoes to posture and show their bellies, steaming in a bowl in the middle of a table, with hungry people all around, staring. How rewarding it must be to feed people and make them feel happy and satiated. All that thinking about their habits befriended me with them.

I hung my bag at a stick and dug the ground with a shovel.

"Look, I found a big one with dirt and roots on it. It looks like a rat. That's why they didn't see it. It's half a pound and *Mutti* can make a whole meal out of it. Look, when I scratch the dirt off I see its beady eyes."

"It looks frightening!" said Helga. "And we need more than one fat one. I'm already hungry."

We trailed along the dug up rows of potatoes. The discarded green leaves, still lying on the ground, would later be raked into a pile and burned. When the days grew shorter and the smoke from the fields would hang like sheets of silk above the land, we would jump across the potato fire and show our courage. That followed an old custom to celebrate harvest time. It was one of the rare evenings when Helga and I were allowed to stay up late and into the dark of the night. We would watch how the embers from the fire flew high above the heads of people. The sparks painted erratic zigzag patterns and died in the dark, as though the black of the night had eaten them. The silhouettes of the boys who jumped across the fire looked like cutout figures from our fairy tale book. Fire was uncanny; one never knew if it were friendly or fierce. When I was older and had longer legs, I would jump across the flames, too. To be able to jump across fire meant that one was almost grown-up.

Other children had already cleared most of the leftover potatoes. I poked the heel of my boot deeply into the earth and felt resistance. Pushing my bare hands gently into the hole I found the mud-crusted ball. The skin, wounded by a spade, exposed the inner body of the potato as if it were naked underneath.

"Look, Helga, how is it possible that the plant can make yellow-white potato flesh out of this dark and mushy earth? How can a plant change dark into yellow and make a potato out of dirt?"

I remembered that my mother once talked about "the banana," and what a beautiful name that was, with three long and delicious a-vowels. "Banana," I had whispered slowly, and asked my mother what that meant. She had explained to me that it was an exotic fruit. One couldn't get it now, during the war, because bananas did not grow in Germany. They needed a lot of sun. "How do they taste?" I had asked, and my mother tried to describe the taste of a banana.

'Sweet and soft and creamy,' she had said, and I realized that a taste could not be imagined; it had to be felt inside the mouth and throat. One could say "green" or "red" and another would understand and get it almost right, but "banana" was just a name, and not a sensation, not the real thing.

Many years later, when the American occupiers imported bananas, I ate my first banana and it was so very different from what I had imagined. And the most stunning discovery was how golden-yellow they were, like peaches without the red. I was surprised that my mother didn't say 'yellow,' although the color was the most important characteristic of the banana.

The light of the day began to hide behind the trees at the edge of the field. I poked my little shovel into the sticky mud and the ground exuded a sweet and heavy smell, like cinnamon and chamomile tea. The body of the earth smelled like the body of a woman, and I imagined the earth being a big mother, and the potatoes being her children.

My knees sank into the dirt. The rain dripped off my eyebrows and ran down to my chin. "Look, Helga. Here's the entrance to a mouse nest. Shall I dig them out?"

"No! Dig potatoes and not mice," Helga mumbled. She was bent over the bag and sounded tired. I observed my sister's profile and how the rain had plastered her hair to the skin of her forehead. It might be hard for my sister, I thought, to always be the older one. She was so serious. I, for myself, turned everything into play, but Helga was already too old for that. *When would I be too grown-up to enjoy playing and talking to mice and potatoes? Does one decide when to stop being a child or does it all happen by itself?* I scooted nearer to her and held the rough bag open. With the other hand, I slowly moved across my sister's forehead so that the hair would not cover her eyes. My finger left a streak of dirt on her white skin. When darkness was too thick we carried the heavy bag home, each holding on to one corner. We were very quiet.

"There's a house burning in *Bergstedt!* I saw it from Marianne's window!"

My sister and her friend came running towards Dieter and me. They were hot and out of breath, panting.

"The whole roof is in flames," she stuttered, " and the smoke is sky-high and, and, and one fire police car was already there and another one is rushing in from *Volksdorf*, people said, and there was a wedding and the thatched roof caught fire, Marianne's aunt had called Marianne's family, she lives near the burning house, and she was upset and she cried on the phone."

Helga turned around, grasped Marianne's hand and scampered towards the village, moving so fast that her socks slid down. The two girls didn't wait for us.

I had been playing with Dieter in the sandbox in front of the kitchen window. Hidden between bushes of raspberries and blackberries, the sandbox was safe and secretive. Small handfuls of sand carried all kind of possibilities, like roads, rivers and steep hills, from where the trucks could roll down by themselves, especially when we loaded them with pebbles or green pears that had fallen off the tree. Sometimes Dieter's truck and my truck would crash into each other and then we had to play police and untangle them and scold the drivers, 'You fool, watch out, you're stupid.' I had just pretended to be the police officer and enjoyed yelling at the driver; now I looked at Dieter and he nodded. We dropped everything, tied our shoes, grabbed each other's hands and ran.

Other people hurried in the same direction. I recognized neighbors, friends and strangers. The smoke of the burning house rose high between the big trees of the village. It waved like a flag and indicated the direction.

A big crowd had gathered in a circle around the burning house. The thatched roof was violently devoured by flames. It looked as if a yellow and red beast lay on top of the house, and it roared. We stood in silence, watching how this beast destroyed a family's home. The heat heaved sparks and burning pieces off the roof and threw them upward into the summer sky. Smoke hovered like a heavy helmet above the entire village.

I had never seen a ravaging fire so close up and was bewildered by the power and force that was eating straw, iron and wood. The beauty of the flames contrasted with the horror of destruction. *Was it the same fire that destroyed my grandparent's house? Did fire have one big body that was torn into parts and scattered all over the country? Did it always need to eat more and more houses to stay alive?*

People ran in and out of the home to rescue whatever they could grab. A woman carried a birdcage and a flowering plant. A man threw burning pillows into the grass and the feathers spewed out in every direction like an exploding swan. Another man ran back and forth without anything in his hands, as if it were impossible to stand still. People scurried erratically. Something had to be done, whatever it might be, to keep hope alive. The circle of onlookers around the fire formed a sturdy dam with their bodies. It held the chaos inside like a container, so that it would not rip into everybody's heart and mind.

I squeezed Dieter's hand so tightly that my sweaty fingers cramped. How vulnerable people were in their soft, fleshy bodies. I feared for them as I watched the people hurry into the hellish yellow and orange heat, carrying out random items as if the objects were living beings. The fire now burst the glass of the windows. The roaring flames stumbled around, a giant with burning feet and hair.

"There was a wedding in this house," said a woman.

"They were just cooking and eating and enjoying themselves, when sparks from the kitchen fire hit the reeds on the roof."

I remembered a wedding in the old village church nearby. The bride wore a white princess gown. She had curly blond hair and white and yellow roses fixed at each side of her head, held together by a crown made out of lace. Now, I imagined such a bride running in and out of this burning house and how her white dress would turn dirty and how the bride herself might catch fire and burn her dress and her veil and her curly hair and the roses in it. In fairy tales, all the problems get solved at the end when the bride and groom get married. But here, in life, the problems had just started.

Suddenly I felt the two hands of my mother on both of my shoulders. My frantic mind calmed down, my feet felt again the ground where I stood. After several hours, the fire police succeeded in squelching all the grasping fingers of flames. The onlookers turned around and went back home, thoughtful and without talking. Gray and black smoke still billowed into the blue afternoon sky.

I had trouble sleeping that night. For years now I had been surrounded by war and fire, but nothing had carved the power of destruction deeper into my awareness than the reality of my senses: seeing, feeling, smelling and sweating in the heat at the moment when fire recklessly devoured a home. It was impossible for me to call it 'bad'; the raging fire was just living out its own nature. I was surprised that I didn't hate it, but felt awe and admiration. Fire was like air or water or earth; it had a character and spirit. There was joy in its dance, a joy that stood in contrast to its greedy destruction and hunger for things. It naturally needed and demanded food to stay alive, like we humans did.

The next day Dieter and I walked back to *Bergstedt* and visited the burned house. Feathery smoke eddies still emerged from the straw roof. Blackened rafters stuck through the holes. They reminded me of the rotting corpse of a dead horse that I had seen last winter at the edge of the wheat field. I had explored it with disgust and curiosity, and I peeked inside the ribcage and into the hollow dark space where once the heart had lived.

When my parents created the garden, they had planted a young apple tree that had three branches. In spring there were white blossoms sitting on them, resembling clusters of butterflies between the green leaves. It was full of humming bees; and then, the wind blew the blossoms away and left small green knots. After some weeks, the knots swelled, and I discovered that they were the buds from which the fruit would grow. Everything already looked like an apple, just very tiny. All during summer, the apple buds grew, but many fell down on the ground, green and hard as if they had given up hope of reaching adulthood. I felt a bit sad and disappointed about them. Why would they not hold onto the mother tree? Why would anybody choose to die when they had such a good chance of growing big and beautiful and bursting with sweetness?

In fall the tree had lost all but three of its fruit. They held the promise of summer in their bellies: sun and rain and bird song, and the northern wind that bent the youthful tree and made the leaves quiver. I watched the apples turn from green to yellow to orange and saw them grow fat like giant marbles. At that time it was rare that we saw apples in the store, there were only turnips and carrots in the wooden crates. In the evening my mother read the story of Snow White to me and I was furious that the queen would use an apple to poison her stepdaughter. The queen's treacherous apple was a lie, its beauty misused for crime.

"Can we finally pick one apple today, Mom? It's the first real apple from our garden and it's so hard to wait any longer." Mother looked out the kitchen window towards the small tree. In the kitchen she was always busy with something, but when she let her gaze caress the green, red and purple colors of the garden, her hands rested and her eyes smiled. I thought that she was really one of the flowers or trees.

"Not yet, Elke. They are still growing. Let's give them two more days to get their cheeks red."

The next morning I hurried into the garden to check out the growth of the peas and to see if anything new had poked through the ground into the light of day. The peas stood tall and laced the sky above me with green light and shade. I picked them from the vines, knowing how to pop and peel them with swift fingers out of their tight shell that resembled a fat caterpillar. Then I wandered and stopped in front of the tree. The coveted apples had disappeared. A thief had stolen all three apples during the night!

"*Mutti*, Helga, come and see!"

All three apples are gone!" I cried and touched the little knots on the branches where the apples had been yesterday. They were wet and sticky, like the scratch at a bloody knee, and gooey drops oozed out of them.

I turned slowly around and observed the neighbor's houses. The curtains on the windows were closed. There was a thief living among us. I cringed and felt anger and fear. When I left the garden, I twisted the tight and rusty lock into the metal noose. It had never been used before.

We didn't start fires in the central heating system in our apartment because we had no fuel for it. During this time of war, in 1944, there was no delivery of firewood or coal, and every family had to take care of themselves. There was only the tiny one-plate cooker that was placed on top of the oven in the kitchen. It gave warmth and served to prepare food or keep the water kettle hot to brew tea and cup one's cold hands around. My mother cherished this stove and gave it the name *die Hexe,* the witch. The kitchen was the only room that was cozy and warm. Our home at *Voldsdorferdamm* had a living room with French doors to the terrace and two separate bedrooms. Those parts of the home were cold in winter and one had to put socks and sweaters on to stay warm. During summer, the whole apartment would be used, and all the doors and windows stayed open. We had to watch out for our canary bird that flew around freely in our flat and it managed to escape several times. Once it escaped and reached the pear tree in a neighbor's yard. Mother and I carried a long ladder all the way to that yard and then she climbed into the tree with the birdcage in one hand. There were at least ten people watching and holding their breath. I feared for my mother, yet I was also proud of her courage. Mother wore her crème colored summer dress and she looked like a giant dove that had landed in the branches. The canary waited for her to reach him and he did not fly away, but stepped through the tiny door back into his cage. Mother closed the gate with a small latch and all the people around clapped their hands and the children giggled and jumped with excitement from one foot to the other. In the evening the whole family had a little feast. We ate *Hefekloesse* with sugar, melted butter and blackberries on top. Everybody had blue teeth as we laughed and talked about the canary who sat now in his cage, all his yellow feathers fluffed up. "Did you see how my mother climbed through the branches and green leaves to find you?" I whispered to the bird. "Did you see how she looked like a bird herself, and how her wings were caught in the tree? Do you understand how much I love her?"

But now it turned into winter and memories of summer didn't warm us. We had no wood and no coal, so the grown-ups deliberated a plan. I sat on my mother's lap and heard it all, eager to be part of the adventure. Mother said yes to my request, and we got ready when darkness fell. All of us women put their warm winter clothing on and then we went into the garage to take the wheelbarrow out. We hid the big saw by covering it with a tarp. I sat on top of the tarp to make it look unsuspicious.

We women tiptoed near the hedges of the neighborhood and then we snaked along the potato fields until we reached a tree that stood all by itself at the corner where two trails crossed. It was nearly dark now. Aunt Gretel carried a small flashlight that cut a cone of light into the night. The women stopped and I climbed out of the wheelbarrow, lifting the tarp and helping to take the two-handled saw out and position it. Mother and grandmother stood on opposite sides of the lonesome tree and put the saw against its bark. Then they nodded and started cutting into the live tree. It hurt. They hurried because the swish of the saw sounded loudly through the night. I realized that they were stealing what was not theirs. This tree had to die to warm our kitchen and to cook our food. I stood in the dark, listening to my mother's and grandmother's heavy breath as they pulled the saw back and forth, back and forth in regular rhythm. I imagined that the farmer would wake up when he heard the *rrrisch-rrrash* of the saw, that he would come and shoot us or throw us into a cage like Hänsel and Gretel, he might bring his big dogs over to devour us or he would....

At that moment the tree leaned to one side and fell slowly to the ground. All of the assembled jumped away like grasshoppers. There were muffled shouts. My aunt Gretchen had grabbed me before she ran away from the falling tree. Now grandmother and mother went back in a hurry to cut it into smaller pieces that could be transported in the wheelbarrow. When they had two pieces ready that were about the length of my body from head to toe, we heard loud shouts and rough curses and swearing at a distance. I wanted to run, but I also didn't want to leave the tree behind because it had been killed for us, to light a fire in our home. I grabbed a long

branch and pulled it behind me as I followed the women. We stumbled along the dark path between the fields, pushing the heavy wheelbarrow with two big pieces of the trunk on it.

The farmer stopped at the site of the fallen tree and inspected the damage. That allowed us women more time to get away. Aunt Gretchen held my hand and pulled me along. I ran and clenched my fist fiercely around the branch that dragged behind me on the ground. I was determined to defend it and all of us with my life. We had stolen what was not ours. We had killed a tree and the darkness around us had veiled the deed. But we had succeeded. I was surprised how satisfying it felt to be bad and to do what was forbidden. I was part of a conspiracy of thieves and the newness of this made me feel elated, enjoying the danger and ruthlessness of this night. I had blood and tar on my hands, like bad people in fairy tales. But I was determined to return to that tree the next night to get the other pieces, because we had earned our booty. I hated the owner for interrupting our adventure, and my biggest regret was that we could not go all the way with our crime.

I didn't really mind the feeling of hunger, because it was so familiar and I trusted that there would always be something to eat and to ease the pain. The moment of the first bite into a piece of bread filled me with ecstasy, it was a sweet as lying down when really tired or going to the bathroom with great urgency. The women around me would consistently create a miracle and feed us. These women were like deep earth, unfathomable and nurturing. I never lost confidence in these sources of nourishment. I lived in a society of women and was eager to share in their strength and grow into one myself.

So I joined Grandma in the battle to attack the giants of hunger that clawed inside our bellies. She was big and tall, and I was small and thin. Grandma carried the spear for the hunt and I was her helper and devout servant. We looked like Don Quixote and Sancho Panza in reverse when we went out food hunting.

I begged, "Please *Oma,* please take me with you. I'll help carry the things and walk steadily at your side."

"Yes, I need you, *min Deern,*" she nodded, smiling. We wore heavy boots and woolen caps and gloves. I reached for my *Oma*'s hand and struggled to keep pace with her long legs and strong stride. The rhythm of our feet scratched in the sand of the road, the wind blew into our faces and colored our cheeks. My hand was entwined with the hand of the tall woman beside me, a most reassuring bond. I was serious and reliable and grandma had confidence in me. I took two strides when Grandmother took one.

We arrived at the farmer's house, and Grandma had to bend her head down to enter the door to their kitchen. It was one of the Northern German farmhouses thatched with reeds. The roof sat like a big old fur cap on the brick basement. The couple knew my grandma and greeted her with friendly grins. The farmer held a sharpening stone in his gnarly hand; one finger was missing and a white scar marked the empty space. His shirt, unbuttoned, showed the skin on his chest, it seemed crumbled like earth after heavy rain and then dried by the sun. His wife was thin and leathery. She was cross-eyed, her eyes turned to each other as if the right one wanted jealously to observe what the left eye saw. Hiding in my corner, I tried to imitate that stare. There was cabbage cooking on the stove with blood and liver sausage in it, and the delicious smell made my stomach clench with greedy desire.

We placed our treasures for barter on the table, occupying the right spots, so that they glinted in the sun and looked royal and desirable. There were china cups and saucers and doilies or jewelry and a precious box with a mother-of-pearl lid. There was also a ring from my mother with a ruby. It looked forlorn and abandoned, as though the joy had left it when it was pulled off her finger.

My grandma was good at bartering and negotiating for food with farmers. Her unrelenting life had taught her how to get what she wanted and how to talk to these people from whom she wanted it. She slapped the man and his wife on their backs and made them laugh with her jokes. She spoke *plattdütsch* with them, the old dialect of Northern German country people and fishermen; it has its roots in the Anglo Saxon language.

Grandma was in no hurry. She admired the baby in the arms of the farmer's wife, and gave helpful advice how to cure its cough. She praised the new bench the farmer had nailed together, and she tied the shoelaces of the little boy named Hansie. Grandmother was real and didn't use tricks. From the moment, she stepped into the kitchen of this family, she participated in their lives. She was at ease with these strangers and treated them like old friends.

On the contrary, I was shy and quiet and felt like an intruder in this house, so I stood out of view and observed. I looked at the treasures that we offered to the farmer and thought they were dead things compared with the live ham, eggs and apples in this kitchen. The farmer seemed to know how much we lusted after his edible goods. He was the king and we were his serfs. He didn't care much for our things. But the farmer's wife was aroused by desire. She sat her baby down between pillows and took the handle of the cups carefully between two of her red and rough fingers. Her crooked eyes became dreamy.

"See, how the cups match the flowery blue curtains you have at your windows," Grandma pointed out. The woman sighed. She sat down and lifted her eyebrows, the fragile cup in her big hands disappeared like a bird in a nest.

"I don't know where to put them," she hesitated. She had collected many precious things from other hungry people. I watched my grandma close-in on that woman. Grandma would never give up; I had no doubt that she would win. She moved other things on the shelves towards the back and put the blue cups up front between the open curtains. The farmer's wife coveted the objects. She peeled herself out of her seat and nodded her head, disregarding her husband's resistance. So, we got two loaves of bread, ten eggs, a big piece of ham, and a ball of fresh butter.

The farmer's wife had now six precious cups on her shelf, placed in the first row. She would take them down from time to time and hold them in her gnarly red hands and she would dream of using them one day, maybe at the wedding many years in the future, when her baby-girl was a grown woman.

And, because the woman liked Grandma, she brought a bag of apples and pears from her cellar and layered them within our backpack without saying a word. The two women had an ancient way of understanding each other. The farmer's wife stood at the open door when we left, and we waved to each other, and all of us were content and happy. I was glad that she didn't take the ruby ring. Soon it would be back on my mother's finger, where it belonged.

On our way home I held firmly onto my *Oma*'s hand. I carried my share in the sling bag over my right shoulder; it bumped against my knee when I slid in the mud. We arrived back home and I was tired from walking for so many hours, but I never complained about the bloody blister on my heel or the stiff shoulder. I dug my teeth into the bread with great delight. There was real butter on it, and I thought that eating was one of the best things in the world, and having worked hard for it made me feel righteous in my satisfaction. The pleasure rippled down from my mouth, through my belly and crotch and thighs, all the way to my tired toes. And then, I dropped contented into my soft bed. The sweater hanging over the chair still smelled faintly of cabbage and liver sausage.

6

PLAY AND POISON

In the beginning our land was covered with wild grass, thorny weeds and scattered rocks, so my mother told me. Dandelions had yellow haloes and puffy white feather heads on the same plants, like grandmother and child in the same house. I walked around naked in our garden, and when I blew the feathery seeds they would rub along my chest and tickle the skin. I chased them when the wind scattered those mini-umbrellas all across the field. Moles dug long trenches that looked from above like giant earthworms with crumpled skin. Mice lived in burrows in the ground; imprints of tiny feet marked the entrance to their dwellings. Giant anthills came to life like cities in the morning sun, when their inhabitants began the work of the day. The ants bustled around, running over and under each other and following some secret call of duty. It seemed to me that each one of

Shadows on the wall
Noises down the hall
Life doesn't frighten me at all
Bad dogs barking loud
Big ghosts in a cloud
Life doesn't frighten me at all.

I've got a magic charm
That I keep up my sleeve,
I can walk the ocean floor
And never have to breathe.
— Maya Angelou, Excerpt from
Life Doesn't Frighten Me
Bantam Books, *Poems*

them knew exactly what he needed to do, even if they appeared chaotic and nervous.

My parents transformed this wilderness into a garden. It stretched out in front of our kitchen window and was a source of our food and wellbeing. They had created it from scratch when they moved into this home, just after their marriage. The work took years. They imprinted their new order and changed the character of the land. They started at one corner and worked their way all across to the other side, turning the earth over with spades. They cleared out the pebbles by throwing the dirt on a big metal sieve in a wooden frame that my Dad had nailed together out of fine fence wire and a wooden frame.

"Wow," said my mother, as he carried it out of his workshop. He supported it on one side with a staff, so it slanted in an angle. My mother wiped sweat from her forehead and tested the sieve. "Look, all those rocks get separated and roll down in front of the sieve, fantastic," she smiled.

My father shoveled those pebbles into wheelbarrows and spread them on the walkways. The sifted earth looked fine like chocolate powder, spicy and promising. My mother shaped the earth into raised beds and planted raspberry bushes and black and red currants, gooseberries and the baby-apple-tree.

When all the raised beds were carefully prepared with dark earth in them, like food for a birthday party, my mother knelt down beside the beds and pressed tiny grooves into the ground with her thumb. She squeezed green, black and brown seeds between her fingertips, like salt, and sprinkled them carefully into the grooves. Those seeds were tiny and I thought that they looked like dead ants. My mother spread the little wall of dirt that fringed the grooves over the seeds and pressed gently with flat hands. Then she got up, shook her dress and rubbed the earth from her knees. She filled a watering can with water and spread it all over the bed. I followed closely with my play can and moved in rhythm with my mother.

After all the seeding and planting was done, I visited the garden every day. Hunkering beside the beds, I watched and listened so that I might hear a sound or rustle of growth. One morning, the first shoots peeked out of the ground, their heads curled up in spirals or bent to one side like my grandpa's leg. They poked and stretched, and soon I was able to recognize some, because I knew the shape of the leaves. There were peas, beans, squash, red cabbage, rhubarb and butter lettuce. As long as they were tiny, they appeared similar to each other as though they were all from the same family. But in a little while they had specific characteristics and I could name them. I would stand at Mom's side and hold her hand as we observed the plant-creatures. I could see them move and stretch like humans or animals, just much slower. They pushed out of the dark earth with great force, and nothing could hold them back.

"Look, *Mutti*. They're small and in such a hurry to grow up, like human children."

I held my finger above the shoots to find out if I could feel them push against my skin. I cleared pebbles away to make it easier for them, or I shaped a small circle around their stem with my finger like a moat around a castle, so the rainwater could gather there.

My mother knelt down beside me and told me the names of the baby plants. "These are peas, and here is a picture of them on the paper bag, so that we know what we planted. And this one in between the carrots, with the curly leaves, that's parsley, and over here, that's squash, and onions, and rhubarb."

"Rhuuuuubarrrb," I repeated, and "squaaaaash" and "parrrsssslyyy." I spoke those wonderfully strange names slowly and enjoyed the rolling, popping and squishy sounds they made. Oh, saying those names was almost as delightful as eating the plants. They triggered saliva under my tongue and made my lips tingle.

"If we know the name of things," I asked my mother, "do we own them, and that allows us to eat them?" Mother looked thoughtfully and nodded her head.

Then she said, "I'd rather think that we make them familiar to us, and they become part of our life and family. We can talk to them and help them grow. We call them by names, like you gave your doll the name Susan, and now she is like your child." When I strolled out of the garden that evening I waved 'Good Night!' to rhubarb and parsley, because they were now part of my family.

My sister still thinks that I "did all those weird things" as a child. She says, what happened at that summer afternoon with Dieter and me was "really bad". My parents had warned me, 'Do not ever touch or absolutely never eat from the mushroom called *Fliegenpilz*.' I understood that they were rare, but where I lived I found them often, because I had an eye for their hiding places.

I protested, "it has such beautiful color. Look at the red hat with white dots and the white stem, like the white feathers of seagulls!"

I knelt down in the grass and looked underneath. "Look, the hat has soft white skins hanging on the underside in neat rows and a tiny skirt around its stem, just like ice dancers."

My father insisted, "It's very poisonous. Don't even get close to it or you might die!"

These kind of dramatic statements always triggered my curiosity. I stood two feet away and watched the flies landing and walking around on it without dying.

That's why they're called fly-mushroom, I thought. I remembered them from pictures in my children's books. Dwarves used them as umbrellas. They built garden benches beneath the red hoods and sat there, smoking their tiny pipes, not knowing how close to death they lived.

One summer day I found two of them in the grass under my favorite beech tree. I watched them grow every day, and I stood before them thinking they were outrageously beautiful and that very soon little dwarves would build a bench underneath to sit and smoke their pipes.

As I always did when I found something especially exciting, I showed them to Dieter. With our knees in the dirt, we admired the white dots on the red hat and threw dry leaves on the sticky top. We observed for a long time, but no dwarves came, and nothing else happened to indicate deadly danger.

So I said to Dieter, "You know, Dieter, my parents warned that if we eat them, we'd fall dead on the ground, immediately. But I think the grown-ups often say things just to scare us. What do you think? Shall we find out?"

"How'd we find out?" he asked.

"I'll break off a piece and give it to you. You chew it and swallow it and we'll see if you fall down dead immediately." I had no concept of death, yet. I was about five and surrounded by war, but death had not entered my imagination. That happened some years later. Dieter thought that I made a reasonable suggestion and we would find out the truth through our own experience.

I broke off a piece and he chewed on it and swallowed it and we held our breath and looked at each other and waited. Nothing happened. So we clapped our hands and laughed and put our arms around each other's shoulders so that they crossed in the back and walked home for dinner, proud that we were so smart. There were no dwarfs, but there was no poison either.

It was Saturday and my mother put my sister and me into the bathtub for our weekly bath. Dad was at home and sat on the toilet beside the tub and we all talked and scrubbed each other and had a good time. I used this intimate moment to share my discovery.

" You know, Dad, those red poisonous mushrooms really do nothing. We found out, Dieter and I."

My Dad sat up straight and his eyes turned cold and green. He squeezed them into small slits. "What did you and Dieter do?"

"Oh, I gave him a piece from the mushroom and he ate it and he did not fall down dead. He walked home and was really well and..."

My Dad jumped off the toilet seat and pulled me out of the tub dripping and full of soap. He put me across his knees and very firmly spanked me with his big and heavy hands on my naked behind for a long time. It all happened so fast and hurt so badly that I forgot to breathe and almost passed out. My sister was stunned into silence. My mom's hands hung down at her sides and the water trickled down on the tiles. She said nothing.

Then my dad stormed out and slammed the door. I heard him rush out of the house and knew that he was running over to Dieter's parents. I sensed a real danger and felt a rift between my charmed reality and another world where things could turn out the wrong way. I feared that Dieter might die and I decided that I would eat from the same mushroom and be buried beside him. I regretted that I had not shared the mushroom with him. It seemed easier to me to be dead than to confront what I had set in motion. I felt helpless and confused. Regret, I thought, was bitter and more poisonous than any other thing.

It was a very dreadful evening. My sister badgered me until I cried.

"It's all your fault," she said. "You always do things that no other kid would do. He's going to die and you'll regret it forever." Nobody comforted me, not even my mother, because I was guilty. After many hours of waiting my Dad came back.

"When Dieter came home he began feeling nauseous," my father reported. " Then he fell on the floor and jerked his body. I told them about the poisonous mushroom. We rushed him to the hospital and the doctor pumped his stomach empty. Dieter still feels lousy." Dad looked at me with piercing eyes, "but he's home in bed now and the doctor said things are going to be all right."

I don't remember what else was said. My sister probably gave me more troubles but I didn't really listen. The next morning, when I went outside, Dieter sat as usual in front of our door, at the second step of the stairs and was waiting for me. I looked at him and my heart grew big and round. It tickled in my chest as if it had a hiccup. He stood up from the stairs and simply said, "What're we going to play today?"

We put our arms around each other's shoulders so that they crossed in the back and walked into the fields. We didn't talk about yesterday, but I understood what true love and friendship really meant. I felt it all through my body down to my toes. Even the top of my neck tingled and I felt like crying and laughing all at once, and I think, I did.

For a whole week the five fingers of my Dad's hand could be seen on my behind, and it was evening entertainment for my family to look at the imprints and the changing colors, from red to purple to bluish-brown, until at the end they faded. I felt humiliated but I chuckled, because I discovered that people really like to laugh after they've lived through a really scary event.

During hot summer days the family would go for outings to the pond, using our bikes. My father had fixed small seats between the handle-bars of the adult's bikes, so all four of us could drive together. Most of the time, my sister would use the seat in front of my father's bike and I would sit on my mom's. It was clear that this was the order of things.

One Sunday afternoon I climbed, for a change, on my father's bike as we were heading towards the pond where we could swim in summer and ice-skate in winter. He was pedaling along and I kept my shoes on the footrest because one could get hurt when toes or heels would stick into the spinning spokes of the wheel. It happened to my sister and she still carries a white scar on her right foot. The sun was shining and larks flew high, weaving their summer songs into the wind. We drove by a monument that had been standing there as long as I remembered. On top of a cement foundation, as tall as I was, stood a heavy iron post. For some mysterious reason, the rusty old post was bent to the left like a crooked branch of a tree. My father stopped his bike, put one foot down to secure balance and pointed with his finger to the post. He turned to me and said with a deep voice, pretending to be very serious, "Elke, why did you mess up this iron post?"

We both burst into laughter, because it was impossible even for a giant to bend the metal, but I was so proud that he pretended to see such power in me. From then on, each time we came by this monument, my father pointed his finger and furrowed his brow and then he asked the same question, "My my, how did you do that?" We made a game out of it. There was a hint of intimacy and connection and my stomach tingled with joy. Did my father really believe I was so strong that I could bend the iron post? I decided that, one day, when I was grown-up, I would show him that I was able to do outrageous things, and I would do it just for him.

One of the best games I loved to play was going to town with grandmother and visiting Hamburg Harbor. There were improvised fish restaurants and smelly shops along the cobblestone sidewalks. The shops had small windows and the smoke billowed out of them into the open air. It clung to the walls and filled the whole street with the odor of fried food.

My *Oma* waited in a long line to get baked flounder and potato salad for us. The man behind the counter rolled two greasy pieces of newspaper into the shape of funnels and filled one with fish and another with salad. We grabbed the bags and sat down on a bench near the water where we heard it gurgle and splash against the stonewalls. Thick ropes creaked and moaned where the ships were moored

I chewed, watching all the hectic activity on the water. Small pilot ships, called *Schalupen*, hurried ahead of the big ocean steamers and showed them the way out towards the North Sea. The little boats had control over the giants' movements and directed them where to go. The men inside the pilot ships wore white caps and yellow oil jackets. They grabbed their steering wheels with suntanned hands, confident looks on their faces.

I got up from my seat and stood behind my grandma, holding on to her woolen scarf, to be sure that I would not lose her in all this hustle and bustle. People squeezed by and pushed against me. The stench of sweat and urine was stinging in my nose. Men and women crowded around the fish place, bartering and selling their possessions. They whispered and held their heads close together, nervously offering objects that were hidden inside their coats.

Most of the houses behind me were half or totally destroyed by bombs. Some walls, still standing, had smoke creep out of basement windows. Human signs were scattered and piled high, a kitchen sink and a piece of mirror, silent stones, a door handle and a single leather boot. Found objects carried great practical worth. A chipped cup or bent spoon turned into precious assets. Ordinary things had value beyond their appeerence. A wall nearby hung dangerously out of balance, leaning as if tired and ready to fall on top of the women who poked in the rubble near its foot in search for anything usable.

The edges of the ruin resembled black teeth. The leaning wall was a remnant, the left-over of a five-story building. My eyes followed the freestanding wall upwards, as if I were climbing the staircase that was marked as a zigzag line in a non-existing hallway. Suddenly I saw a bright red blotch of color up there, on the fourth or fifth story. The glass in the window was shattered, but on the windowsill stood a living geranium plant. A red flag in the heartland of death. Yesterday, this geranium was inside a home, I imagined. A woman had watered it and a family sat around the dinner table near the window. Today, it was waiting for someone who might never come back.

"Look, *Oma*, look behind you," I whispered and pointed.

My grandmother turned around and wiped across her eyes with her big hands. The lines beside her mouth dark and sharp, she slumped forward and dropped her food. A scrawny dog devoured it in seconds.

For a moment, the length of a heartbeat, a curtain opened in my naïve awareness. The blotch of red color in the middle of a naked, blackened wall jerked this child into the center of war's reality. She reached for Grandmother's hand and turned back to watch the ships. The curtain closed again; there was no talk, but what she had seen would not be undone. The red color on the wall etched itself into her brain and would remain there like a stain.

My sister often ran away with her friends, when I wanted to play with her. I was the little one and she had more important things to do than hang out with me. So I was delighted when she asked me one day, "Shall I show you a trick, a special trick that makes you win against boys? I learned it in school," she added and I was impressed.

**Heartland of Death. Photograph from *The Fire* by Joerg Friedrich,
courtesy of Columbia University Press.**

"Yes, hmmm, sure," I said, trying not to seem too eager.

"That's how you do it; first you kneel down." Helga cleaned a place on the ground for her knee and to make the performance more dramatic. "Now stretch your arm, put it over my shoulder and turn the inside up, this way." I did as she explained.

"Now, I pull slowly." She held my wrist and pulled. It hurt and I jumped to release the strain. My sister let go.

"If you do it with boys, you can pull harder. They have strong arms, but the more you pull the more they whine and you impress them and they will never bully you again."

I didn't feel bullied by boys, really, but I wanted to impress them and show them a new trick because they always knew many games and I was eager to play with them. It took courage and wits to keep up with boys. I thought I had both. I was sure that in climbing trees I was even better than they were, because I was little and could squeeze between branches like a squirrel.

I was eager to show off my new trick. There were no boys around, so I ran to my girlfriend, Siglinde, whose mother was an opera singer. She lived on *Grenzweg*, a dirt road with blackberry bushes along one side that separated it from the fields.

I found her balancing on the pedals of her bike in front of her house. I shouted already from some distance, "Do you want to know a trick that my sister just taught me? You can use it to win against boys and they give in."

"Yes, I want to," she said, eager and curious. She believed that I had many good and funny ideas.

I knelt in front of her and gave her instructions, just as I learned it before.

When she had her arm across my shoulder I pulled and then, I felt a slight snap.

Crack! A muffled sound that made my heart stop.

Siglinde screamed in pain. She ran inside, to her Mom, who shrieked with her high singing voice, and ran to the phone.

I was horrified, fear sitting in my neck like a vulture with sharp claws. I ran home, hoping that somebody would undo whatever it was I had done, and make my friend not hurt and me not get into big trouble. That was a silly hope, because it was already too late. Many kids had gathered now, after they heard the screaming of Siglinde and her mother. They saw how frantic I was and followed behind me like fishes in a net. Glad not to be in trouble, they were eager to participate in mine.

I ran and found my father in the garden with his shovel, turning the earth for new potatoes to be planted.

"Dad, I have…I did…Helga's trick and…and…and Siglinde hurts… and I think…I think I broke her arm!"

My dad dropped the shovel. He grabbed me and jerked me upwards. And then he hung me over his knees like he did with our rabbits before he killed them for our Sunday brunch. I hoped he would hit my head with a hammer, because that was better than what he did when he pulled my underpants down in front of all the kids. He smacked his big hands on my naked buttocks faster and faster, until I thought the lower part of my body would fall off. I smelled the musty odor of my father's body and saw the crusted dirt on his shoes. I didn't mind the hurt, because I wanted to hurt, too, after I had injured my friend.

My father finally put me down. I stood with my panties around my ankles and faced the kids staring at me as I pulled them up and walked into the house. Shame sat like a bag of boulders on my shoulders. I hoped it would make me disappear into the earth. The kids stood frozen. I thought they would never love or respect me again, and I was not sure if I, myself, would be able to, either. This world was so hard to live in, when innocent tricks could turn so bad.

My father ran to Siglinde's house and they rushed to the doctor's. I had dislodged the joint of her elbow and she needed to wear a cast for two weeks to make it heal in place. I visited daily and brought her gifts and sweets and told her how sorry I was that I had hurt her. She enjoyed the attention, and our friendship continued. Our bond grew even stronger because we had gone through a challenge together. But other people, who were not involved, made a big story out of the event.

For me this was a key event in my relationships with my father. I felt raw and petrified about the hurt I had inflicted. I needed help; but instead, I got an instant reaction of cold revenge. I wondered what clicked inside the brain of this man who takes his small daughter, less than half his size, and shames her in front of her friends, not only beating her mercilessly, but taking her underwear off. He pounced on me. He thrashed me around and I became the target of his wrath. I asked myself if my father just played the role of an enraged father. He punished because that's what German fathers are supposed to do when they play this role? He didn't know how to invent a new way of relating to his daughter or a more effective way of teaching her. He had no clue how to be a father in a compassionate way. Was he brutal or just thoughtless and habitual in his actions?

As for myself, I doubted if being a child was enough of an excuse that would release me of responsibility. I had harmed my friend out of pure curiosity and pride. I had caused pain unintentionally and had to face the despair and regret of an action that could not be undone, realizing that true remorse tasted bitter and painful. I was ignorant and careless. Both traits together proved to be a poisonous concoction, like the mushroom offered to Dieter. I was also terrified to discover how easily one could do harm to somebody whom one loved; and war, I thought, was happening when people purposefully wanted to harm and hurt the other. Or not? Maybe it was always an aberration, a mistake, a surprise?

The dragon lived at the end of our garden path in dense hazel bushes. This green dragon was the hero of my secret ritual play, only my sister knew about him. He was not a dragon that spit fire and burned down houses or people; he was one of those that guarded princesses and treasures. He was not a dangerous one that would smash you with one paw and thrust his claws through your chest and eat what was left of you, licking your intestines from his claws. This one was a gentle dragon, friendly with children, especially those born on a Sunday, as I was, on the fourth of September. This dragon could shape-shift from cloud into tree or into a green snake with black marks on his back.

The gate to his dwelling could only be penetrated by force and speed. To succeed in that, I used the old baby carriage from our garage that served us to transport potatoes or firewood. This shaky wagon was my chariot. My sister and I placed it at the top of the garden path that was slanting towards the hazel bush where the dragon lived. And then I climbed into this chariot while Helga clutched the handle with both hands. I hunkered down on the mouse-damaged mattress, put my head on my knees and my arms over my hair.

"Your elbows 're sticking out at the sides," Helga said and pushed them inside the small space.

I took a deep breath and whispered, "I'm ready!"

"Hoooow, hoooow, here we goooow!" she shouted and pushed me down the path with increasing speed towards the hazel bush. Then she gave the chariot a last fierce shove and I sailed downhill straight into the mouth of the dragon. I pierced the green veil and his feathers tickled my neck. His jaws split open, yellow and green flecks sparked between fleshy folds. Sticks and leaves jotted across the gate of purple flesh in the depth of his throat. The dragon's long black teeth scratched my arms before I disappeared into his dark belly full of shadows. The chariot stopped with a jolt, and then there was only silence.

I lifted my head very slowly from my knees and lowered the arms from my hair. Blood drops trickled from the back of my hands and the red ribbon that held my braid was undone. It hung along my leg like a deep wound from a sword. Green light specks peeked through the leaves and branches; a ladybug crawled along my little finger. I had found my way into dragon-land and wondered *was I still alive?*

"Elke, Elke are you well?" My sister pulled on the handle of the carriage to free me from the tight grip of the embracing bush.

The Dragon. Photography by Shanti Elke Roessner.

"I was afraid you might never come back," she sighed and wiped the blood off my arm. She peeled me out of the old wagon that creaked and swayed. "What'd you see?" We sat down, picking the leaves from my hair.

"He has three heads, and snakes in his mouth, and green specks of light inside his belly, and it smells like moss and rain. I think that's what they eat, those dragons — wet earth with all the small and weird creatures that live on it." I gasped for air. I was Odysseus, the traveler, and my sister, Helga, was my companion and confidant. She held my sword and spear and called upon the winds that would carry me to new territories. I prepared myself for anticipated battles. I believed if I faced danger by my own choice, I would be strong enough to face the future perils that awaited me in my life.

Looking back today, I am surprised to realize how the games of childhood predicted my future. During all those later years of adult life, I would, again and again, enter into the 'mouth of the dragon' to get familiar with the mystery of unknown people and cultures. I would travel and immerse myself into new situations and countries. I would enter places of wilderness to find the hidden soul in untamed creatures and beings. Through experience, I learned to trust in their benevolence and friendliness. Throughout all those explorations I found my belief confirmed that our home, this earth, is a great mystery and she yearns to be discovered and made familiar, hoping to be approached with awe and curiosity.

And so this child grew up and learned that she was part of a network of relations with people, landscapes, creatures and even the elements. As a child, she lived easily inside that unifying web without any doubts about her belonging and kinship. Later, she became more shy and secretive about those experiences of unity. But as I age, I delight in the freedom of a child again; I rejoice in the seen and the unseen magic of this universe without hesitation and with great abandon.

One summer afternoon, when I was five, I was stuck on my girlfriend

Siglinde's porch. The rain poured down on the roof as though a barrel in the sky had been kicked over. To avoid ruining my new sandals, I sat down on a bench and settled to wait out the storm. My legs swung back and forth, and the fabric of my skirt rustled. As the rain pulled close around the place, it spun a curtain made of water. I was alone and felt dreamy and safe inside this fluid tent. The raindrops hammered on the roof like the fingers of God. I breathed slowly and listened to the pause between inhale and exhale.

Oh, and I heard how harshly the water hit the trees that encircled the house. Every drop said *blingg!* as it fell on the wet leaves, and then again: *blingg!* The earth slurped the water and steam lifted off the grass. Rain in fall or spring was gentler, it spread into misty pellets as if it were flowing through a sieve. But this summer storm was full of threat and secrets, guttural roars burst from the throat of the wind.

Suddenly, the rain stopped and it was still. Very still. The silence extended, forming a hollow space that sucked me in. It swallowed the rustle of my skirt and wrapped itself all around me so that I felt its touch on my naked skin. The hair on my arms stood upright and I wished I were back in mother's kitchen where she would be cooking dinner. Jumping off the bench to go home, I pressed my doll against the chest, knowing that I had to pass beside the towering beech trees to reach our door. All noise had settled like falling leaves on a pond. I stepped warily into the dense substance of silence outside the porch.

Walking along the path I looked towards the trees to my left and there, hovering in the tangle of branches, was the living presence of stillness. This stillness crouched between the leaves with shiny eyes; it was a breathing creature. Its soft, long fur swallowed every sound. It stared at me and I peered back.

I slowly pulled my shoulders up. Some single drops fell from the top to the lower branches and made *blingg*, and *blingg*, with long pauses in between. Blades of grass trembled. Occasional thuds pierced the silence. I was small, and everything around me was enormous. I panicked, wanted to run, but I only dared to slowly put one foot in front of the other to avoid stirring the stillness. No wind moved the heavy leaves. I took my sandals off and scurried with bare feet. The squishy cool earth stuck between my toes as I slithered along the ground that was scarred by the rain. The tree-giants beckoned me, but I wished to be invisible. The trees and the stillness gestured and reached out towards me, luring me into their wet, green, opaque space of vibrant silence. I held my breath and then, I ran.

My mother was at home in the kitchen. Climbing up on the chair beside the table, I watched how she held tomatoes in her hands and cut them into small pieces. Her hands were like big leaves as she closed them around the ripe tomato. She was taming all the red in the world, containing it between her two hands, so that it would not set fire to every other color and to my heart.

Should I tell her about the stillness that crouched in the branches like a living creature? With two eyes to watch you? No, I thought, I will keep it as one of my secrets. Secrets revealed get so easily damaged, like spider webs. I will not tell anybody that my panic tasted as sweet and bitter as ginger bread, and that I ran away because I feared I could not resist the lure of the trees. I feared, and hoped, being transformed into a tree myself. Trees are calm and safe and they are always in the company of other trees, and the young ones grow in the sheltering branches of the grown-ups. But if I were a tree and had roots that reached deeply into the ground, I would never again come home to watch the two hands of my Mother cradle those red, those fiery red tomatoes that marked the center of my world, a world in which I could not imagine existing without her.

7

LUST FOR LIFE

On May 8, 1945, a radio announcement declared the end of World War II and the women of the neighborhood got very busy. They made huge pots and bowls full of green peppermint tea and red berry juice and they prepared plates of dry bread and cooked potatoes, whatever scarce food they could find in their pantries. The women washed their hair and put lipstick on. They colored the upper lip in the shape of a heart and then they rolled the lower lip against the upper. They smiled and leaned their heads back to pluck their eyebrows into fine, thin lines. They cut their toenails and took colorful dresses off hangers to hold against their figures, turning in front of mirrors which they hadn't looked into for a long time. Some painted with brown pens and steady hands, a long seam from their heels upwards to their buttocks to pretend they were wearing silk stockings. My mother fixed a red tulip flower in her hair.

Sadness, scarab
with seven crippled feet,
spiderweb egg,
scramble-brained rat,
bitch's skeleton:
No entry here.
Don't come in.
Go away.
Go back.
—Pablo Neruda, *Ode to Sadness*
University of California Press

All wars produce scarred
minds and ravaged spirits.
—Larry Dossey, *Healing*
Beyond the Body

We had heard the news about the end of war from the small radio in our kitchen, which was fixed to the wall like a little altar I'd seen in church. It was called *Volksempfänger* – people's radio – and had only one station. It often scratched and moaned like a sick animal, especially when *Der Führer* bellowed his speeches and filled our home with the heavy stench of madness. Carved wood ornaments on the front had brown fabric behind them that trembled when his voice poured out. But today, a different speaker announced that the war was over and that the Allied Troops would soon be marching into Germany.

I don't really remember if my family commented on the news or showed emotions, so I didn't know if that declaration was good or bad for us. The war was something strange and ever-present for me, and I assumed it was a normal part of life. War was a backdrop for my childhood. War's presence hid in the corners of our home and wafted like a foul stench behind the curtains and underneath my bed, but we had gotten used to it and did not talk about the war. Nobody explained to me what the 'end of war' meant - and so many things had already ended before the end.

In front of our house was a triangle of grass between three merging streets. The women had gathered there and set up their drinks and food in this place, and then we stood and waited. Soon a rhythmic scraping sound rolled towards us and then soldiers of the German army appeared. They poured and rolled by, a seemingly never-ending murky river of men. I stood in front of my mother and held her hand. She wore the blue-and-white dress that I loved so much. I hadn't seen it on her since the time of our family vacation at the Baltic Sea, years ago. I leaned my head backwards against her belly.

The German soldiers who staggered in front of us were dirty, wounded, tired, their eyes glazed and their movements helpless and awkward. Some sat on horse-drawn carts, others on bikes, but most walked. A man with only one arm and a bandaged hand tried to cling to one of the wagons, but his bloody hand slipped off and he nearly tumbled to the ground. He caught himself and slouched forward.

The women leaned into the street to offer drink and food; I could see the soft, white undersides of their arms and chins when I looked up. The soldiers grabbed the gifts hastily. They continued their march as they ate and drank, and some sent an exhausted smile back to the person who had extended this gesture of caring. The stream of tired human bodies was pushed by an invisible power towards an invisible goal. A feeling of utter futility hovered above them. It seemed as if they were moving from nowhere to nowhere. Everybody was quiet, like during a funeral. Only the boots of the soldiers scratched along the sandy road.

After a long time, the last of the military men dwindled away like dry leaves blown into the corners of this destroyed country. But the women stayed and waited — I didn't know why. And then they came, the next river of men, the English and American soldiers, the occupiers of our burnt earth. They looked clean and shaven, their belts and boots sparkled. They carried healthy limbs and unbroken self-esteem. They smiled at the women who greeted them with the same gestures of lifting their arms with drink and food in their hands, leaning towards the men and exchanging smiles. The women's naked arms reached across me towards the soldiers like flowers towards the sun. There were shouts of 'Hello!' and 'Thank you!' The men waved and the women brightened. The whole world was sucking in air and exhaling after holding tight for too long, inside a suffocating clench. I wondered if the losing German soldiers were the wrong and unworthy ones, and the victors were the good ones, just by the fact that they had won the war? Their prowess and unbroken-ness was attractive and seemed to charge the group of women with electric and glistening desire. I, too, thought that they looked splendid.

I moved the tip of my shoe back and forth in the dust and rocks of the road, back and forth, scraping a little half circle in front of me. What was the meaning of these strange parades? Both, losers and winners, had faces and hands and feet; they looked very similar. Why were some men enemies and the others *our people*? And the enemies were so friendly and kind. They gave us kids chewing gum, something I had never tasted before. It stuck to my teeth and made my mouth drip with pleasure. It was a miracle food, I could bite and bite on it and it never got smaller.

I liked these soldiers—they made me smile. They were not frightening. Were these the men who threw the bombs on my town and burned down Hamburg until the houses looked like rotten teeth?

I held tightly onto my mother's hand as I watched the manly legs marching by in front of me, my eyes at the height of their belts and dangling pistols. I feared if I let go, I might fall apart and scatter into pieces, like a puzzle that couldn't be assembled into a whole picture. My head rumbled with all the things stuffed inside which I didn't understand. I was too young to know what I know today, that we were witnessing the last aching gasps of the most widespread war in human history. I didn't know that over seventy million people were killed over six years, most of them civilians like us: women and children. We were standing at the sidelines, watching the last convulsions of the deadliest global conflict ever. The majority of the world's nations had spent their most precious human, economic and scientific resources on the destruction of human cultures and lives.

We women and children hovered at the edge of the river of men-of-war in front of us. We were standing like a living wall. The soldiers were flowing by, their movements brushing along our hips, our bellies and our breasts. We were like a riverbank with roots and rocks in it, and they were the current, whirling and changing the shape of the ground. We had an appointment with history, and we knew it in the marrow of this very moment. Out of the corners of our eyes we recognized the slanted landscape of an unknown future, a future when we women would sit together and would become quiet and struggle with words and stare out of the windows, holding on tightly to each other's hands. A future when we would say: 'Do you remember' and 'It was bad' and 'It was good,' and so…and so….

Heavy sleet fell on the trees and bushes at Christmas Eve. When darkness crowded outside the windows, my mother stood up and walked slowly around the tree to light the candles. The soft glow made her skin shine, and there was a smile on her face. I couldn't sit still, jumped up and hugged her, and after crawling into my *Oma*'s lap, I grabbed my sister's hand and wiggled on her braids. We gathered on the couch that was turned around to face the Christmas tree. On top of the tree presided an old angel to bless us all. It wore a lace dress and curly white hair encircled its porcelain head that had a crack. That damage changed its perfect beauty into an expression of fierceness. It was the face of a fallen angel that looked more human than divine.

The house smelled of punch and freshly baked *Christ-Stollen*, made with yeast-dough, raisins, nuts and candied fruit. The outside was shaped like a baby rolled in a blanket to honor the baby Jesus' birthday. Traditions were still taken seriously, even though millions of people had died. Familiar customs crept out of the ground and came back to life, they provided a feeling of normalcy.

There was a trace of fuel mixed into the scent of cinnamon and hot cider because an oil-burning stove heated our living room. My father had built it by welding all the single pieces together following his own design, so we could use this room for special events and would not have to restrict ourselves to the tiny space in our warm kitchen.

My sister and I ran back and forth. I felt like a spring that was tightly wound up, whenever I sat down, I popped up seconds later. My mother warmed herself beside the stove. She wore her silk jacket with flower patterns that she had saved for these occations. My grandmother toasted towards her daughter with a glass of hot rum. Her mighty breasts were contained inside a black blouse sealed with a brooch. My grandfather leaned forward against his walking stick; his white shirt underneath a festive suit that was awkwardly mended on the elbows. Uncle Albin and Aunt Gretchen clunked with pots and lids in the kitchen, cooking a celebratory meal. My father was not with us. Even at Christmas he was busy with work. I didn't know where he stayed and had stopped asking. I didn't miss him and I felt ashamed as I caught this thought.

There was a knocking at the door and my mother hurried to open it. Our new friend, Tom, an officer of the occupying English army stood outside. His coat was wet with heavy snow and rain, and the brass buttons of his uniform reflected the light of the candles. He walked into the room and greeted everybody with a hug or shaking of hands. 'Froulicke Wineact!' he sang in German.

Tom was slim and young, but his coat seemed big and bulging. He hesitated to take it off and simply sat down on the couch. Drips of rain collected in the folds and fell on the carpet. We children stood in front of him and put our hands hesitantly on the bulge that protruded from his chest, because it moved. We reached inside his coat and that's when Tom burst into waves of laughter, like a truck being started, and he made puffy barking sounds. His black hair fell into his face, his eyes sparkled and his tongue appeared between his teeth as if he tried to contain his joy. We pulled the coat from his chest and found a puppy dog, wet and squealing.

Helga and I held him with four hands and danced around. I fell into Tom's arms and lap and couldn't stop laughing, my joy so intensely that I cried simultaneously. My grandmother grinned and took the puppy into her big hands to hold him up above her head. "He's a boy," she said and then she looked into his small face and decided, "He looks like my brother Kalli." And that's how our doggy got his name.

We built forts out of pillows for Kalli and fed him with milk and cookies. He peed on the rug and we fixed a diaper around him but he wagged his tail constantly and that tore the fabric off.

We all gathered around the table to eat roasted rabbit with red cabbage and potatoes and drink hot cider. I gave the best piece of my roast to Tom. The oil-heated stove that my father had installed kept us all cozy and warm during this cold night, and it was one of the best of my life.

Helga and I threw a coin and I won. I took Kalli into my bed. He slept beside me and he snored with tiny raspy sounds like a grasshopper flying. Everybody was asleep, but me. My grandparents had moved into the corner room, my aunt and uncle were in the attic, and Tom was in the bedroom with my mother.

I woke up in the middle of the night and heard small puffs of breath, whiffs of air tickled my ear and neck. It was still in the house; I lay motionless and listened. An enormous feather duvet covered me like a warm cloud. I turned my head gently to the right and my cheek touched Kalli's cold, wet nose. I nuzzled my face into his furry flank. He smelled a bit like our rabbits, but his hair was much shorter. I felt his beating heart at my cheek.

"Kalli," I whispered, "Kalli, you are so warm and real, my play-mate and friend, my dearest creature, my snoopy little brother!"

I put my hand very lightly on Kalli's back and thought about how much I loved Tom with the black, slick hair. He was slim and tall and could bend in every direction, like a willow tree, easily laughing about anything. As officer of the English Allied Troops, he brought us boxes of Army food every week. He rolled around on the floor with us children and played Dominos and hide-and-seek. He joked with our grandmother and slapped her behind — and she permitted that. I think she liked him. I taught him some words in German and he pulled me up to sit on his lap. We both giggled because of his clumsy pronunciation. He could never say sugar in German, which sounds like "*Tsucker.*" I showed him how to stick the tongue just behind the front teeth and breathe firmly to make a sharp "ts" sound. He tried and failed and thought this was very funny. He could wrinkle his forehead so that the two thick bows of his eyebrows met in the middle, like a bridge. I leaned my head against his shoulder, the rough fabric of his uniform scratching my cheek. He put his arm around my waist and sometimes, we just sat there quietly not doing anything. And those were the moments when I loved him most, because he treated me like a real person and friend and didn't play the role of an adult.

Kalli turned and sniffled on my cheek. He huffed and puffed a bit as if he were dreaming. Tomorrow we would show him to our friends, none of them had a dog because people needed the food for themselves. We would tell them that our friend Tom brought Kalli to us as a gift. Tom had effortlessly become a part of our family. He dropped in at least three times a week during the day or in the evening. I saw my mother's smiles and happiness and felt grateful that she shared him with us. I didn't want a life without him and feared that he might disappear when my father came back, because there was no space for both of them.

Secretly, I wanted Tom as a father, but believed that this was a very sinful desire and that God would punish me for it. So I whispered in my mother's ear, '*Mutti,* you know, I love Tom more than *Vati* and I want him to stay with us all the time. But please, please don't tell anybody about this; it's our secret.' She nodded and her face was tense, as if she tried not to cry.

Three brick steps led up to the store of the milkman; one of them was loose on the right side and made "click" when somebody stepped on it. We usually had to wait in line for an hour or more to get to the clicking step and receive half a liter of milk per person. I liked to stand in line because I hid in the skirts of my mother, my grandma or aunt and listened to the women's talk. Frau Zimmerman had her hand all bandaged up. She said she had a nail infected, it was full of puss and she had spent a whole morning in the doctor's office. "He slowly cut off the infected nail and gave me a cigarette to smoke in between because it hurt so much." She turned to my mother and said, "That was more painful than giving birth to my daughter. When she came, I pressed and pushed three times and out she slipped and all was over and done. But this infected nail, it was hell." I felt nauseous just listening to her.

Frau Kant stood so close behind me that I could smell her warm body odor. She leaned towards her women friends and whispered. "My man is home and it's like a dream. In the middle of the night he comes on top of me and I think I'm dreaming, but it's real, and he climbs up on top of me again an hour later and he fills my sweet bucket to the brim. God, it's so good to have a man at home!"

I squeezed to the front of the line and watched how the milkman measured the milk by dipping a half-liter metal scoop with a long handle into the can. What was too much dripped back into the can, he didn't even have to level and watch it. He gave exactly the same to each of the women and it felt fair. He poured it with a curly swing of his arm from some distance, so it looked like an arc made out of fluid white. He was a real artist of his trade and delighted in the women's admiration. They told jokes and laughed, but I didn't understand why. He poured five measures full into our old and battered milk can and made the same long ark of milk, and he even turned his head, because I giggled, but he didn't spill one drop. Then he handed a piece of butter and cheese across the counter. We waved goodbye to the women behind us in line and trotted over to the candy store.

Frau Berger had old-fashioned lace curtains at the windows of her candy store and the shadow of the pattern fell on the floor. I walked on this pattern like a queen on a precious rug. All those glasses with candy stood in a straight line along the walls; they were my ladies-in-waiting. They were eager to be chosen, and I sent royal nods of consent to them as I walked along to choose one or two.

I had twenty pennies to spend, so I selected a piece of my favorite nougat and a *Cremehütchen* in silver paper and two coconut balls covered with chocolate. Frau Berger leaned forward and I could see the blue veins under the white skin of her breasts. Her décolleté was low cut and her flesh shone like the marzipan on her counter. She asked me, "Can I pack it all in one bag?" I nodded and reached across with the pennies on the palm of my hand.

My aunt Margarete stood behind me and grabbed my hand when we left the store. Suddenly she bent down to me and whispered, "I heard that you love Tom very much, even more than your father." I stared at my shoes and my face burned and I didn't know what to do with my hands. They felt heavy and awkward, like the broken wings of a wet bird. I dropped the bag with candy and ran home ahead of her. I realized that I couldn't trust grown-ups anymore, ever, if I couldn't even safely tell a secret to my own mother.

Several months after Christmas, Tom came on a snowy day. He brought his last package of army food and said goodbye to us because he was leaving Germany and returning to England. Tom hugged me and lifted me up to his face, smelling like cigarettes and a bit like the warm fur of a horse. I was glad that his skin was wet, too, so he wouldn't see me cry. He put his arms around everyone in our family, though not my grandfather; he only took his hands between both of his. Grandfather smiled, and that happened rarely. We all stood around Tom in the kitchen, and it was warm and tight and really dense when all our bodies were so close together. Then he walked down the path in front of our house and we never saw him again. Kalli stayed with us and grew taller every day.

My mother said: "Tomorrow is *Waschtag.*" Laundry day happened twice a month and moved in on us with the regularity of the seasons.

She gathered dirty linens and underwear and layered them into the huge copper cauldron in the basement; then she added water and soap and let it sit there during the night. Next morning she would get up early and wind a blue scarf around her hair. She put on old clothes and started a fire underneath the cauldron. It had to burn for two hours to heat the water, which my mother would stir every so often with a long wooden stick.

"*Mutti,* can I help you?"

I sat on a little chair in a corner, shuffling my feet along the tiles. Steam bulged out of the window where it turned and rolled like a twisting snake before it dissolved, eaten by the wind. The whole room was filled with vapor, and my mother looked like a witch brewing potent potions.

"You can turn the crank on the mangling machine," she said. It had a long wrought iron lever in the shape of a swan's neck and the wooden handle was shiny from wear.

Soapy, hot water squeezed out of the big sheets and ran back into the cauldron to be used for another soak. It carried the sweat of the night and the musty grime of daily work and life.

We hung the big sheets outside along the ropes which were strung back and forth between hooks on the wall of the house and the beam for our swing. I held the wooden poles and my mother placed them underneath the ropes to keep them high up, so that the sheets would not wipe along the ground when the wind played with them, making them dance and squirm. I walked inside the alleys between the blinding white sheets and stroked them with my hands, singing a ballad about the princess who lost her way as she was seeking the prince Kalifa, in a strange Oriental town somewhere in Tunisia or in my dreams. It was a ballad where at the end all came together again and life was restored to beauty and joy. Oh, how I loved good endings, I sang that part again and again:"...*und sie liebte ihn bis in den Tod.*"

We took the dry laundry down when darkness fell. I helped stretch the edges and fold them into neat squares. My mother unwound her scarf with a tired, slow movement, her brown hair falling down and covering the high forehead. Mother's arms were red, and the skin on her hands looked white and bleached from being wet most of the day. The regular laundry day was a ritual that set a marker during the flow of the month; it promised security and normalcy, confirming order in our life. At the end, all the sheets were clean, and we could start a new cycle, unblemished by old stories.

Our food supply was scarce. No more army rations would be delivered by Tom to nurture the family. But hunger was easier to bear when everybody felt it. There was something comforting in the communal sharing of misery.

Helga was nine years old, and one day she came home from school with an order from the nurse on a yellow slip of paper. "Helga Roessner is extremely undernourished and is ordered to be sent to a *Landheim*, a Country School Home, so that she will gain weight." Helga handed it to our mother, and we all sat down in the kitchen and discussed what it meant. My grandma joined in, and so did my aunt Gretel and Uncle Albin—everybody had an opinion and talked at the same time.

We had heard about those homes, where thin kids would be assembled to be fattened like Hansel and Gretel in the fairytale. That note meant that Helga had to leave home. I knew she would get homesick, because she wouldn't be able to play with our dog Kalli or with me.

"I don't want to go, *Mutti*," she cried, "I hate to be stuffed with food and have to take a nap in the afternoon, like a baby. I'll be so homesick that I'll come home thinner than before. All my friends are bony and nobody else has to go there. Don't make me go," she whined and fussed, and I felt sick to my stomach when I imagined my life without her. So I joined into her wailing.

After everything was said and repeated and said again, we came up with a solution. My mother summarized it this way, "You two girls go together to the *Landheim*, because you, Elke, need some flesh on your bones, too. You can sleep in the same room and sit at the same table and play together. The time will be over soon and then you come home. And in the middle of the four weeks, I will come and visit you." We looked at each other and thought we could manage that. That I was capable of easing my sister's homesickness made me feel good and important.

Mother packed a small bag for each of us and brought us to the North Sea on the bus, to a village called *St. Peter Ording*. The Country School Home was sitting like a duck in the middle of green fields near the water. It was an old straw thatched house with a big veranda, glass all around, so that the wind would not blow too strongly in the space where all the kids had to take their naps, all in a row and on their backs, like sardines in a can, packed tightly into gray blankets with their arms inside, so they could not play or gesture to each other.

Helga and I soon realized that this was not fun, but it rather resembled a prison and the *Oberin* was the prison boss. The food that was supposed to make us fat was horrible. I could hardly swallow it and thought that the women in my home would have never imagined how anybody could create something so disgusting out of real ingredients. There was brown stuff that was slimy and green stuff randomly mixed into it, resembling old leaves in a potato field where snails had left their shiny trails.

The dining room was a torture chamber. It smelled sour and stale, like a cold potato soup with a greenish skin of mold on top. We had to sit straight in our chairs and were not allowed to talk with each other. So we just made faces and signs and that made us laugh, and the *Frau*

Oberin would walk slowly around with beady eyes. She slapped the back of the head when one would not expect it with a sharp upward stroke. She sneaked up from behind, aiming at each kid that would wiggle or giggle, and I was always startled by her attack.

"You have to eat every little bit on your plate!" She looked like a terrier dog with her curled gray hair and I was afraid she might bite. I had never thought that it could be a punishment to have to eat, but I learned soon that the world in my kitchen at home was heaven and this was hell. In this place, food was taken in under the dread of threats and shame.

"If you don't eat your plate empty, you will sit on your chair until you have done so, even if it takes days!"

The menace in her voice made me aware how difficult it was to follow such rules when eating. The fodder was forced into my body but my stomach had its own ideas about what was acceptable, and I didn't have any control over it. During the next days the drama around meals increased in a way that changed my love for food into fear and loathing. During every mealtime, some kids would throw up, and the stench in the room was penetrating. The food that went into the body through the mouth looked too similar to what came out at the other end.

There was sunshine outside and the wind bent the long grasses so that they reflected the light, but we sat inside this house as if we lived in a different reality. We were damned ghosts and I doubted that we would ever be allowed to leave. One day it was my turn to suffer embarrassment. I stuffed the grayish pulp into my mouth and swallowed. But my stomach was eagerly pushing upwards to press it back out through my throat. I held my breath and swallowed again, but the push upwards was stronger. I lifted my hand and just had enough air to whisper, "I need to throw up. I can't hold it down!"

I wanted to run out and to the bathroom, but the terrier-faced *Frau Oberin* held me down on the chair with an iron grip at my shoulders. There were all those different pushes and pulls inside and outside my body and my thoughts got stuck in between and wanted to be free and my stomach said a total and firm 'NO' to the food, so it squirted out through my nose and mouth in a big arch all over the table. I thought I'd rather die right now, but before I die I'd kill this woman who clutched her hands into my shoulders. I had never known how to hate somebody, but I detested the prison guard behind me with a force that stunned me.

My half-digested meal looked gray and yellow and spread across the surface of the table. I could see the square pattern of the oilcloth show through it. The other kids pulled their plate back and stared into it. My throat hurt like fire, and the smell was disgusting. *Frau Oberin* had me clean the slimy brew with a towel that stank already from another job.

"Helga," I whispered under the covers in the evening when the lights were out, "I hate *Frau Oberin* and have never felt such hatred before. It sits in my neck and squeezes my shoulder blades like a trap. I am glad that I created a mess with my vomit, because it's all her fault. I wanted to throw up on her, but she stood behind me."

Helga was quiet, she, too, was very unhappy and she was right, we didn't gain weight. We missed our mother and grandma, our familiar bed and our dog Kalli. We could think about them, but thoughts were fluffy and empty inside, they didn't have the scent and touch of the real thing, like the warm sensation of two arms around loved-ones.

There were about twenty other bony kids and we all were homesick. In the evening we cried under our covers or pillows, so that the *Frau Oberin* could not hear our sobs.

Visits were allowed on Sunday of the second weekend. My mother came as she had promised. She wore her blue angora sweater and a scarf around her head and her whole face was smiling when she climbed out of the bus. We ran towards her and I started crying because I remembered how much I had missed her, and now she was here. Struck by happiness I burst into tears.

She brought some homemade quince jam and real self-baked bread. We put our fingers into the glass and licked every little piece out of it and the lid. We broke whole chunks of the bread loaf and chewed it and the quince stuck to our palates. We three sat in the grass of the dunes in a small circle. The wind blew a fresh salty scent from the North Sea and it ruffled our hair and skirts. The grass was sharp and poked into our legs, but the sand surrounded us warm and soft.

"I need to tell you something sad," my mom whispered and she put an arm around each of us. I felt a pinching squeeze in my throat and turned away. This moment with her was so very precious; I didn't want anything to disturb it.

"Your sweet Kalli-dog was run over by a big truck. You know how much he liked to chase cars, and he always was risking too much. So, yesterday the truck was faster than he was and he got under it, and we had to bury him in the garden where we already have the little grave for Toby, our canary bird."

My mother held us very tight. My wet cheek stuck to the fine hair of the angora sweater. The world was hard to live in when what we love can disappear so fast, without a warning.

Mutti left and we stood and waved with our hands until the bus was only a dot at the horizon. That night, Helga and I crawled secretly into each other's bed and we cried in the dark under the covers. I held onto her shoulder and she carefully covered my back so that I would be protected from the cold.

We had not gained any weight when we came home. I walked slowly through the garden and touched the peas and apples, I sang to the blackberries and stroked the pears all around their round bellies. I knew one or two things about life and about families, I thought, and I had learned something new about food and about the loss of a beloved creature. All of that experience would find a place in my mind and settle inside my body. When I nestled into my bed and mother sang us a lullaby, I believed I was in heaven. I had not expected it to be so ordinary and familiar.

On the right side of my parent's bed was a nightstand and a framed photograph had been placed on top of it when we came home from the Country School Home. The picture showed a man in uniform, his arm around his wife, and on each side of them leaned a child against their shoulders. His name was John, said my mother, and he was an officer of the English Allied Troops in Germany. His absent family was bundled together inside the wooden frame, smiling at us from the side of our mother's bed. The man in the picture was a quiet and gentle Englishman, and he visited us regularly. He, too, would become part of the extended tribal community in our home.

I got used to John's presence and crawled into his lap when he visited. First he would set down the brown cardboard box with army food on the kitchen table, and then he shook everybody's hand very formally. All the women in the kitchen watched Mother as she cut the string and paper strips off the box. She opened the flaps, and we put our heads together to look inside. There were chocolate bars and cans with cheese, crackers in boxes, coffee in cans and sweet cookies. The soft white bread was already sliced, something I had never seen before. What I loved most was the chocolate powder for cocoa. When I sat on John's lap to enjoy a cup full of this delicious drink, he slung his arm around my waist and I leaned my head against his shoulder. I imagined that we looked like his happy-family picture in the frame and was a bit shy.

John felt somewhat stranger than Tom, because he did not play funny games with us or roll around on the floor. He was a real grown-up, calm and elegant. I had loved Tom better, but welcomed John, because he, too, shared his own food rations with us very generously. He helped us survive, and my mom seemed very happy, so I was grateful.

John stayed overnight with my mother in her bedroom, and usually he went back to his officers' house in the early morning. I did not mind that. Though the war had ended, my father was still gone for long periods of time.

There was nothing clandestine about the English Allied soldiers in our house. Tom, and after him John, came and went by daylight or in the evening, and they stayed overnight. I didn't know if the neighbors talked about it, and I was not listening for gossip, assuming that our arrangement was normal and good. My mother was happy and there were no secrets or hidden stories. So I enjoyed those new members in our house and did not give it much thought. As children, we love in a radical, unorthodox way, not the people we *should* love but those to whom we feel drawn. Until this day, my sister and I don't know if our father was aware of these arrangements.

My forehead leaned against John's back. His uniform shirt was rough and scratched my skin. He had said he wanted to take a nap and I had asked, 'Can I come, too, and have a nap with you?' He had nodded, but when I climbed up into my parent's bed, he had turned his back to me. I felt lonesome and kept my eyes open.

The room was drenched in a yellowish afternoon light that covered everything like fog. The small alarm clock beside the picture of John and his family ticked, the silence in between tick-and-tuck seemed loud. I sensed the presence of absence; I felt what this moment did not contain. There was no father, and no familiarity. Thinking about my Dad, I missed him; *he would not have turned his back to me, he would have put his arm around my shoulder.* I wondered why he was still gone, now, that the war was over. My feet were cold but I didn't dare move because this man was sleeping in my parent's bed, and I was trying to get warm, cuddled in behind his back. His head was turned towards the nightstand where his whole family looked at him from the photograph inside the wooden frame. They all seemed to love each other. They looked a bit stiff and didn't smile. My grandma had told me that the English were serious, and they always kept good manners and polite speech.

I remembered how it was different in the past; when my father lived with us, summer was family time. We packed our bags and took off for a week or two to the North Sea or Baltic Sea. Both were big waters that almost merged with each other, only separated by the slim tongue of land that leads up towards northern countries with names like Denmark, Sweden and Norway.

The Sisters at the North Sea. Drawing by Isolde Roessner.

My sister, Helga, and I loved the North Sea with a passion. There were long stretches of sand, called *Wattenmeer*, that lifted out of the water when the tide was low. But when it returned, the incoming water swallowed and covered the sandy stretches again. We had to walk for miles to get from the dunes to the edge of the sea, and little shells in the sand poked into the soles of our feet. Helga and I complained and whined, "*Mutti, Vati,* can you please, please carry me, it hurts my feet so much to walk on the shells."

But our parents had to lug the bathrobes, the food, the shovels and towels, and there was no chance for me to sit on father's shoulders. I knew that, but I loved the ritual of the same thing happening again and again and knowing the outcome. When we arrived at the water's edge, Helga and I immediately hopped into the waves. We looked out for jellyfish, because they burned and stung and felt so slimy when stroking along our skin. But soon we thrashed around and got lost in the magic of the open space containing water and sky and sand. It was fantastic to be little in such a big world.

Helga and I looked in every direction, and if nobody was close Helga suggested, "Let's take our bathing suits off and be naked in the water, it tickles the skin as if the water has fingers". "Look Helga, how I can swim already," I shouted, both hands on the ground and my feet floating on the surface. Suddenly, there was a face directly in front of me with a big mustache and round, piercing black eyes the size of plums. I screeched and ran and heard Helga laugh. As I turned around, I realized that the face belonged to a seal. He had come close and wanted to play, but his face had such a human expression that I felt embarrassed to be naked as he was watching.

When the tide returned, we had to hurry, because the way to the shore was long and the water fast. One afternoon we played too long out there and had to run not to be caught by the rising waters that followed swiftly and licked on our heels. I got scared and was surprised that a sweet and familiar place could suddenly become dangerous. The North Sea had this changing character. At times it was inviting, expansive and glorious. But it could unexpectedly turn into a destructive force that threatened land and fortifications and the lives of those near by.

Every year we rented two rooms in a fisherman's house near the big dike that curved all around the peninsula of *St. Peter Ording*. The dam separated and protected the land from the wild and storm-beaten sea. Reeds and wheat fields hugged the thatched-roof house of the fisherman. I often sat on top of the dam and looked in both directions, towards the water and towards the land, like the captain of a large ship. The wind blew incessantly and created wavy patterns in the dry dune grass and in the waters that stood in pools where wild ducks, seagulls and herons bred and raised their young.

There was one unforgettable night when, for the first time, I experienced *Meeresleuchten*, the phosphorescence of the sea. Our family had arrived at the North Sea at about midnight, but we couldn't wait to take our first bath, so we ran towards the edge of the water, following the sound of the waves. In the darkness of the night, we saw the sparkling plankton in the water, as my father explained to us. Every movement of the sea turned into golden light like exploding fireworks. My sister and I threw ourselves into this golden flood, sending showers of stars into the air by shaking our legs, paddling our feet, diving and coming up. The crests of incoming waves were crowned with sparkling globes and they burst into light as they rolled over our shoulders. Water, air, golden sparks and fireworks merged into the enormous dark space of the night. Surrounded by night-angels we created the world by transforming black water into detonations of luminous, quivering light and we danced inside this magic.

Early in the morning, when we were still asleep, the fisherman would sail out to sea and catch heavy nets full of small shrimp. He heaved them home and threw the load into boiling salt water. When we woke up, Helga and I went into the kitchen where the fisherman rolled triangular cones out of newspaper and filled them to the top with fresh and warm shrimp, one for each of us.

My sister and I would find a sheltered place near the top of the dam and wiggle a seat in the sand with our buttocks. We put the newspaper bags between our knees and started the slow and delicious work of peeling the shrimp and eating them. It took so much time to fiddle each one out of its armor that I was always hungry for the next one. Peeling and eating unfolded in a perfect rhythm, never reaching the point of satiation. The desire was always kept even with the new supply of fresh, warm little shrimp between our teeth.

I returned from my dreamlike memories and listened to the regular breath of John. Looking down along his back, to the blotch of light near my cold feet, where the cover had slipped away, I felt a deep sadness. Everything seemed bent out of shape and out of place and nobody knew how it all had come to this. How did this man get into our bed and why was I here, behind his strange back, hoping for warmth and closeness?

I was in the wrong place, or was he—and where was my father? Could anything ever be again how it was in the past?

I unwrapped myself very carefully from the covers and slipped down from the bed and out of the room. The late afternoon light had turned almost brownish. My mother sat in the kitchen with a cup of real coffee from John's military rations in front of her. She looked up at me and smiled, but her eyes were heavy and appeared closed, like the curtains in the bedroom. She was quiet and focused on wrapping an old brooch with garnets into a small handkerchief. She knotted it all together with a piece of ribbon from her red sewing kit. She never had worn this brooch, but she had shown it to me once and told me: 'This is a piece from your great-grandmother in *Aussig*, your father's mother's mother.' I remember this grandmother as a big and round woman all clad in black, with a white lace collar and white lace gloves. She smelled like eucalyptus when she bent down to kiss me. My father told me that she used this oil to massage her joints, because she was hurting all the time. He talked about her as if she were a neighbor or a visitor.

I sat down beside my mother and watched, pulling my legs up and resting my chin on the bony edges of my knees. My head was heavy and my throat hurt as though I needed to cry, but I squeezed the tears back down. The coffee water winced and gurgled in the old battered pot.

My mother got up and walked into the bedroom to wake John. They talked for some time, and when she came back, the small package with the brooch was not in her hand any more. She made some real coffee for John and put the cup on the table beside her own. Then she turned slightly toward me, her face a bit wretched and gray, and said, "John is leaving. He's going back to his home and family in England. Tomorrow."

My feet were still cold and I held them with both hands as I sat on the chair, my body tightly folded up into a lump. I unfurled myself and put boots on to walk out in the last faint light of day. I didn't want to say one more good-bye, not to John or to anybody else. I was embarrassed about my tears and I didn't even know why I was so sad.

157

When I came for the last visit with my grandmother in 1982, before I left for America, she told me about the family heirloom, the brooch with garnets.

"When the English officer, John, left to go back to England, your mother gave him the brooch from your father's mother's mother. She gave it as a goodbye gift for John's wife. She wanted to make a generous gesture to the woman whose husband she had enjoyed during the brutally hard time after the war's end." And she told me the rest of the story, too. It was an uncanny story that has lingered in my imagination, because it is one of those that will not be resolved and nobody is alive to tell the truth. I wonder today if I even desire to know what happened.

"Your father came home one day from one of his long trips, and somehow he asked your Mother about the brooch. They were both estranged from each other, and your Mother lived her life very independently. I wonder, even today, if your father knew about the Allied soldiers, Tom and John, in our house. Your dad was a very quiet and secretive man, and he talked little about himself, especially not to me.

"So, he found one thing to hang my Dolly on a hook. He had his suspicions. That day, he asked for the brooch and, you know how your Mother is, she didn't make up lies. She told him that she gave it away, that she gave it as a gift to the man who had brought us food and visited our home. She said that is was a gift for his wife in England. They stood there in front of each other in the kitchen when she said that."

Grandmother wiped her long fingers over her face as if to rub away the images stored inside her brain. "I see them as if it were today."

"Hans got these ice-cold green eyes and clenched his jaws without saying a word, you know how he does that."

I did.

Grandmother sighed, "He points to their bedroom. It's so tight in this apartment because many people live here, no privacy for anybody. He points to the door without a word and they both go in there and he closes the door and locks it. I'm holding my breath, standing in the kitchen and am really afraid for your Mother, my Dolly. I listen, and you know, there's not one sound I can hear. It's so silent that it's creepy. I would love to step in, but don't dare to do it. Your father frightens me." She pauses.

"It's dead silent inside, for long time. It's one of those moments in my life where I want to help my Dolly, but can't. I hurt for her and feel so…so helpless, and all happens just in the next room and I cannot imagine what's going on and what's he doing to her in this icy silence in the bedroom."

I listened to my grandmother and felt a grip around my neck that was painful and heavy, like an old and familiar chain. I wondered about the mystery we are to each other, even in the small web of our loved-ones. Our families shape us and wound us and imprint themselves into every cell of our bodies and minds.

Grandmother looked pained. "After a long, long time, your Mother comes out of the room, alone. She is white in her face like a sheet. I look at her and she doesn't look back at me, avoids my eyes. She leans over the sink and starts cleaning pots, wildly, as if she needs to grip something hard, and hold onto something to feel that she's alive."

"And you know, *min Deern*, she never told me what happened inside the room, she told neither me, nor her sister Margarete. We don't know what he did to her, but I think it was very frightening and humiliating. Maybe he took revenge. We'll never know."

8

ASHES AND ASHES

My father picked us up in Hamburg at the end of 1947, so we would join him in Munich, situated in the south of Germany and far away. We left home, and I was torn out of the web of the familiar tribe that was cramped together in our small apartment— my beloved grandparents, my aunt Margarete, and uncle Albin. I also left behind my dearest friend, Dieter, and the familiar trees, the companions of my childhood. At nine years of age, I felt raw and uprooted. But underneath the anxiety was excitement about the new start for us four. Moving south prompted us to depart from everything well known and trusted, but it also contained the promise that we would bond again and grow together as a family.

The American Allied troops had hired my father to take inventory of the war machinery that the retreating German army had abandoned at the airport Munich

*Everything is far
and long gone by.
I think that the star
glittering above me
has been dead for a million
years.
I think there were tears.*
— Rainer Maria Rilke, *Lament*

*People ought to be told…
ought to be taught that
immortality
is mortal, that it can die,
it's happened before and it
happens still.*
— Marguerite Duras,
The Lover
Pantheon Books New York

Holzkirchen. His contract said in English language: 'Mr. Roessner is the representative of the German Government and will arrange for the removal of scrap stocks that are located on your field.' Signed by Captain of Infantry, Richard Dunsmore, and Captain W. Thad Lovett, these documents dated from September 1945. This order was confirmed with the stamp of the Allied military government. My father was proud to be one of the first to receive employment and income from the occupiers of the destroyed Germany; it was an acknowledgment of his skills.

We looked toward a future where food and shelter for the whole family seemed secured.

Munich is close to the Bavarian Alps. Some peaks have snow and glacier ice on top all year round. I had never seen mountains before so I asked my father, "What are they made of? If they are dirt, they would crumble when it rains."

My father said, "They are giant rocks, much harder than earth, and they have been there for thousands of years without falling apart."

That gave me a lot to think about as I sat with my sister in the back seat of his car. We were driving south, all four together, to our new home. We talked and joked, imagining this and that, and it felt as if we were a real family again. My mother told us that the American troops occupied Bavaria, and since there were black people in America, we would also see them in Munich. I was afraid and excited to meet Negroes, and I decided to beg them to let me touch their skin and rub my fingers over it to see if the color came off.

My father attained permission to rent an apartment for us in a three-family house that had survived the bombings. We were lucky, most families were forced to share one room. The street was called Hirsch-Gereuth Strasse. The house, surrounded by a small garden on three sides, sheltered a chicken coop in the back. There was a wheat field adjacent to the house, and the chain-link fence was torn enough for the chickens to sneak through and eat the seeds that were supposed to grow and bear fruit. Herr and Frau Sorg, this name means sorrow, were the owners of the house, and they pretended not to notice their chickens in the farmer's field, so they got them fed without having to care for them. In summer, it became obvious that the chickens ate the seeds because there was no wheat growing all along the fence. I thought it was not fair to intrude into someone else's territory. Fences were obvious boundaries and needed to be respected. Sometimes I was very opinionated and righteous.

The apartment had just enough space for all four of us. We children didn't need to share bedrooms with the grownups any more. My sister and I slept in bunk beds in a very small room, but my father and mother had a real bedroom for themselves. There was a kitchen with a wood burning stove and a balcony along the front of our living room, because we lived on the second floor. Upstairs lived a blond girl my age, named Christle. She was nine years old, like me, and she became my best friend. Downstairs lived Herr and Frau Sorg and their daughter Isolde, the same name as my mother's. She was eleven, my sister's age. My father called our house the "*Vier-Mäderl-Hause,*" the four-girls-house, similar to the title of an operetta. We laughed and I enjoyed his joking.

Helga and I went to the new school and we felt awkward. The Bavarian dialect was like a foreign language. In the northern part of Germany people pride themselves in speaking High German, but in the south of Germany the local dialect is well-loved and bonds all the Bavarians into one big and raucous family.

The kids in school observed us from a distance, as if we were strange animals, because we looked and sounded different. The children in Bavaria wore unique clothing, colorful blouses and skirts for the girls, called *dirndel*, and *lederhosen* with suspenders and white shirts for the boys. The suspenders had edelweiss and blue enzian flowers stitched on them. The boys put their thumbs underneath the suspenders and protruded their bellies. *This stance seemed to be characteristic of Bavarian boys,* I thought, remembering those pictures from a children's book, where dwarfs wearing Bavarian hats sat on little benches under mushrooms and smoked pipes.

It slowly dawned on me that we would now be spending our lives here. Exchanging home and the familiar hum of language for new ones was similar to wearing unfitting clothes that pinched and scratched and had the wrong color. 'Home' was a felt-sense in my body, triggered by smells, weather, sights and sounds. I observed a new self, walking beside me, and I was ill at ease, because she was shy and clumsy and I didn't like her. My memory of home had become liquid, and hard to hold on to. I missed my grandmother and her funny stories. I missed my grandfather and his crooked walk with the cane. Mother, father, my sister and I were the same four people in our family, but the container was different, and that transformed us, too. We needed to yield into the mold of a new environment at the same time as we were trying to compose a new life with each other.

Now, my father was with us daily, and that felt awkward. Even the presence of his physical body felt strange to me: his scent, his hands, his way of moving around and watching us, his habit of imposing his opinions and orders. He was my father and I didn't know him well. My sister and I had grown through several years without his company and I felt hesitant touching him. But Helga was very happy. She had missed our father and suffered severely when the Allied officers visited our home, but she didn't talk about that. She climbed into my father's lap, and they held hands when walking along together. But I cuddled in with my mother and watched him with apprehension, feeling sad and guilty to be so estranged.

The children in school and neighborhood cornered my sister and me, pretending to teach us the Bavarian dialect. They pronounced slowly the most difficult words. Those words scratched in the throat and we stuttered and blushed, but they laughed and slapped their thighs, jumping up and down with amusement. One of those words was "*oachkatzerlschwoaf*," which means a squirrel's tail. The Bavarians frequently use the ending *–erl* at the end of words to make them sound endearing. They were very proud of their land and wished to declare Bavaria a kingdom, separate from the rest of Germany. It was obvious that we northern people would not be considered part of that kingdom.

In school we learned about the colorful history of Munich and all of Bavaria. The teachers told us about the kings and the aristocracy, of bloody battles and the building of graceful castles, like *Hohenschwangau* and *Neuschwanstein*. But our teachers offered also a hesitant glance at the more recent disasters that weighed down on the town, before, during and after the war. Munich is the third largest city in Germany, following Berlin and Hamburg. After suffering through more than seventy air raids, it was very severely destroyed at the end of the war. This town was the cradle of Hitler's National Socialism and called the "Capital of the Movement." But it was also the birthplace of resistance to the *Führer's* madness. Students at the University founded the movement *"Weisse Rose"* — White Rose — inspired and led by the siblings Hans and Sophie Scholl. They distributed leaflets on campus, informing people about the atrocities of the Nazi regime. Brother and sister Scholl risked their lives for their passion of truth; consequently, like many other resisters, they were caught, imprisoned, and executed by guillotine.

And there was a man named Georg Elser, who attempted to assassinate Hitler in the *Bürgerbräukeller* in Munich, November 8, 1939. He planned the attack for a year, and in thirty days of work, he single-handedly and secretly hollowed out a wooden column beside the place where Hitler would be standing during his commemoration speech. Elser hid a bomb inside this column and timed it to go off during the Fuehrer's speech. But Hitler appeared earlier at the place, and had already left when the explosion occurred, killing eight innocent bystanders. Hitler triumphed, 'Now I am content. The fact that I left earlier than usual shows that Providence intends to allow me to reach my goals!' The devil had protected the devil. Elser died years later in the concentration camp Dachau, ten miles northwest of Munich, the first camp to be installed.

At the end of the war, hundreds of thousands of refugees from Sudetenland were directed to settle in Bavaria. My Aunt Hannie and Uncle Ernst, my father's brother, were among them. Expelled from their hometown, *Aussig*, they arrived in 1947 at our doorsteps in Munich to live with us for short time until they found their own space to rent. I scarcely knew them from a former visit to Hamburg. We offered to them our small kid's room with the bunk beds and we children slept on the sofa in the living room.

Uncle Ernst and Aunt Hanny were bitter and outraged when they talked about being 'chased from their rightfully owned homes and country,' where they had lived all their lives, and so did several generations of our paternal family before them. A dark and confusing history overshadowed this territory. I didn't know about that until my uncle explained the story to me.

In 1938, Hitler had invaded and annexed the Czech country of Sudetenland. At that time he acted with the agreement of British Prime Minister Chamberlin and French Prime Minister Eduouard Daladier. Mussolin, the Italian Prime Minister, took the initiative, inviting these leaders to a conference in Munich, on September 29, 1938. They signed the infamous Munich Agreement on September 30, and the big war machinery began to roll.

Sudetenland lies at the eastern border of Germany, and in 1938 it was part of Czechoslovakia. The ruling powers agreed to Hitler's takeover, without even consulting the Czech government, in an effort to appease Hitler and to prevent his movement towards a general war. Little did they know that they were throwing a piece of meat to a ferocious lion. As a consequence, the lion had tasted blood. After that fateful agreement, the Czech inhabitants were ruthlessly expelled. They had to leave their homes and country in ten days!

But after Germany's capitulation at the end of World War II, the Potsdam Conference turned that arrangement on its head and determined that this time, the German population would be forced to leave because Sudetenland was re-claimed by Czechoslovakia. In the early phase of that exodus, the number of German refugees was estimated to be 500,000. During the organized phase in 1946, a total of 2.2 million were exiled from their homes in Sudetenland and sent to Germany. Their possessions were confiscated and claimed as war reparations.

There was so much repressed rage and resentment on the side of the Czech people against former Nazi behavior, that mistreatment and even murder of the fleeing Germans were common. The exodus of refugees was later called the 'Brno Death March' or *Brünner Todesmarsch*. It is assumed that about 24,000 deaths were directly related to the expulsion, caused by suicide, murder, disease and old age.

Aunt Hannie and Uncle Ernst were part of this death march towards the west. They arrived in Munich without possessions, and the few things they salvaged had immense meaning for them. My uncle Ernst was my father's only brother. He was a gentle and warmhearted man and he rarely talked about their ordeal.

My aunt cherished a small milk can with a smooth handle made out of dark wood. She had carried it all the way from her home in the east. "For refugees," she told me, "it was sometimes a question of life or death to have a container for the food that was offered along the long and painful march.

"Occasionally, there were trucks that provided rations for the thousands of famished homeless who streamed westwards. Those trucks would appear suddenly, with nurses offering boiling hot soup and ladling it into the cups or containers that people carried. We were desperately tired and hungry," she told me once when we sat together in the kitchen waiting for her apple-strudel to bake.

"Your uncle Ernst had soldered it himself, this simple milk can, he made it from a piece of pipe. We guarded it like our most precious possession, because we could collect food in it. So this tin can means more to me than the jewelry we hid in the hollow heels of our shoes. This container held the food that kept us alive and going." She rubbed the wooden handle with her slightly arthritic hands, and polished the metal with the sleeve of her sweater. I sat very quietly and listened, because she rarely allowed me a glance into the landscape of her sorrow and loss.

After two months of living with us, my Aunt Hanny and Uncle Ernst found a furnished room to rent in a repaired house not too far from us. They moved out of our home and my sister and I had our small bunk-bedroom again for ourselves.

On February 23, 1948, my mother left to go away for a day and night without indicating her destination. All four of us were in the kitchen, the only place that was heated and cozy during an extremely cold winter, our first in Bavaria. I thought that she looked so beautiful when she said goodbye, wearing a dark blue coat and a turban made out of the same fabric. She had sown her clothing herself, as she was very skilled in creating something attractive out of almost nothing. She wore bright lipstick and waved a rabbit-fur muff in one hand, laughing and happy. When she put her arms around my shoulders and kissed me, she looked directly into my eyes and said, 'I'll be gone for a short time and tomorrow I'll be back with you!'

The skin of her face was radiant and her eyes twinkled. I put my hands on each side of her face. My thumbs placed in the dimple on her chin, my middle fingers touched the lobes of her ears. Her high forehead was bright, as if light shone from the inside out.

Oh God, how much I love her, I thought, and happiness stirred in my whole body like a gentle fire that would always burn and never leave me.

I stood at the window and waved until she disappeared when she took the seat beside my father in his car. My breath clouded the icy windowpane. I painted a heart onto it with my index finger.

The doorbell awakened me in the middle of the night. I opened my eyes and stared into black space. It was like in a movie I had seen where the deep ocean was so dark that the fish had little lights on their fins and tails. My sister in the lower bunk bed sighed and stirred in her sleep.

Is this about mother? I wondered, my heart racing. *I am afraid! Something is very wrong.*

The bell rings again. I hold my breath and hear my dad scramble out of his bedroom. Sharp alertness cuts like a knife into my sleepy mind. There are steps on the wooden stairs outside. A person comes to the door and whispers. Someone stumbles up and down the stairs in a hurry. Heels clunk on the metal edges of the stairs and arms scrape along the walls as though carrying something heavy.

I breathe in puffs. The air scratches my throat. A thought grabs and chokes me, scarring like an iron trap that snaps shut around a living limb: *Mother is in danger. Something bad has happened to her.*

I lie on the sheets, frozen, my body stiffens. Blades of light cut through the slits between the door and its frame. The blades slice the darkness into sharp blocks. The blocks pile around me and compress the air. I stare without blinking. And then, and then I lift – slowly - out of my body, floating above a self that is broken open. *Whatever happens to my mother will penetrate me, too. I am bonded to her. Enfleshened. Tied and woven into her life. Knotted inside her being.*

The whispers outside sift through the keyhole. Murky, scratching breath and sound reach into the room, squeeze between books, toys, and night pot, wrapping around me.

Mama, is it you who groans and whines? Mama, is it you who cuts the light into slices? Mama I don't want to be separate from you! Mama, this fear is so cold and hard.

I am entangled, curled into the whispers, severed into two. One part is frozen stiff and trapped inside my body; the other is fluid and without shape.

The fluid self escapes and swirls upward above the roof of the house, expanding into the wide star-filled darkness of the night. An enormous soft shadow embraces me like the supple wings of a black bird.

I am weightless, stretching into the feathery space, becoming space myself. Stars rotate and swirl inside me. I am part of the sky and of the silvery light that filters through the dusk. Darkness and light meet inside me and fuse. There's no separation. I am weightless, without shape or form. Crossing a threshold, I am offered a choice at a forking path in front of me. One path pulls me gently upward to drift higher and higher. I can float and become radiant, star-stitched into night's fluid darkness. The other path leads down, merging back into my body made of flesh, to face the terror of this night with its secrets and whispers and scratchy moans. So, I stretch and extend towards the stars. I want to dissolve in the fluid light. I unravel the tentacles of my life from my form and know that this is the end of everything familiar, fleshy, pulsating and warm.

Suddenly, a force seizes me and plunges me down with the furor of a waterfall. I drown in this force. I am swirling inside a wildly driving mass that holds me with its relentless grip, collapses me back into form and slips me into the girl's petrified body on the crumpled sheets in the black room where the blades of light around the door cut into the sharp blocks of darkness.

My sister's breath sounds from the lower bed. I lift my arms slowly and feel their weight. I heave my legs up and climb out of bed, my body stiff and awkward. I am a hundred years old, a changed person, twisted inside myself. I scramble into bed with my sister, I need another body to touch and sense that I exist.

I pull the sheets all the way up over my head, fragile and bloody like a skinned animal. I don't dare go outside the room, unable to expose the thin ribbon that tethers me to life.

Early in the morning, before the light had penetrated the curtains, my father walked into our room where I lay half asleep and half awake, because everything inside me was ripped and raw after a restless night. His eyelids were heavy and he had his jacket on; the wrong holes joined with the wrong buttons, he looked out of sync and crooked. Father bent down and said to Helga and me, 'Get up and put warm stuff on. Your mother is not well. I will bring you to your aunt Hannie and uncle Ernst so that your mother has some quiet and can rest. Rest,' he said once more and turned around.

I felt split into fragments, a puzzle with pieces missing or the picture torn off. My brown sweater was inside-out and my socks, bigger than the shoes, made folds at my heels. Helga was sleepy and stumbled a bit. I trembled in the cold. The fire in the kitchen had died during the night. I knew how to light a fire and stuffed some paper and kindling into the oven to heat milk and to postpone our departure, giving my mother time, hoping she might suddenly open the door and walk in. But I also sensed that all doors would stay closed.

My father, urging us on, held my winter coat, and I slipped the arms into the holes and threw the shawl around my neck, without lighting the fire. My mother had worn a shawl yesterday, when she left and held me in her arms to say goodbye. I had rested my chin on her shoulder and inhaled her scent, and that's when I saw that her earlobe threw a small shadow against her neck and her blood was pulsating underneath that place of shadow. Her blood was so close to the surface of the skin that I felt it beating against my eyelashes as I leaned my head into that place of warmth.

Father locked the door and we clambered down those creaky stairs. When we opened the door, the cold hit across my face like a whip. It squeezed tears out of my eyes, and my body quivered like the dry grass in the dunes of the North Sea where we used to walk together in happy times in what seemed a thousand years ago.

My father backed his car out of the driveway. He had to open the garden gate, drive and then close it again after he passed it. Helga and I usually squabbled as to who would be faster at reaching the gate to do this job, but this morning we both sat together in the back seat and held so firmly on to each other that my shoulder ached and I could not breathe. The engine sputtered and choked in the cold. My father drove down the *Obersendlinger Strasse*, and there were few other cars on the road because it was so early and extremely icy. Most window shades were still closed, and even the milk shop at the corner had the metal guards still locked in place. Four milk cans stood in front of the chain like soldiers in armor, their lids like helmets.

When we passed by the *Sendlinger Park*, my father drove the car to the side of the road, its tires scratching against the curb. Then he turned

171

around toward us and opened his mouth. This mouth appeared like a black hole in the middle of his gray face.

I didn't want this to happen. I wanted him to stop. I wanted to sink deep into the earth or fly away. But I could not move from this cold seat. My father spoke slowly and it took a long time for every word to travel from his mouth to my ear. From far away I heard him say one sentence: 'Your mother is with the Angels in Heaven.'

After these words memory is stalled, as though black curtains inside my brain had separated those hours. Memory has been abandoned in chambers in a vault deep inside a mountain, and the entry is blocked. I only recall that my sister and I were lying in our Aunt Hannie's bed. We were intertwined into each other, our hands clawed together, crying for days, sinking in and out of reality. We ingested the loss of our mother in small and bloody chunks.

I never saw my mother again. The night of her death sealed the end of my childhood.

My sister and I came home to a cold and empty house. The following day I went back to school and told my teacher: 'Sorry that I missed class, but my Mother has died.'

She looked at me, her face turned white. She was silent, and her breath slowed. Fräulein Hendling was a beloved teacher of mine. She had large, rolling hips and gray hair, like my *Oma,* tied into a small bun. She always wore dark dresses with white collars made of lace. Soft hair covered her chin and a mole extended her left eyebrow. I trusted her. As her eyes locked into mine, I felt a heavy iron door inside my chest open. A searing stream of anguish shot through the opening. It burned its way across my inner fortifications and a thousand years of loneliness lined up in front of me. Fräulein Hendling's compassion lifted the thin skin off my wound and it ruptured to expose raw flesh. I started weeping and felt very embarrassed, because the other children in class where watching us, eyes wide open.

"You need some time at home," she said softly. "It's fine that you stay home as long as you want and come back when you can."

I grabbed my school bag and scuttled out, weeping all the way home.

In later years I understood that children are able to deal with trauma if there is at least one person in whom they can confide. If one adult listens and helps to understand, the child can integrate tremendous loss and encounters with death. Fräulein Hendling was one of those people. That morning, when she looked at me with compassion, I dared to touch the bleeding wound inside. But I had to close the trapdoor immediately, because there was nobody at home to talk to or to continue the devastating journey of mourning. My sister was as traumatized as I. We stumbled like shipwrecked travelers through our lives. So, I created a soundproof chamber around the scream inside, and it took years until I had the maturity to open the gate again. When I finally did, I found decomposed pieces of my childhood memory in a deep well of grief.

At age seventy, I still have not reached its bottom. Grieving is an art and we need to learn its expression like a foreign language. Most of us feel insecure and clumsy, because people avoid speaking this language. If we face loss as children, we watch the adults around us and helplessly adjust to the message we get from them. In my case, it was not only in my family that we were lacking words of truth and consolation, but my whole country was mute and deaf to its inner cries of mourning.

I would have thought, today, that the constant presence of war had prepared me for death and loss. But the loss of hundreds of thousands was too enormous to be integrated. We protect ourselves against such a reality by denial and survival instincts. In contrast, when one person who is an intimate part of our life, is ripped out of the familiar web, we are bleeding and broken as though a knife had cut a piece out of a living organism.

I hid in Helga's and my room, pressed my forehead against the cold windowpane and watched the snow fall. It slowly covered the barren apple tree and the muddy road and traces of car tires that looked like scars. Winter storm pressed its fists against the glass.

My mother had died. The ground of my life had shifted as if rattled by an earthquake. The devastated landscape had turned into an unrecognizable chaos of rocks, dirt and deep craters. I blindly walked around in this moon-like territory and tried desperately to make sense of the events. But being nine years old, making sense of the screeching pain inside was a task I could not handle by myself.

My father's voice came from the kitchen.

"Helga, Elke, come here and sit down with me."

When my sister, Helga, and I came into the kitchen, my father sat in the corner on a stiff wooden chair. We climbed on the bench beside him that was covered with red and white-checkered pillows that tried to look homey and Bavarian. We waited. His face was pale. We three were clustered together like a group of marionettes with hanging limbs, tangled in their strings. I looked at him and felt a small flame of hope inside, hope that he would speak words to create some order and meaning in the middle of this chaos.

"Our neighbors and your friends might ask how your mother died," he said, being factual and short. I held my breath so that the small flame of hope would not die at the slightest draft.

"I want to explain to you what to tell them," he continued.

He put his hands down on the table and watched with great attention how they shifted the checkered cloth and created valleys and peaks in the soft surface. All three of us stared at the play of light and shadow in those crinkles.

"Tell them that your mother walked barefoot in the garage and a rusty nail poked itself into her sole. The wound got infected and created blood poisoning. It went to her heart and there was nothing that could be done as it happened so fast."

I turned my eyes to the window and I imagined my mother walking barefoot in the snow. I knew that this story was a lie. The hope vanished and my helplessness made me very small as the lie weighed down on my shoulders and heart.

I remembered how movie scenes were filmed, by starting with two arms of board that snapped together. They were striped black and white and looked like scissors or a barking dog. I decided to change scenes in my head. I snapped the boards and then I created a new movie all by myself, right at that moment.

There was the infected foot of my mother, and the poisoned blood snaked inside her body, and inside her veins, and towards the heart, and then the snake ate her heart and she died. But behind the movie screen sat my sister and I and we were holding the biggest questions of our lives, like an empty begging bowl—'What really happened that night?'

My dad got up from the chair, he straightened out the ruffled tablecloth, stroking with his hands across any unevenness. He walked towards the door and pulled the cloth off the table with his right hip. It lay on the floor and reminded me of a pile of stinking guts that I once saw in a butcher shop. My father closed the door behind him.

Never again did he talk about the death of my mother. The story of her death was the black hole in our family that sucked anybody who would circle it into its void. This black hole also sucked the life energy out of my relationship with my father. His presence was like a no-man's land that did not provide comfort or a place to talk. I retreated into my own world and closed the door.

Even my sister and I rarely talked about mother. We crossed this desert of our grief in silence, as we could not decipher the runes and hieroglyphs that marked our path. But having Helga at my side was essential for my emotional survival. She was part of me, she was familiar, and she was my living companion.

That afternoon my father had lain down an unspoken law: 'We don't ask questions or speak about Mother's death. We don't cry or whine.'

That unspoken law settled into every crack of my brain and became part of my reality. I understood the rule that I was just a child and had no right to ask questions. I succumbed and fell into silence, accepting that my longing for truth was against the family order. My mother had died and a secret was born. The questions around her death haunted me for most of my adult life.

Nearly forty years later, when I saw my father for the last time, I was still afraid of asking him the truth about my own mother's death. In the years to come, the wrestling for answers in my personal life merged seamlessly with the search for meaning and truth about the war and its atrocities. Our personal secret mirrored the denial of German actions during that time. The intimate and small story of one family merged with the dark cloud of lies and secrets that overshadowed our whole culture.

> *Like the low-hanging moon*
> *O I think this vessel is heavy*
> *With love's suffering.*
> —Micheline Aharonian Marcom, *Three Apples Fell From Heaven*

They thought I needed a pair of black shoes and a black coat and a black hat. They borrowed the clothes from our neighbors and hung them all around this small, cold body so that I would look appropriate, how one has to look at a funeral, even a child. This was the funeral of my mother and I was nine.

What I really needed was a hand to hold onto. My father folded his gloved hands in his lap. I didn't know how to reach over to him because I could not move. There were yellowish tiles on the floor and blind crystal lamps along the walls, like scratched glasses half-full of sour milk, their light didn't penetrate the gray darkness of this crematorium. My legs were too short; I couldn't lean against the back of the bench and the edge of the seat cut into my thighs.

My father, my sister and I sat in the first row. Nobody else was with us in the first row because these seats were reserved, *Reserviert!* for the ones who hurt the most. There was an empty seat where my grandmother should have been. I ached for her.

In the next row were my Aunt Hannie and Uncle Ernst, my father's brother. Their faces were pale and gray like the dirty snow outside. In the following rows sat neighbors, but only a few. They didn't really know my mother, because we had just moved to Munich and people were still strangers to us. Those strangers sat further away from the big brown wooden box in the middle of the stage. My mother was inside the box — that's what my father had told me.

I would never see her again. She was alive some days ago. She smiled at me, and I smelled the sweet and warm scent of her skin and hair and saw the little shadow that her ear lobe cast on her neck. I observed it as I nestled my head between her shawl and her hair when she held me in her arms to say goodbye. The memory of this little shadow behind her ear was now frozen inside my brain as if to prove that my mother was real, some endless time ago.

I hoped that this memory would stay frozen. If it melted, I would catch fire and burn me to cinders.

I was so close to the box that I could have touched it, but didn't dare to reach out. Ice crystals stuck to my skin and to the black coat that I wore. It was my friend Christle's coat. She lived in the apartment above us and went to school with me every day. Right now I didn't go to school because I couldn't look into the faces of my classmates without sobbing. They were filled with fear. Christle and I never talked about my mother's death. I think she, too, like everybody, was afraid of saying words like "death" and "forever."

A man in a black cape stood near the box, twisting his hands and mouth. He lifted his heavy eyelids and folded his forehead into layers of skin. He said things that I couldn't hear or understand. I wondered if this robed man still had a mother, and if he talked to her like to us, uttering sounds without any meaning. His words slithered out the door into the cemetery where they gathered like dry leaves in corners between the granite-covered graves.

Two men in black suits with black gloves walked slowly toward the box. They put their glove-covered hands at the corners of the box and pushed it gradually towards the big door.

The box moved on rollers and I knew — how did I know — that my mother inside this box would now be burned and turned into ashes and smoke. The little shadow behind her ear would melt and would only be real as long as I lived and remembered it. But I didn't even want to live without my mother's ears and smells and warmth. Why would any child in this world want to live without the warm body of Mother to fold into and to know from inside that place in the mother-fold that life made sense?

The gate opened in two pieces, like two dark wings, and uttered a muffled screech that punched into the silence like a fist.

I assumed that there was a fire behind the next gate made from iron, which I could not see. The box slid into the dim space behind the black wings. The wings screeched again, they flapped and shut closed and I thought that this might be the moment of "forever."

My mother would now turn into fire and light and smoke, but I was drowning in ice crystals. They poked through my eyes and throat and pierced my body like nails. I wanted to be sucked into the big black hole that was inside me. I wanted to coil into my own black middle and never come out. The black winter coat from Christle slid down from my shoulders, and my father lifted it back into place. I had forgotten that he was there, that anybody was there beside me.

Scattered music fell from the organ on the balcony like smoke that choked my throat. My father, my sister and I were signaled to get up. We stood beside each other, arranged like puppets on father's left and right side and flanked by two white columns.

People slouched by in front of us and shook our hands. Some had tears in their eyes and uttered small clouds of words that stood in the cold air, hesitant to dissolve. I had to lean my head back to see their faces underneath the rim of the black hat that was pinned with a clamp to my hair. Some looked as if they knew about those boxes that disappeared in dim spaces with fire waiting to devour them. And some had no face at all, and I would see through them into a far distance where everybody had lost somebody they loved.

The black, shiny shoes from my friend Christle were too small for my feet, and I felt my toes clenching together and screaming for space. The pain called my attention downward and I woke up to the sensation of my own body and to the strange place where the soles of my feet touched the ground. I saw the black shoes standing on yellow tiles scratched blind by the shoes of hundreds and thousands of people who had shaken hands here with others after their box rolled through the "forever"-door and caught fire. I was part of a long line of children and grown-ups who had stood here over the years. They had touched each other's hands and had passed by, looking into the eyes of people who didn't want to be there. Their hands were intertwining and holding on to each other so that they wouldn't drown in ice crystals or turn into ashes. My feet ached and signaled to me that I was still alive inside this small and numb body.

My mother's feet would never hurt again because she was right now turning into smoke and the tiny shadow behind her left ear disappeared forever. Her warm smell dissolved in the heat; it mingled with burnt flakes of her skin and twirled out of the long chimney into the winter air.

The mother-smoke staggered along the roof of the building and lingered in the barren trees along the path where we now walked in silence, because there were no words that could pierce the loneliness in a world where my mother's body and the shadow behind her ear had dissolved in the fire.

My father found a shop where they enlarged a black and white photograph of our mother. He framed it and fixed it on the wall of the living room. Then he bought two small glass vases shaped like balls that hung on strings from wrought iron holders. He fixed one on each side of the picture, just at the height of mother's bright smile. My sister and I arranged fresh flowers in those two glass balls and filled them daily with new water. The living room was usually without heat, so our hands were trembling when we stuck the flowers into the vases. This ritual was our clumsy recognition of her absence. We performed these meager gestures, but no words were spoken to bridge the gap between life before and life after her death. I had never actually seen my mother dead, there was no experience of her in a deceased body. *Maybe it was all a lie, or a nightmare. Maybe I was mad and I would never be normal again.*

The interactions inside our family were frozen. The ritualistic gesture of fresh flowers in those two small glass vases confirmed, 'Yes, it's true, our *Mutti* is dead.' But the silence about her death made it unreal. The silence gave it the seal of something bad and embarrassing, so we could not talk to others about her. We lacked a real live person who would listen and comfort us and stroke our hair with gentle hands and kneel down to our size and whisper in our ears.

Part of me lived a 'normal life' as a child. The other part was petrified and hidden, buried in sorrow. The reality of death, not acknowledged through words and healing gestures, was like a heavy yoke around my shoulders. This fragmented family had fallen into a deep sleep and there was nobody to wake us up. My whole body longed with a clawing hunger for my grandmother, for touch, for somebody who would help to untangle the chaotic strands of this nightmarish and ghostly web of loneliness.

My sister Helga and I learned to keep our small household going. We cooked potatoes and mashed them. With some butter on top and salt and parsley, it was a dinner. We mainly ate rolled oats. Rolled oats with raisins, rolled oats with apples and cinnamon, rolled oats as leftover from the day before. One day, when I was cleaning the pot where I just had cooked rolled oats, I found in the fold, where the handle was fixed to the pot, some dried up and crusted beans. I stopped and remembered that we had not eaten beans for weeks; so, I thought, those remnants were from the time when my mother had prepared a meal. She really had lived in this house, I thought, she had cooked beans and now she did not any more. I didn't dream that she was not here or that she would not stand ever again here in this kitchen. Everything was real, those beans confirmed that she existed, and now she did not exist any more. Ever. I sat very slowly down on a chair and held the pot between my two hands, and then I licked the crusted beans because my mother had left them there. I stared at them, and then I licked again and then a whole river of terror tried to push itself through my throat, from the inside out. But I held tight, pressed my lips and my breath and then my whole chest into one sturdy shield that separated the inside from the outside. I stood, and then I cleaned the dry beans with a knife off the pot and pushed the pot into the very back of the kitchen cabinet and the metal clinked and clunked like an iron gate being closed.

I opened the door to the closet and found my mother's coat on a hanger. Her scent clung to the inside like a piece of her skin, between the lining and the rough wool fabric. I embraced the coat with both arms and pushed my hands into the pockets, where I found her crumbled handkerchief. I sucked on it and swallowed the tiny shreds of her life, contained in her smell. She was dead and had vanished. And I was dead, too, the child I was when she was alive, did not exist any more. That child, when she existed, was seen by her eyes, stroked by her hands, held in her arms with fondness. But when she ceased to create this child, everyday anew, through her awareness and her love, that child was wiped from existence. That daughter disappeared with her mother. That girl sensed the disappearance, but there was no comfort for that death-of-self, that death of daughter-hood, either. There was no medicine or gesture to purge the horror called loss of selfhood, a loss that could not be spoken in words and had no name.

Instead, there was another girl, an awkward child, unknown to herself, a stranger in her own body. And that stranger realized the death of the child that was once herself, the child that had lived in tandem with her mother and had received every day the affirmation that she existed, through the simple and natural presence of a mother who saw her and spoke her name. The stranger, the new "I" had been tossed at the shores of an unknown continent, called adulthood, and she had no tools or map to wander this foreign land.

Helga and Elke. Photograph by Hans Roessner.

When I came home from school, our house was quiet and lonesome. The rooms were empty and cold. Without my mother's presence moving around in them, they had changed shape. They did not fit or comfort, but strangled like a dress that was handed down to me from a stranger. Love needs a body to be expressed. Love is physical. Love needs two hands to cook or take the hot bread from the oven, it needs hands to bind and stroke a wound, it needs hands to brush the hair of a child, it needs hands to kiss and hold a child's face, it needs arms to embrace a child, a mouth to speak of love. These hands, this mouth had disappeared and with them the gestures of love, their scents and their touch.

At that time we wore our long hair in a complicated style. Little strands all around the head were braided into a main strand and that looked like a wheel with rays of a sun. Many girls wore this hairdo. It was very difficult to arrange by oneself, especially in the back where one couldn't see what was happening. So my sister's and my hair often looked crooked and weird because our fingers were clumsy and sad.

"Helga, would you please help me," I asked her in the morning.

"Our *Mutti* could do it so easily," I said tight-voiced. "She knew how to make strands and sling them into the braid around my head. And it felt so good when she brushed and combed my hair. But now I am getting it all tangled, and my arms hurt from keeping them up so long."

It was the first time I spoke the words that seemed forbidden in the presence of my father. Saying "our *Mutti*," felt like entering foreign and dangerous land that was mangled by an earthquake, the number of casualties still not accounted for.

"When I say, '*Mutti*' I think she might open the door and walk in," I said. "And what is much worse, when I say '*Mutti*,' I fear she might never again come through that door." I looked in the mirror and saw my pale face surrounded by frenzied hair, like the thin branches of trees in winter.

"Come and sit down," Helga said, "I'll try. Don't know how to make it look good. I'm tired of failing, I'm tired of being sad, I'm tired of being hungry and cold and alone."

The dark rings under her eyes made her look older than the eleven years she was.

"Helga, do you think it's real?"

"What do you mean by it's real?" she said, as if she didn't know.

"Is it real that our *Mutti* is dead?" I dared to say.

"No, it's not real 'cause I don't want it to be."

"Can we make it unreal by not wanting it?"

"Yes. No. Hold still. Don't talk."

"It hurts," I whispered. "It's all tangled, it's all fuzzy and it's impossible to straighten out."

"I'm clumsy, and you are stupid to think that one can make real things unreal." Her chin quivered.

I sat stiffly upright as she fussed with my long hair. Then she dropped the comb and pressed her gangly body beside mine on the same chair. We leaned our heads together and cried without a sound.

The death of my mother exposed me to such a violent change that I liken it to an alchemical process that cracks the molecular structure of an object. Many years later, I studied ceramic arts and learned to fire in the Japanese style called *Raku*. This method is very radical and mysterious, and the artist cannot predict the outcome of the ware. The glowing red-hot piece is taken with tongs out of the scorching flames and immersed into organic material, like dry leaves or sawdust. That material catches fire immediately, and black smoke emerges from underneath the lid of the container, where the piece is now cooling down. The rapid change from hot to cold cracks the surface of the piece, since it is shocked into cooling faster than the whole inner clay body. That produces innumerable fine crack-lines all over the surface, and that texture gives the piece a look of blood vessels holding it together like a natural, fragile net.

As a child, I was unable to adjust to the abrupt transition from heat to cold, when my mother disappeared so suddenly from my life. I was forever cracked open, exposing fine lines on my surface. Even at a mature age I would easily burst into tears as if the deeply buried grief had its own mind and forced its way to the surface through the broken skin.

My mother had survived the firestorms of Hamburg, but not the fire of her personal fate. The raging energy of flames that had destroyed my hometown had also eaten the body of my mother. The truth is that as a child, I did not weave a connection between those events, because the personal always seems so much closer to the heart than the historical. The dimensions of our individual story are human; the numbing pain of a personal loss shrinks the world into one single focus and wipes out the awareness of anything else surrounding it. Such a death is an all-consuming event. With the help of time, the personal can be integrated into the saga of a specific family and its members. The loss of my mother was personal fate, but it was also overshadowed by history, by the facts about the war and the monstrosities that my people had inflicted on others. I was already broken open when confronted with the Nazi's horrors beyond imagination. In later years I would find out that the perpetrators are scarred and distorted, too, like the victims. I belong to both sides, imprinted by my culture of origin.

9

ANGUISH AND
APPLESTRUDEL

Two weeks after mother's death, my sister and I returned to school every day and lived as if things were normal. I discovered that one survives loss by continuing all the habitual motions as though being moved by mechanical forces. Watching my environment, I found my inner landscape reflected in the outer world. Munich was destroyed. The splendid churches lay in erratic piles on the ground. Former *Bürgerhäuser*, the homes of wealthy citizens, had only the chimneys standing upright, like masts on a sinking ship. Parks were vacant of plants and visitors. People vegetated in the basements of their ruined dwellings from where they emerged like ghosts from the folds of a nightmare. They gathered in groups to clean up and rebuild their homes. The *Münchners* loved their city and they decided to reconstruct the gorgeous historical buildings according to the original plans that

For into nothingness we
*   must again build a Yes.*
Houses we must build . . .
*   over the abysses,*
the craters and the slit-
*   trenches*
and over the open mouths of
*   the dead.*
—Wolfgang Borchert
The Man Outside.
Rowohlt Verlag GMBH

had been preserved in archives. Munich is one of the most architecturally interesting cities in Germany and was for centuries a splendid bastion for kings and aristocrats. But when we moved here in 1947, it was a carcass of its former beauty, and nobody knew if it would emerge into splendor again.

The four girls in our house shared the same road to school every day. We took an adventuresome short cut and drove our bikes down the flanks of the enormous *"Trümmerberg,"* a rubble hill that stretched for more than a mile. It was piling high at the edges of the *Theresian Wiese*, the location of the yearly *Octoberfest*, shaped out of debris from destroyed buildings that covered most of Munich.

We usually stopped our bikes at the top of the hill and put a foot down to rest and keep the bikes balanced. From this place we observed an endless line of trucks approaching, releasing their dusty load and turning around when empty. They heaped the broken dwellings of a tortured city, layer by layer, unto the hill, until the landscape itself was changed. This hill would later be covered with earth and grass and used as amusement park for children upon which to sled and ski or run with balloons and kites tied to their hands.

A dirt road for the trucks wound down this hill and towards our school and the Isar River Valley. We used the decline to gain momentum on our bikes. We pulled our feet up, resting them on the frame, and sped in breathtaking tempo downhill. Dirt and dust shot from beneath our tires, and we enjoyed the audacity, ignoring the danger of falling and scraping our knees or breaking our necks. The wind blew in my face, and it flashed through my mind that we were crossing the remnants of living rooms and furniture and bathtubs from destroyed apartments. There were decayed bones and hair and teeth and eyeballs and fingernails of the dead in the rubble. History's edge between past and future was at this very place, at the thin line where my tires hit the wreckage of war. We young girls were the next generation driving across the shattered pieces of the past and racing towards the promise of a better future.

The jagged, post-war topography of this city was familiar to me and reminded me of my hometown, Hamburg. Rubble and dust became a natural part of my reality, a symbol for my own life. The grown-ups around me involved themselves with grim determination in *Wiederaufbau*. My family, as well, as the whole country of Germany, were driven by the ideal to work hard and not look back and mourn.

> *My aching heart found a bigger aching.*
> —Carson Mc.Cullers, *Ballad Of the Sad Café*

The signature melody of Radio München was composed of the beginning tunes from the song *"Solang der alte Peter, der Petersdom noch steht..."* which means, "As long as the old St. Peter's church is still standing things would be fine." But the St. Peter's church was rubble, it's beautiful columns and altars piled into heaps of dust and bricks. The Saints looked like wounded soldiers with amputated limbs. To honor these facts, the radio signature melody was played in a crippled form: *As long as the old St. Pe...*, it ended there and the last tune hung in the air like a tattered ribbon. The inhabitants of Munich made it their prominent goal to rebuild the St. Peter's Church in the heart of their town. They were convinced that, if this church could emerge from brutal destruction, then everything else could come back to life, too. All over town, people rattling brown metal cans collected donations for the beloved St. Peter's church. The clinking of the coins was part of the familiar noise in the streets. After many years, on that glorious day when the church was rebuilt and inaugurated, the station *Radio Bavaria* played the full melody: *So lang der alte Peter*. In the streets, people hugged and danced with tears in their eyes.

My Aunt Hannie's name was really Johanna. After my mother's death, she came once a week, cooking and cleaning for us. When she appeared, the house was warm, the table set and the smell of warm food greeted me at the door, making my heart flutter. For a short moment, the great gaping hole in my life was covered and I felt at home in my own body.

Aunt Hannie was a fantastic cook of Austrian pastries and Hungarian specialties. She simmered the paprika flavored goulash for hours, the aroma causing my stomach to ache with desire. Onions, meat and potatoes swam in the spicy red sauce and when I swallowed a spoon-full, it heated my throat as though the sun had rolled through it. And the next morning, when I went to the bathroom, it warmed my other side and made me laugh. Aunt Hannie knew by heart the original recipe for paprika-chicken. She made it with wild mushrooms and added the chopped liver of the chicken. Just before serving, she poured sour cream into it, which made it silky and soft, so the red paprika would collect in patches on the surface, looking like small floating islands.

Aunt Hannie baked the best traditional Christmas *Stollen*. She took it out of the oven when it was still hot, and then she brushed it with fluid butter and rolled it in powder sugar. The butter/sugar crust was so thick that the *Stollen* stayed soft and juicy for a long time after Christmas, and it was her tradition to preserve the last precious piece for Easter Sunday.

Before she left to return home in the afternoon, she often asked us, "What do you want me to cook when I come next week?"

"Apple Strudel," I said, and looked forward to assisting her, like an apprentice who served a true master.

My aunt prepared herself for the baking of Applestrudel like a priestess in a temple. First, she took off her rings and placed them in a glass at the windowsill, and then she strung an apron around her waist. She forcefully kneaded and fluffed the yeast dough until she ran out of breath. She sprinkled it with flour before she covered it with a clean towel and placed it near the warm oven, until it had doubled in size. I could see how it was expanding, because the flour showed cracks in its surface, like dry land without rain. She rolled the dough flat and then she pulled it gently with her skilled hands in every direction, like fabric, spreading it over the table that was speckled with flour to keep the dough from sticking to the surface. She stretched it until it was so transparent 'that one could read a newspaper through it,' she said proudly. Then she spread thinly sliced apples on top and I helped to cut the apples and fill any place that was not evenly covered. Raisins and chopped nuts settled on top of the apples and sugar and cinnamon completed the filling. The whole piece of delicious art was lying on a big kitchen towel. She pulled on one corner and lifted it very slowly, so that the dough and all the wonderful stuff on top would roll itself into a log. With firm fingers she folded the ends like one would do with the paper around a birthday package. Then she took a brush and spread egg yolk mixed with sugar and milk on top of it. In the oven it went and soon the most delicious scents spread through the kitchen and the whole house. When it was ready and cut open, it steamed and burst its contents onto the plate, as though it was bragging and exploding with delight. The scent and taste of this familiar dish made me feel safe and loved, and it made small curls of joy spread from the belly to the heart.

One day, when Aunt Hannie was visiting, she asked me to buy half a liter of milk from Herr Oberwiler, who had reopened his dairy shop in his garage, at the corner of our street. I took her precious milk can, put my woolen hat and gloves on, and ran out into the cold. On the way back I met my friend Christle. There was a whole mound of snow at the corner, so I put the can down to help her with the building of a small city on top of this mound.

"Let's build a bridge and make trenches underneath," she suggested. We got busy shaping walls and turrets with our bare hands. We laughed and rolled balls of snow down the mound and into holes at the bottom. Then I marched home. But at the door I realized that I had forgotten the milk can under the tree where we had played.

I hurried back. The can with the milk was gone; I found only the small, lonesome, circular indentation in the snow. I had to admit to aunt Hannie that I had lost her most precious possession, the container that had provided food for them; the one object that had shared their fate and had been such an important companion during a gruesome march into exile. When I told her, she sank down into a chair and sobbed.

I felt painful shame and regret; and I learned that objects could become precious representatives of an event in time. Those objects had ceased to be themselves, they had become part of somebody else's life story. I had nothing, I thought, that really could stand as symbol for life with my mother. Yes, there were pieces she had worn or held in her hands, but I would not even consider that they had the power to mirror her personality or our togetherness. Her physical body had turned into ashes, and no "thing" could be a symbol of her warmth and vitality. No object carried the sound of her voice and no sign was equal to the sensation of my love for her.

When alone in our quiet home, I often stood at the window, leaned my forehead against the cold glass and stared outside. When I did not breathe or move, standing like a stone, there was no proof that I existed. The trees and branches swung in the wind and their gentle gestures scratched at the frozen surface of memories, buried in my internal landscape. Imagining obsessively how my mother held me in her arms when she said her last goodbye, I was unable to believe that I would never see her again, not alive and not dead. There was a gap between life and death that seemed so wide that I was incapable of bridging it. The soft and safe reality of my life with Mother seemed like a dream and I wondered if I had just awakened into an alternative life where she did not exist. *Maybe she never was real and I had been dreaming her all along. Or maybe*, I thought, *her death was a dream, and I would wake up and find my mother alive and well.* The adults around me were mute. They seemed to walk inside the abyss, packed in felt and fur, all sounds muffled. Nobody taught me how to mend this split. I was voiceless and blocked from speaking the language of grief.

I found myself hanging in the empty space between those two realities, vanishing into non-existence. I was a ghost myself, scuttling around without a sense of this body that I did not inhabit. I had lost the ability to know and sense a Self that carried my name. I hoped I would wake up and discover myself in either the realm of the living or of the dead. If my mother lingered in one of them, I was incapable of connecting with her. Abandoned, I could not produce the substance that would unite me with hers. I tried to dissolve into nothingness by sheer will. Sometimes I sat motionless, hoping I could simply disappear by not doing anything, just waiting for time to move on without me, not realizing that it had left me behind. To fall out of the boat of time, what a comforting thought.

Longing for my grandmother, I fantasized her presence. '*Min Deern*,' she would say and press me towards her enormous chest, 'I am sad, too, and we can cry together, I will hold you and warm you, I am always here for you.' And I imagined she would say, 'you lost your mother, *min Deern*, and you see, I lost my daughter, it hurts the same, very much, very much.' Or, I hoped, she would whisper, 'One day you'll be happy again. One day your broken heart will mend, I promise that to you.' But Grandmother lived far away in the north. I had no way of reaching her, as the public trains were destroyed or overcrowded. I was locked into a vast silence, in a vacuum devoid of motherly nurturing, I was drowning in a chaotic world with nothing to hold on to. Trapped inside myself, the world around me jerked and moved in bizarre ways.

Grieving was not practiced and accepted in my culture. Germany had experienced and created loss in an expanse that was unimaginable, but an unwritten law denounced collective grief or expression of pain and regret. Human despair was hidden from view; people were busy cleaning rubble and rebuilding their homes and cities. The memory of loss was suppressed for the sake of survival, all energy invested to just live one day at a time. I learned, in my family and country, that sorrow and loss were underground night-creatures; they visited people when nobody witnessed the agony. It seemed that there was no adequate language in Germany that could communicate anguish and remorse.

One day, when Aunt Hannie arrived in our home to cook and

care for us, she was pale and agitated. She took off her coat and hung it carefully inside the closet, stroking the front straight, and neatly arranging the sleeves before she closed the door. She made herself tea and sat down. I sensed that she wanted to talk and stood beside her.

"There was an accident, at the *Stachus* place, where all the streetcars cross and meet," she said. "It was very busy, so many people and so few street cars, everybody pushed and tried to get into the cars that were already stuffed full of folks. It was horrible," she sighed and wiped a strand of gray hair out of her forehead. "I was close to the curb and hoped to get into the next car. People poked their elbows into my back. There was a woman beside me with an enormous bag full of stuff. Suddenly, somebody must have pushed her from behind, because she slipped and fell directly on the tracks in front of the approaching streetcar. The driver rang his bell wildly, the brakes screeched and everybody shrieked," she wiped sweat off her forehead and her hands trembled.

"Her legs were crossing the tracks and she could not move fast because the bag bogged her down. The iron wheels of the car stopped about two centimeters from her right leg and people howled with relief. I stood there and was horrified. I imagined how the wheels could have cut her legs off and how the blood would have squirted high up into the air, and my new winter coat would be totally ruined with all that blood!"

One morning in spring I woke and stood in my nightgown at the window. I saw piles of decaying vegetables and faded leaves from last fall in the garden, but I saw also the first green triangles of tulips and iris poking through the murky surface. The garden appeared to be dead, but new life forced itself through the crusty remains of winter. From a tiny place inside my chest came a voice. *'Elke'*, it whispered my name, *'go out with bare feet. Let the mud squish between your toes. Kneel down and free the new, green shoots from the rotten leaves that keep the sun away.'* The voice rustled like wind through barley and made my body tremble with delight. I opened the window and, in that moment, envisioned how trees and flowers, clouds and oceans are all saturated by the energy of life, the same that flows also in me and in rocks and beetles, too, and in swallows and sunflowers. I remembered how — in the past — I used to go to the forest, when I was sad or lonesome. I would sit in the branches of the mighty beech tree and hold on to her trunk and she would take on my sorrow as if it were her sustenance; she would simply absorb it and let it trickle down through her body into her roots where the earth soaked it up between grains of sand. She rejected nothing.

Perhaps we are a generation full of arrival on a new star, in a new life…
Perhaps we are a generation full of arrival at a new love, at a new laughter,
at a new God.

— Wolfgang Borchert *The Man Outside*.
Rowohlt Verlag GMBH

I reclaimed my life on a Sunday afternoon during the summer, a year or two after my mother's death. The four girls from our house had planned an outing. We rode our bikes to the nearby *Starnberger* Lake, about an hour from our home. We swam in the sun-warmed water and ate our liverwurst sandwiches. I lay on my stomach and looked towards the Alps, fresh grass pressed against my skin and left stringy imprints on top of my knees. I showed the pattern to Christle, Isolde and my sister Helga. We giggled, tanned our legs and engaged in girl talk.

"Let's go to the swings, let's sit on the wall and hang our feet into the water, let's play ball and run around the outhouse to catch dragonflies, give me a bite from your apple, can I try your bathing suit, I lost my sandals and your bike has a flat, I can dive longer under water than you, your hair is wet and drips on my back, listen how I whistle on a blade of grass, watch out for the wasps, what's the time?"

It was a hot and humid day and, in the late afternoon, a thunderstorm formed and gathered bulging black clouds above the mountains. The sun disappeared, and a grayish darkness stretched across the lake. We quickly packed our towels and sandals in bags and began the ride back home. But the weather caught up with us, and a severe rainstorm forced us to huddle underneath a huge oak tree that thrashed its branches in the wind. Thunderbolts shook the ground and lightning burnt the air. The rain drenched us thoroughly. "I think we should not seek shelter under this tree, when the lightning flashes like that," said Isolde, the oldest of us. So, we decided to rather enjoy the fierce weather and continue our way home instead of hiding out, because we didn't see any sign that the raging rainstorm would end.

We splashed through puddles and the mud surged upwards sticking heavily to our legs and bikes. An electrifying euphoria of abandon to the forces of this storm gripped us. There was no dry thread on our bodies. We shrieked and laughed and got out of breath as we crossed water channels and circled piles of wet leaves and branches. Torrents jumped over rocks at the side of the road and carried sticks and pebbles along with the flood. The rain united everything into one expansive and untamed eddy, and we whirled and twisted in the center.

A lightning bolt clashed into the ground near our path, and the electricity rolled like a wave across my body. Brightness blinded me, as though I was emerging from an unlit cave. I heard a deep hum, like the engines in an old steamboat, everything around me roared with a voice. The water gurgled and ran into my shirt, down my belly and into my crotch. My tiny nipples and breasts protruded under the wet fabric. Lightning lit the scene with bluish flashes. A powerful force rushed through me like blood circulating furiously after one's limbs unfroze. This torrent of energy hurt, but it also electrified me with ferocious pleasure. An irresistible yearning to be alive jerked me out of numbness and forced me back into the flesh and senses of my body.

And then, a heavy rock bolted away from the gate to the dark cave where I had been hiding out. My whole body vibrated as I burst through the opening. I jumped on the train of time, asserting my place. I reclaimed my life. It was mine and I had a right to existence, even as a motherless child. Or was it life itself that claimed me back? I was being birthed, groaning like an animal. My youth demanded to live, with mother or without her. A raw and wild voice echoed inside me. An enormous bird was beating her wings, forcing her way into freedom. I clenched my fists and leaped forward into the future, pulsating with blood and spit and the odors of the earth and my own body.

We grew into adolescence. Thin arms with edgy elbows, long legs and a bony neck. My sister and I were eagerly checking for the first, itchy pubic hair. I was envious of Helga's breasts, the size of summer plums. She was shy about them and sent her little sister to buy her first bra; and then she burst into tears of embarrassment when I admitted that I had told the neighbor's woman in the store that, yes, this bra was for my sister and it was her first.

We were clumsy and confused about our emerging womanhood. There was no mother who would laugh with us about these awkward investigations, or to help and explain the changes in our bodies. All my girlfriends had already their periods, indicated by their sitting in the sidelines of the gym every four weeks and not participating in sports activities. So when I finally found some drops of blood in my panties, I danced in front of my sister, swinging the underwear in my hand and giggling with glee. Now, I too, would proudly sit at the side of the gym and just observe. I was becoming a woman, and every girl in my school would know.

"We will move to Frankfurt, soon," said my father one day. "I was hired as an engineer in the *Opel Werke*. The Americans have taken over the firm and I will have good work again. I'm sure you'll like it there." We packed and said goodbye to our dear friends, Christle and Isolde. This move indicated the beginning edge of a new period in my life. The move to the unknown place pointed to an outer and inner shift, challenging as well as promising.

Entering high school at a time in the fifties when we young people and our teachers faced the reckoning with Germany's recent past, I was waking up into truth as if emerging from a nightmare of personal and collective stupor. My teenage years were burdened with wrenching disclosures about the past and rattled by harsh argument between the generations.

"We had spent our lives watching and listening
with the constant sharp attention of
children lost in the dark.
It seemed that we were bewilderingly lost
in a landscape that, with any light at all,
would be wholly familiar."
— Marilynne Robinson, *Housekeeping*
Picador, New York

10

FIGHT AND FLIGHT

When I was a teenager in the 1950s, my stepmother, Helene, took over the reins in our house. My father married her when I was fourteen. Under her influence, he became even more aloof and rigid. Helene was a fiercely devoted Nazi and retained her viewpoint, even after the end of the war, until she died, forty years later. My father supported her values so easily, it seemed that her encouragement brought his to blossom. I never knew how much of a Hitler follower he was, because we didn't talk politics when I was a child. But that would change now.

Helene had designed the interior and rearranged the house according to her own plan of appropriate style and order. At that time, the physicality and idea of home didn't mean much for me, especially after Helene eliminated most of our furniture and replaced it with her own. The living room had lost its character. Everything was

...we are the generation without restraint and without protection – thrown out of the playpen of childhood into a world made for us by those who now despise us..., made of us a generation without farewell...
We are a generation without homecoming, for we have nothing to come home to, and we have no one to take care of our hearts.
— Wolfgang Borchert,
The Man Outside.
Rowohlt Verlag GMBH

somewhat neutral, not hot or cold, not too glaring or too faint. Our little green parrot, named Pucky, was not welcome any more because he left colorful feathers and tiny, dry turds behind.

The furniture was stiff, as if holding its breath. All the objects surrendered to Helene's rigid German discipline. The pieces, shy and intimidated, didn't talk to each other in lively conversations, but mumbled in muted whispers. Even the air that lingered in the open spaces was plain and without scent or spice. No clock ticked, no bird twittered. Flowers wilted with resignation. The fringes along the edge of the rugs were tense and straight, like lines of soldiers. I lifted my legs automatically, to prevent my feet from stepping into their invisible battlefield. The rugs, docile and well-behaved, prostrated themselves in muted shades of beige, the sandy color of deserts.

The drapes, wavering in their indecision to look either royal, with fringes and tassels or modern and straight, hovered somewhere in the middle between classic and new-look. The whole room shunned expression or liveliness because that would be "loud" and considered ordinary and plebeian. In a country where so much brutality had ruled, Helene's search for "style" seemed absurd to me.

The only sensual piece of furniture was a new acquisition, a combination of radio, speakers and record player. At that time, in the 1950s, it was the hottest achievement of home technology. Curved and slick, it dared to bulge into the neutral middle space of the room with two round outcroppings that were shaped like a heavy woman's voluptuous thighs. With loudspeakers hidden inside the swaying forms, this piece of furniture was intrusive, shameless and gleefully devoted to its purpose of breaking through the whispers in the salon. I assume my father had bought it without input from Helene. He loved things that worked well and he didn't care much for the looks. In contrast, she dampened what she touched, castrated it and reduced its personality. But the loudspeakers disregarded the decency of the decor, they were young, vital and self-possessed.

I was about fifteen and addicted to roaring and ecstatic organ concerts, for example, the *Toccata and Fugue in D-minor* by Johann Sebastian Bach. When I needed to escape the neutral, odorless and tasteless atmosphere of the house, I would put a record onto the turntable and lower my head between the thigh-shaped speakers. In this musical cave I was happy and protected from intrusion. The arousing music provided an acoustically closed door with a sign that said, 'Keep Out! Leave me alone.'

The salon was used as the official place to receive visitors and have conversations. It served to impress and convince the guests that we were "higher class" and had culture. In those years after the war, any loud declaration of wealth or status was *nouveaux riche* and considered profane by those whose former wealth and status was in shambles.

My stepmother, Helene, had cherry-wood bookshelves designed and built to fit exactly underneath the two large picture windows facing the garden. She put her leather-backed books there in orderly rows and allowed my father to add some of his. One day, alone at home, I sat on the floor in front of the books. I haphazardly grabbed one with the title *Die Stute Deflorata*, The Mare Deflorata, by Arthur Heinz Lehman. The companion book was placed just beside it, *Der Hengst Majestoso Austria*, The Stallion Majestoso Austria, telling the stories of two passionate horse lovers and their unfolding romance. I opened to a random page and landed in the middle of a fiery love scene between a man and women. With hot cheeks I devoured the lustful description of lovemaking and orgasm from the very sensual viewpoint of a woman. Being sexually inexperienced, I followed willingly as the heroine metaphorically took my hand and guided me into the mysterious caves of a woman's body. She described every move, sensation and vision of her ecstasy, as if the cells of her body were talking. She told me how she knotted her legs around the hips and back of her man and moved in the rhythm of waves in the ocean. She sank to its bottom and readily drowned in her pleasure. She yielded to her lust as if she were willing to offer her life in exchange, and so she revealed to me the secrets I yearned to know. She was the initiating mother whom I missed so much.

She kindled my imagination. I had earlier explored my own body with shy and fumbling fingers, experiencing feelings of pleasure mixed with guilt, as if it were not mine, my own flesh and juice, my own home in which I lived. She encouraged me to treat my womanly body like an exotic continent, full of secrets to be released and delights to be discovered: blossoms and honey, trees and wind and ocean waves and salty skin.

After this initiation, the rigid living-room was flooded, for me, with the colors of flesh and the scents of armpits and thighs. The orgasmic music of Johann Sebastian Bach and Friedrich Buxtehude aroused in my fantasy the visions of silky hair and a woman's legs around the back of her man, pearls of sweat rolling from his shoulders. I had a secret and private garden of my own in between the stiff furniture of our salon. Vibrant flowers had emerged out of dry and neutral desert grounds. Sandy plains burst open to allow space for secretive and lustful flights of my imagination.

I took this book repeatedly off the shelf and envisioned with sweet arousal and anticipation what was waiting for me in my own awakening sexuality. I felt deep gratitude to this unknown narrator who had initiated me through storytelling into the art and ecstasy of lovemaking. My only introduction at that time, besides nightly whispers with my older sister Helga, had been a pamphlet that our pastor handed to my father who deposited it without words on our nightstand. It had the title "What you need to know…" and was as neutral, tasteless and odorless as a deep frozen dish.

Because the "*Stute Deflorata*" was missing from the bookshelf, my father found out that I had read the book. He felt obliged to confront me with a sermon and serious talk, stating that I was not allowed to take those adult books off the shelves, and how could I dare to, and why did I not have more respect, and I was too young and I should be ashamed and so and so on. I forgot what he said and delighted in my secret alliance with the hero and heroine.

During those dreadful teenage years, I found a clandestine way to attract interest from my estranged father and to bond with him under disguise. I had inherited a good technical sense from him. He worked at the *Opel Werke* near Frankfurt, and when the Americans annexed this car manufacturer, he was one of the leading technicians and inventors. He spoke English well, and a whole new career opened up for him with the introduction of foreign staff. His work shaped his identity and made him fulfilled and happy. Finally, he found himself recognized and respected.

There was little that we had in common, but if I asked him questions about his work, his eyes would lighten up and he would take out a paper or use the corner of a magazine to scribble drawings and explain to me what he researched. I understood his demonstrations easily and we would get very involved, putting our heads together and discussing the options for how to solve a problem or how to improve a technical device. There was an unusual sense of intimacy between us in those moments, fragile, like soap bubbles. I had found an opening into his attention. When he explained the newest model of the upcoming Opel car, he talked about it with the passion of an artist or hunter, happy to have in me somebody with whom he could share his enthusiasm.

Those newly designed cars had to be kept under disguise until the date of the great "coming-out" announcement to the public. The Americans were skilled at stirring intense attention for such an event. Because of the secrecy, my father had to drive the car for research during the dark of the night, or cover it under a foreign chassis that would not reveal the brand underneath. He loved this kind of game, and I was the only one outside work who knew about those clandestine cover-ups.

He would produce drawings of how the brakes worked and how he had mounted a camera underneath the car. "Look how I placed the camera on the frame of the car," showing me a photograph, "and when I drive around a tight curve with high speed, it takes pictures during the process, so one can observe how the tires gets distorted." He looked at me for some kind of response or approval and those times were the only ones when our eyes met and connected.

Father test-driving Opel car. Photographer unknown.

His ideas were good and made sense, and I wondered why nobody else had realized them before. He had a creative mind and it gave him great pleasure to use it. He was passionate about his creations. I observed his serious face and felt a tinge of love, hoping that he would be honored and praised, since he was so hungry for recognition.

When I leaned towards him across the table, following the lines on the paper with my fingertips, there was a new sense of equality between us. I usually experienced my father as remote and cold, like fog in a valley; or as painful as a sharp rock in my shoe. I wondered if he would have loved me more if I were a son instead of a daughter. This thought made me miss my mother intensely. It was hard to grow toward womanhood in the shadow of this stern father, without a mother at my side to model the process.

When my father retired at age sixty-five, he received a medal from the "Deutscher Erfinderverband," the German Inventors Association. It was the revered Rudolf Diesel Award. On the front of it was engraved *Ehre dem Verdienst*, Honor the Merit. Made from embossed brass and placed in blue velvet, a small lock in front of the case held it together. I regret that I had reached this man so rarely and only across the bridge of our technical discussions. Who was he besides that? What dreams did he carry and what regrets burdened him? He was a dark stranger in my life.

Rudolf Diesel Award. Photograph by Shanti Elke Bannwart.

In a bundle of old documents that I received after his death, I discovered with surprise a diploma signed by *Der Fuehrer* Adolf Hitler himself on January 30, 1944 in Berlin. The paper named him as receiver of the *Kriegsverdienstkreuz*, the cross of merit in war, a highly coveted medal. It carried also a signature by O. Meissner: the German Chancellor for three regimes: from the Keiser and the Weimar Republic to the Third Reich. The medal was a cross without swords, which was given for efforts not related to armed battles, awarded for service in the war effort, be it political, diplomatic, economic or industrial. He never talked about it and never wore the medal either. The reason for this decoration will remain a mystery for me.

IM NAMEN
DES DEUTSCHEN VOLKES
VERLEIHE ICH

dem Diplom-Ingenieur

Hans R ö ß n e r

in Hamburg-Volksdorf

DAS
KRIEGSVERDIENSTKREUZ
2. KLASSE

BERLIN, 30. Januar 1944.

DER FÜHRER

The Iron Cross of Merit. Copy of official document.

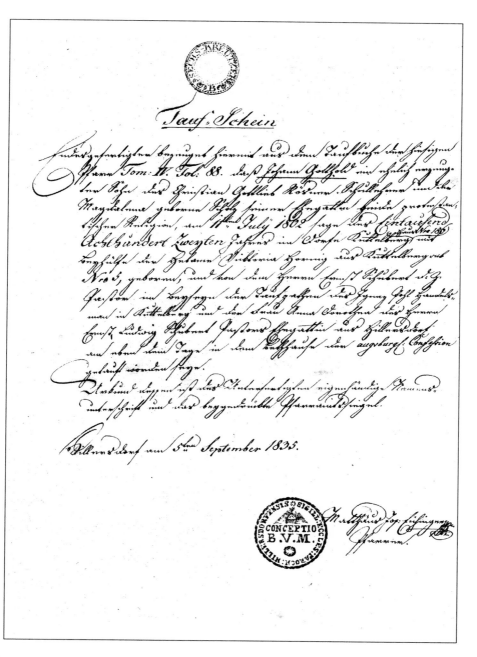

Baptism Document, dated 1835. Copy of official document.

I own a compilation of original papers dating back to 1835 or even to 1717. The example here is a certificate of baptism. Most of them were birth and death documents and marriage announcements. They were obviously obtained to prove that we had no Jewish blood in our family. These beautifully hand-written originals were carefully collected to confirm what we were *not*—which was more important during the Third Reich than what we were and where we came from.

The future enters into us, in order to transform itself in us,
long before it happens.

—Rainer Maria Rilke

Dr. Toit Riesler was in his mid fifties, about my father's age, very tall and lanky, with a face deeply marked by lines, and full, puffy lips. There was something almost intimidating and grotesque in his expressive features, intensified by elongated arms and heavy, powerful hands. He assumed a commanding posture with a laid back attitude; his movements were out of sync and erratic, as though he wore a royal cape that slid repeatedly down from his shoulders. One day in August he arrived from northern Germany to participate in a trip to Italy, where my father would have to observe tires under conditions of a hot climate. Dr. Riesler occupied a high position in a German tire manufacturing company and was very interested in the results.

The men used two cars, and since it was vacation time, my father invited my sister and me to join them on this trip to the Mediterranean. Naturally, Helga, as my father's favorite, settled into his car and I escorted Dr. Riesler in his.

We drove south through Switzerland and over the *Gotthard Pass*, climbing up winding roads through the mountains and back down on the Italian side of the Alps. We stopped at *Lago di Como* for coffee and ambled through villages and towns that nestled into brazenly green valleys, marked by names sounding like songs: *Airolo, Lago di Piazza, Bellinzona, Piacenza* and *Parma*.

Our road snaked up and down along the flanks of the mountains in switchbacks so tight that the suitcases in the trunk shifted. Whitewater creeks crossed under old stone bridges, rocky hiking trails accompanying them.

The trip lasted more than a week and during those days, together in the intimate, small space of his car, Dr. Riesler and I talked extensively and shared very personal thoughts and insights. Reflections about ourselves and about our lives were interrupted by funny remarks about the black-and-white cows along the road or the sighting of crows tearing on the cadaver of a sheep. Sharp political opinions collided in opposition or merged in agreement. We looked at the dark history of our culture like physicians at a corpse. To my astonishment, this man was truly curious about my inner world, and in return, he freely shared his own experiences and conclusions with me. We were true partners, equals in search for meaning and mystery. It seemed totally natural and appropriate for him to treat my youth with respect and esteem.

I was sixteen years old and had never before received this kind of authentic attention from a mature man, had not encountered such a smooth exchange of reflections and thoughts. There was a fiery engagement and pure joy in our connection.

At that time I had just been reading Dostoyevsky's *Brothers Karamazov* as well as Wolfgang Borchert and Heinrich Böll.

"Do human beings have personal freedom or are we slaves to fate?" We considered and my face flushed with shame for anybody who would dare to negate personal responsibility. I was fiercely opinionated.

"Does religion open doors to truth or does it block them?" he asked. There were long and comfortable silences between us; lively silences with the texture of wind-ruffled water, spaces to spin thoughts or linger with questions. We had time in abundance.

"How is Borchert's statement possible," I wondered, "after he was broken by war, he said: *Whatever comes tomorrow, and be it sorrow, I say*

YES! How will my generation find a YES again, as we look towards that tomorrow?"

As if it were the wing of a bird, he stroked my hand with a gesture of compassion, "the YES will grow out of your youth and unbridled life energy, trust it," he said.

We took breaks and, looking down steep cliffs, we observed frothing waterfalls plunge into deep rock basins, leaving misty clouds in the air. We stood shoulder to shoulder without touching. From time to time one of us shared a statement. We probed it, and added a new one, as though constructing a building, stacking bricks or staking wooden poles. Then we stepped back and looked at it. We delighted in the structure of our musings, leaving doors and windows open, so that the wind could blow through, and the air inside would not stagnate but keep tearing away the curtains that usually separate the older and younger generations.

He drove for days, his large hands directing the car. When it grew dark outside, he turned on the lights to observe the road ahead of us. Strings of colorful lanterns decorated restaurants and shops in villages we passed. Never before had I encountered a man like him. He was like a Martian without age, or a Tibetan Snow Tiger, a mystical man, a longed-for man, moving with grace through uncharted territory. Inside my heart, a tightly closed space began to unfurl. A frozen field melted. I longed to grow into adulthood, into *his* kind of adulthood, and I realized that just that was already happening, in his presence. We had a secret that joined us in *statu nascendi*, in this very moment, as his authentic regard allowed me to be vulnerable and to blossom into an electrifying sense of feminine self.

Our weaving of curiosity and sharing excluded physical intimacy or even the extended touch of hands. I was so young that the passion of copulating minds was as ecstatic as I imagined that of our bodies would be. He respected and protected that attitude.

Our encounter was contained within the structure of beginning and end of the trip. I addressed him as Dr. Riesler and he spoke to me as Fräulein Rössner. To my surprise, these formalities provided boundaries that allowed a safe flow of warm and relaxed intimacy. Something grew and stretched inside me and it soon filled me with a never before known power. I was exhilarated by its brilliant presence in every cell of my body.

Inspired by this man with heart and soul, I was glowing. My unusual friend had initiated the first deep and lasting experience of love for a man in my life. I had peered and stepped beyond the bars of my rigid family. Traversing snowcapped mountains, at the end of the week we reached the sunny coast, and I did not resemble any more the shy young woman I had been some days ago.

The 1950s were excruciatingly painful years. I repeatedly confronted my father and stepmother about the past. At that time the revelations about the Holocaust seeped into German consciousness and penetrated the atmosphere inside families. They split the generations apart and overshadowed gravely the next generation of Germany's youth. We were left to dig through the rubble of a horrendous past. My father and stepmother represented for me the guilt-burdened perpetrators. I was so on fire in my rage and righteousness that I almost burned in its flames. It hurt to be young and alive during those years of reckoning.

The discussions and battles in my family occurred with a suffocating redundancy. My stepmother, Helene, and my father usually gathered in the formal living room to drink tea or a glass of wine after he came home from work. The light-blue velvet sofa was stiff and forced them to sit upright. Father and stepmother presided on the sofa like judges in court; I crouched on the Moroccan leather pillow across from them. Any trigger would start the inquiry and attacks. I could have just avoided the futile confrontations with my Nazi parents, but the fights allowed some release of fury, and I was also naïve enough, like every teenager, to hope for change in my parents.

"How could you not have noticed, " I asked, leaning forward, "that your Jewish neighbors' shops were destroyed? The owners disappeared overnight. They were familiar to you all throughout your childhood. You saw their kids grow up. Suddenly the houses were empty, the windows busted, the children were missing and not in school with yours?"

Stepmother Helene waved her right hand as though shooing flies away from food. She sighed, "Ough Ough!" shaking her head as if doubting her stepdaughter's sanity. My father shrugged his shoulders. He was annoyed; the muscles in his jaws clenched and marked tense lines in his cheeks. The skin tightened and the extra tooth created a small bump under his lip. At some undefined moment he had become her husband more than he was my father.

"We didn't know anything, nobody did," said Helene, waving her diamond-clad hand erratically like the lame wing of a dying bird.

She straightened her back and raised her voice. "The reason is simple: the stories about the German concentration camps are invented by the Americans. They even posed pictures and arranged those corpses for the purpose of making the Germans look bad." With hasty strokes, she cleaned some lint off the lace tablecloth. "No one ever, ever should believe such nonsense. No one with a brain," she added, and looked straight at me.

I stared back at her and my father. They sat upright, as if they were visitors in their own home. I sensed the unwritten pact that tied their opinions together and made them impenetrable. I felt nauseous.

"All occupying armies took pictures," I responded, "and there were eye witnesses. The stories are horrendous, I feel sick and broken. We young people are informed. Our professors discuss the events of the past with us in high school. We friends gather in the schoolyards, and in the evenings at home, and we talk about it, all the time. You left us this burden of shame and guilt, it overshadows our future. I wished you would at least once, just once, say ' Maybe it was true,' or 'I feel sorry.'

My father cut in with some short and redundant remarks. "You are too young to understand. You just repeat what they tell you. Let the past rest and take care of your own business. It is sickening to hear those lies." He supported his new wife, but he looked bored.

Helene waved her hand again, irritated and ready to leave this familiar courtroom. "Your teachers brainwash you students, they are instructed to do so by the occupiers of this country." She pulled her left eyebrow up and leaned her head slightly to the right. Dark facial hair grew around her chin. I stared at it and observed how it moved as she talked. "There is no morale in people today, no pride, no honesty. This is called *Nestbeschmutzen*, to dirty your own nest. You dare to put your own country down without shame?"

Shadows of Fear. Photographer unknown.

She got up, stretched and straightened her dress. She was only about five feet two and wore her hair brushed upwards from her forehead like Queen Elizabeth. One of her rules was *Eine Dame geht nie aus ohne Hut,* which means 'A lady never leaves the house without a hat.' She lifted her chin and left the room. She expected her husband to follow, so that their protest would be more demonstrative, and my father did. Helene had run out of arguments, right now, but she would unbendingly insist on Germany's honorable behavior until she died, forty years later. Her life was frozen in time and viewpoint. She had lost her young first husband soon after their marriage. He was an officer and was shot in the line of duty during the early years of the war. He never saw his second child, his daughter. She was born after his death and died, at age three, very tragically by suffering severe burn wounds after she fell into a fire in the garden, where she played with dry leaves. Maybe, I thought many years later, when I was a mother myself, maybe it was impossible to bear such grief without the crutch of worthiness and honor that gave meaning to the sacrifice of her most beloved ones. To honor the memory of her deceased husband, she had to believe in the war and its righteousness. In rare moments, I felt compassion, but I was unable to lift myself out of the hatred that darkened my perception of her.

There was never a satisfying end to our mutual attacks. I was aware that these political and personal confrontations exploded in thousands of families. I could not restrict myself from throwing this topic into the heated cauldron of our family dynamics. It had become an obsession. Possessing a strong sense of justice, I felt called to wield the banner of truth, driven by the conviction that I followed a divine mission, like Joan of Arc or St. George, the dragon killer. I wanted to force the 'yes, the atrocities happened, I am sorry,' out of my father. I craved for his admission of guilt. These three words 'I am sorry,' would have softened my fixation and opened my heart. I wonder today if the obsessive search for truth had a deep root in the unresolved mystery of my own mother's death. The political and the personal secrets seemed hopelessly entwined.

The second generation inherited not only the un-mourned traumas of the parents but also the psychic structures that impeded mourning in the older generation in the first place.
— Eric Santner, Scholar of German film and literature

Archangel Gabriel. Photograph courtesy of Cliché Leroy Stephany.

During those painful years of confrontation with our recent German history, we young people often gathered in the evenings. We assembled in the home of one friend, Dietmar. His mother was the opposite of my parents. She was liberal, laid back and a devoted explorer of facts in search of truth. She represented hippy-dom before the concept and ideology was born. These were the fifties in Germany. We teenagers made fierce demands for ground to stand on and justify our existence. Dietmar's mother often joined our heated discussions and offered us beer and cigarettes. Her hair curled wildly around her head and she cackled at her own jokes. She leaned against the frame of the door, listening to us. Her apron slipped down, exposing the strap of her bra. She spoke with a raspy voice, and the smoke of her cigarette came in puffs from her mouth when she got agitated about a topic. We were allowed to call her by her first name, Lilly.

Dietmar and the whole circle of friends were classmates from high school, or, as it was really called, the *Johann Wolfgang von Goethe Gymnasium*. This group was my family-of-choice and saving grace. There was Alex, tall, bony and blond, who would be the first to be bald-headed. He became a diplomat sent on international missions. Ursula, the calm one, with dark eyes and rolling round hips, would later marry Dietmar and work as a researcher. In the big chair sat Ernst Metzger, the class genius. He could embarrass our teachers with his knowledge, and he became a well-known professor. Karin would study pharmacology and Barbara, my closest friend, would leave Germany, like I did, and move abroad to Canada. In later years I found her again and visited her in Vancouver, after I had moved to the United States. The most rebellious and cynical among us, Horst, became a writer and fighter for justice. And of course there was Dietmar himself. He enjoyed the fact that his home was the cave and abode where we'd feel safe to be ourselves and lick our wounds.

We young people of the fifties were full of a furious and explosive pain. Our rage and anguish about our parents and country was so intense that we lashed out and grieved. This pain did not push us to act, because there was nothing to be done, yet, besides reflection and the gathering of horrifying information. Another ten years were needed before young students all over the world would gather for public protest against old and new wars and atrocities. The second half of the sixties would ignite rebellion and action.

"You are my family," I said, looking around the circle. "Without you, I would go crazy. Our parents' generation invests their hearts and sweat into the *"Wiederaufbau,"* into the reconstruction of Germany and its economy. They go on as if nothing happened. But we young ones, we are trapped between the past and the future."

Lilly stretched one arm towards me to offer a sip of her beer.

Dietmar sat at the corner of the sofa. He leaned into the middle and spoke slowly, "We will think new thoughts and give birth to new ideals. Since everything is broken into pieces, we have the freedom to create from scratch. Our freedom is born from chaos."

Alex stroked the bush of his blond hair with his bony fingers. "I want to be part of the *Wiederaufbau* of justice. I want to be politically powerful and have a say in the shaping of a new relationship with other countries. I will kick the old farts in the ass and help to shape the future, not only mine but this country's."

Baerbel leaned back in her seat and rolled her eyes, "I am so sick of fighting, confrontations and lies. I will leave as soon as I can, find a better country and enjoy myself."

The room was lit by just one candle, painting sharp lines on our faces, as if we had aged before our time. "We were burdened with a story we've not created, but we're also free to dare something new," said Ernst. "In the stinking rubble of this culture we'll find some worthwhile pieces to make it attractive, or at least bearable, to be a German citizen."

"Look at you all," added Lilly from her corner near the door, she whistled as she exhaled and filled the room with wobbling smoke, "you have the brains and courage to get involved. I trust you young folks to speak up and act on your beliefs. God, how much I envy you, that you can say your truth and not get shot for it. I wish I had owned that freedom when the big *Führer* terrorized humankind. Look at what kind of friends you are. You're bonded by your anger and by your urge to find new and better answers about right or wrong."

These friends still live in my fond memory, even after we lost contact from continent to continent. These classmates were profound support in a time of desperation and reckoning. They were my tribe, my foundation for sanity, my hope and nurturance for mind and soul.

It was the heart-wrenching task of my generation to seek and create a new mythology that would justify being alive in Germany as a descendent of this country's culture and history. This longing had the intensity of a life-or-death struggle. I found myself drifting, floating on a current of horrific disclosures. During those years after the war, there were pictures in newspapers, and posters on trees and movies about concentration camps that made me topple over, weeping. And still, at mature age, I cannot talk about the Holocaust without sobbing and a deep shame.

My father was a last remnant of the old mythology. We stabbed into each other's wounds and it was a bloody mess. I refused to perceive him as just a damaged and flawed human being. No, he was the enemy, the representative of the Nazi horrors, and I used him to unleash my rage. I lashed out with ferocious despair as I searched for my own place in the devastated landscape of my shattered homeland. I needed somebody to blame and to tear apart.

My father was lonesome. I don't remember ever having seen him in close friendship with another man, laughing and slapping another's shoulder, or putting an arm around a colleague. Perhaps he had hardened himself not to break or yield. I assume that he was basically apolitical. An engineer at heart, he focused on his research and technical inventions, but he did not care about questions of political guilt and responsibility. Wherever he could shine with his skills, that's where he would serve with precision and dedication. Maybe he posed as an example of typically German devotion to skillful service and obedience. It seduced a whole country into the aberration of "well-functioning" war machinery and concentration camps, where human beings were turned into numbers and smoke.

My relationship with my father was deeply bruised and wore itself out during those years of conflicts. We did not find appeasement because we were too distant and in too much pain to meet and see each other without protective masks. But, mysteriously, our antagonism forged a negative bond that is still charged and ties us together, even beyond his death in later years.

My father's and country's darkness made me resistant to exploring my own flaws and shadows. Thus, I avoided the fear that I, too, might someday become infected with the contagious disease of evil. By accusing the Nazis and being outraged about their behavior, I asserted the belief, 'I'm not like them! I would never act like a Nazi.'

The ghosts of my childhood and youth have cast shadows over the rest of my life. These shadows posture and threaten. But, like the grotesque guardians at the gate of Asian temples, they protect the pilgrim's journey towards that destination which the Sufi Poet, Rumi, calls: *The space beyond wrong-doing and right-doing.* Driven by deep yearning, I am still seeking this peaceful place beyond *wrong-doing and right-doing,* where I would be able to take a stand, without being locked into rigidity and righteousness. It might be the assigned journey of my personal life to seek, and to arrive one day, in that compassionate realm beyond judgment. In the end, this gift may not be granted through my desperate effort, but rather through maturity and a moment of unexpected grace.

Our fears are like dragons guarding our deepest treasures.
—Rainer Maria Rilke

Like a bird that breaks out of a cage after years of captivity, I flew out of home and country in 1959, with quivering wings, singing. I had obtained my diploma in chemistry, was twenty-one years old and a free person. Electrified by joy, I caught myself bursting into snorts of laughter, just for being alive and soon to be free of that household where we had fought the war all over again, inside my family.

My teenage years had been restricted, crippled by guilt through association with my culture. Intensely caught inside the identity of the post-Nazi generation, I had gotten used to the bloody cage in which I had lived. Feeling like a convalescent of Germany's post-war darkness of the fifties, I was ready to fasten a bandage over the psychological and spiritual wounds of my youth.

A new energy blew fresh wind into my life. It opened its arms towards me and invited full-blown participation in an emotional rebirth. Germany with its newly emerging position in Europe shifted to the periphery of my awareness. Lighthearted thoughts and plans occupied my brain. I peeled away the layers of the past and saw myself as a woman beyond nationality, a citizen of the world. Waking up to the possibility of happiness and freedom on my terms, I forged a path towards a future without the constant identification with my country's past. It seemed possible then to take off the old clothes woven out of guilt and shame and live a poetic life, not overshadowed by politics. The burdens that I considered to be my fate dissolved in the sparkling waters of excitement, from whence they would emerge again at a much later time in my life.

After celebrating my graduation all through the night with dear friends, I left the next morning, euphoric and aflame with joy and excitement. A door to the future opened wide: Leaving Germany, I would move to Switzerland, a job was already waiting. It would provide income and independence.

From then on, I envisioned, everything would be different.

I closed the books of the past and moved enthusiastically into a new phase of my life. I was intoxicated by the lure of joy and a physical, sensual way of living. Life offered its embrace as a recovery from a deep illness of the Soul. The grief and rage of the 1950s turned into the optimism and awakening of the 1960s. For the next twenty-five years I was dancing on two feet, grounded in the joys of wife-hood, motherhood and women's liberation.

Many years later, in 1983, I traveled to Wiesbaden for a last visit with my father before leaving Europe for the United States. During those days, there was an opportunity for a walk in the early morning light, without the hovering presence of Stepmother Helene. I held my father's arm. The touch felt rigid. We were not used to closeness. Our connection was thin and broken, like threadbare fabric. The trail we walked was full of gravel and sharp rocks. He stumbled, his steps insecure. Parkinson's disease had made his firm stride wobbly and frail. The sounds of our shoes scratched into the web of silence.

A strong wind spread feathery clouds, like giant hands that grabbed the gray sky above. The trail was empty. It was early morning and the window blinds of nearby houses were closed. We strolled beside a fence covered with lilac exuding a scent so intense that I closed my eyes for seconds and inhaled deeply.

I remembered how my mother loved lilacs. As a child, on the evening before Mother's Day, I would break stems of lilac from a bush at my friend Dieter's house. I'd hide the bouquet in the basement in a can of water. The next morning I'd sneak downstairs to the dark cellar and tie a ribbon around the three or four twigs of lilac before I carried them upstairs to my mother. I opened the door a small slit and said, "Now close your eyes, *Mutti*. And now just inhale through your nose!" My mother took a deep breath, inhaling the heavy scent, and a smile appeared on her face, spreading softly like the rings on water when a dragonfly dimples the surface. As I watched her, I became the pond that held the smile on its rippling surface. Then Mother opened her eyes, saw the lilac, and reached out with her hand. With the other arm, she picked me up and lifted me towards her, leaning her face against mine. And then she kissed me and both of us thrust our noses into the blossoms. I remembered how my mother's skin took on a faint purple hue, because the morning light was shining through the blossoms and carried that color onto the soft hair on my mother's chin and cheek.

The father at my side slipped and grabbed my arm briefly, but let go immediately, as one would pull away after touching a stranger in the subway. I glimpsed at him out of the corners of my eyes. He seemed lonesome, a floating iceberg in arctic water. We entertained small talk, but the words slipped unattended through my mind. It was the first time in years that we were together alone, without his second wife guarding our conversation. I was gripped by one overwhelming thought that occupied my brain since starting this walk with my ailing father.

This is my chance, I thought. *This is the one and last moment to learn the truth about my mother's death when I was a child, during the cold winter of 1948. Today, I will ask the forbidden question.*

I raised my eyes and saw a single lilac bush at the end of the fence, its clusters of blossoms so heavy that the branches drooped like a billowing purple cloud towards the gravel.

That is the marker, I promised myself, *At that lilac bush I will open my mouth and say one sentence. I will count to ten and take a deep breath and at the corner there, where the lilac bush leans over the fence, I will ask the question, just four words: How did Mother die?*

I clenched my fists to carve those words out of the ancient rock of silence that had covered the event. I struggled to shape the question, pregnant inside me for thirty-five years. I knew that this stranger at my side, this frail father, was the only living person who held and hid the truth about my mother's death. My grandmother, my sister and I believed that she died in the night of February 24 in the office of a doctor who performed an abortion procedure and made a fatal mistake, but we never had this assumption confirmed. I yearned deeply to find an answer before it was too late to ask.

I took a long breath and the lilac scent spread inside my chest and filled it with memories, and also with sharp terror, because I knew I had to speak now. We arrived at the bush at the corner and at my last chance to hold the question up to the stranger who was my father.

I opened my mouth and only emptiness fell out like crumbs of frozen earth. They dropped to the ground in front of our feet where the wind had strewn single lilac blossoms between the pebbles.

Silence.

An unspoken law constricted my throat. The law was carved into the barriers that stood between a father and his daughter.

In a flash of memory, I saw my mother on the last afternoon when I was nine years old and did not know that I would never again look into that beloved face. Mother held me close and I breathed the sweet scent of her body. "I will be back soon!" Mother said, looking at me. I cradled my head into the tiny warm cave underneath Mother's chin.

And now my father and I passed the lilac bush in silence. I pulled my eyes along it like a rake that tore the blossoms off the stems. I clung desperately to this last chance. I didn't want this moment to pass. The father at my side was frail, and death clung to his steps like a tired dog at the heels of his master.

I was deeply humbled by my inability to speak. *How often*, I thought, *how often do I counsel others to resolve frightening situations, how often do I say 'Just go, just leave, just step forward, speak up and break the spell!' But here I was, a grown woman, and I was lame and meek at the side of this old man who had frightened me for so many years! At his side, I was still an anxious child. He had a key to the family secret, but I was incapable of wrestling it from him before he died.*

I lifted my head and saw the long fingers of clouds gathering into clusters, resembling clenched fists. We passed the lilacs silently, and turned toward the house where my stepmother already was waiting at the door. *They have a conspiracy of secrets and they have created a web of lies*, I thought. *But, maybe, not even she knows the truth.*

I turned to look back before entering the gate to the house. The lilacs twisted in the wind as if breaking. The restless storm blew dying blossoms over the trail, like flowers tossed into a fresh grave before being sealed with earth.

I followed behind my father as he stepped through the door. His back was bent and he swayed like a willow tree. His head hung forward, too heavy for his spindly neck. I took the coat from his shoulders. It contained the warmth of his body as I pressed it towards mine. And then, miraculously, an angel walked through the space, brushing me with its wings. I felt a sudden wave of tenderness towards this old man and an urge to touch his cheek. Looking into my father's eyes, I saw the loneliness inside. His pupils seemed like scratched windows covered by a thin layer of frost. In this moment, I realized, that there was no more key to unlock the family secret because the last witness had discarded it and he nurtured no desire to open a door to the past. And so it happened, that an old iron trap inside me released its grip smoothly, as though this freedom had been available for me since long ago. The bloody trap had clung to my neck, and I had carried it like our family's coat of arms. But here, finally and mysteriously, this moment of release offered itself, beyond effort and will, a gift of grace from the core of my life. *Beyond wrong-doing and right-doing, there is a place, I'll meet you there....*

I hung my father's jacket on a hook and reached inside its pocket to spread some crumbled petals from the lilac bush that I had clutched in my sweaty palms.

The next day, I left the house with the old man. I also left the old country to start a new life in America. As the plane lifted off, I looked back at the town where my father lived and where he soon would die. An image from Thoreau's *Walden Pond* flashed through my mind. It reflected the story of an old farmhouse that was inhabited singly by a huge lilac tree. Its gnarly branches had spread across the open spaces and reached from wall to crumbling wall. The tree's roots held the stones in place like arthritic fingers, fiercely clutching the soil. The history of that house and its former inhabitants was long forgotten, but the tree still lived and stretched its uncanny and heavy beauty across that desolated place.

I wiped the fog of my warm breath from the windowpane and leaned back. That was the moment when the plane broke through layers of clouds into a clear sky with shimmering views towards the horizon.

Many years later, after my father's death, I received a whole bundle of old documents, and there was a letter from 1945, signed and stamped by the American occupiers. It established that Hans Roessner was *politisch*

unbelastet — politically unburdened. This sought-after and highly valued paper indicated that my father was *entnazifiziert* and free of any Nazi involvements that were against the Geneva Convention.

As part of the documents I found the job contract he had signed with the American Allied Troops. It was also dated from 1945, and that meant: for more than two years after the war had ended, he was absent to work for us and make an income in Munich, all by himself, when we still lived in Hamburg. I did not know that as a child, when I wondered why he was gone, and I was deeply sad about this ignorance.

My father died in 1985 or 1986, I forget the exact year, and I don't know the location of his gravesite and I never had the urge to find out. When I received the announcement of his death, I felt neither grief nor any other emotion, just a sense of completion. After my last visit in 1983, he had stopped responding to my letters, in that way he quietly disappeared from my life, even before his death. Living on a different continent helped me to release the bonds-of-blood to him and to our joint history. The memory of my father surrounds me now with a detached softness, like dry moss clinging lightly to an old tree.

11

SEX AND SENSUALITY

Sex is a full-body experience like giving birth or swimming in the ocean, or hearing music or dying, words cannot transmit its intrinsic sensations and ravishing power. My own sexuality was shaped by the influence of mother and grandmother and all the women without husbands, because they served at the front—and under the pressure of family history and the shadows of that war. For me sex, in its first manifestations, was braided into the experience of war and its aftermath. In my observations as a child, war and sex coupled and embraced each other.

As I age, sexuality mutates gradually into a rich sensuality, aroused by the body's senses and nurtured by the poetry of language, by music, by natural environments and the beauty of the whole universe. The mystery of sex and sensuality does not reveal itself by direct approach. It hides like a

All the true vows
are secret vows,
the ones we speak out loud
are the ones we break.

There is only one life
you can call your own
and a thousand others
you can call by any name
*   you want.*

Hold to the truth you make
every day with your own
*   body,*
don't turn your face away.

Hold to your own truth
at the center of the image
you were born with.
       —David Whyte, from
     "All the True Vows,"
          River Flow,
       Many Rivers Press

mythological animal, a Unicorn in the forest. We talk and dream about this Unicorn, but it remains only a fable until we have experienced it in personal encounters, have touched its wet fur and inhaled its warm creature scent. I will approach that Unicorn by circling the wilderness where it lives and by entering the forest via my personal trail.

One afternoon in August 2004, I sat in the tent auditorium of the International Book Fair in Edinburgh during a longer stay in Scotland. A gusty wind blew fine rain through the open flaps. The tent seemed to burst out of its seams, every seat was taken by eager visitors: gray-haired ladies and gentlemen with coats and hats as well as young people in punk-outfits baring bellybuttons. They were engaged in animated conversations. The expected celebrity was Doris Lessing.

The Grand Old Lady of literature appeared on stage with a shopping bag full of her books, smiling and enjoying the enthusiastic welcome. She read, and then she answered questions. As always, she was well-informed and not shy in expressing her rebellious opinions. In her eighties, she seemed timeless in stature, the gray, curly hair tamed in the back and the beautiful face fiery with passion. She embodied Georgia O'Keeffe's axiom: 'We are not really growing older; we just become more of who we are.'

At one point during her presentation, becoming somber and pensive, she said with a sigh, 'I don't know why, but the older I get, the more the two big wars are in my mind. I am occupied with thoughts and questions about their cause and effect.'

A book signing followed Doris Lessing's presentation. When I stood in front of her I said, 'Your statement about the wars touched me to tears. I am a child of war, and I am experiencing the same urge to reflect on its presence and roots. I suffer a gnawing hunger to understand the past and to find answers for questions that I carried around all of my adult years.' She looked up from her book, and said, 'I cannot explain where it comes from, but it calls me back to that time. This dark history has a power of its own, it stirs and cannot rest.' We looked into each

228

other's eyes and there was a bond of sisterhood that united us two elders.

An hour later, she walked out of the tent with the shopping bag clutched to her side; young people surrounded her, talking, circling and buzzing like bees near a pie.

A steady rain drenched the lawn outside and crowded the spaces in between the tents. Visitors thronged to meet authors who read and discussed every imaginable topic. There were boardwalks that allowed passage without sinking into the muddy black earth of Scottish soil. *Harry Potter* author J.K. Rowling, attracted a queue that stretched along the sidewalk of a whole block in this so-called New Town, built in the eighteenth and nineteenth centuries. It borders on the rose-filled parks around the mighty Royal Castle on top of a steep rock, in the heart of Edinburgh. This rock resisted the grind of glaciers, thousands of years ago. The core of a volcano, it consists of the most enduring stone formations. What a daring place to construct this marvelous palace that mirrors the traits of the Scots: enduring, poetic and feisty.

I walked along rows and rows of books in the tent of the Book Fair that sprawled all over the lawns of Charlotte Square. The books stood like candy jars on the shelves, in all colors and shapes, brimming full of human imagination and stories. The immensity of thought and artistic expression in this tent dazzled me. People with wet coats walked in and out, drying their hands on handkerchiefs and reaching out toward the shelves. Book lovers from all over the world handled the works with respect and eagerness. Opening them at random places they got caught in the tales and visions of human fantasies and rumination, swaying like trees with bent tops, holding books in their branches.

As I was ambling along the bookshelves, I stopped in front of a large photo book with pictures of Europe after World War II, the cover displaying the photograph of a street in Berlin: a row of young soldiers from the occupying army plowing through a rubble-strewn urban landscape of decay. Between each of the young men walked a German woman.

They all had their arms interlinked and smiled. They hurried, forming a phalanx and bursting with erotic, ravenous energy. Like an untamed river forcing its path through rocks and wreckage, they pressed forward without hesitation. It seemed that nothing could hold them back. Mocking the destruction that surrounded them, the women looked beautiful in their fake fashion made out of rags and remnants, wearing bright lipstick and little hats tipped to one side. These women had survived the war and had traveled through hell, but now, they emerged on the other side of it, bursting with life's fierce longing for itself.

I held the book in my hands and wept, one of thesis women could have been my own mother. How familiar I was with their burning determination for enjoyment in the midst of total destruction. That image on the cover symbolized her spirit. She was one of these women who, after the war, seized the new chances for joy and pleasure. She, too, was full of desire for healthy, young and victorious men who still had all their limbs attached to their bodies. Men, who had survived horrible battles and were hungry for these famished women, in a country that twitched on the ground like a trapped and dying creature.

Yes, my mother was one of those fierce women who satisfied her own desires and life's yearning to counter death. My mother, too, had bonded with the victors and invited them into our family home and into her marital bed. War had twisted and changed the rules. Life's ruthless drive for survival of the species knotted her into lusty embrace with the former enemy. Deprived of intimacy, she ached to satiate her body's craving.

I sat down with the book in a canvas chair near the flapping tent corner. The steady sound of rain on the other side of the fabric kindled memories of early years. I had lived as a child through the bombings of Hamburg and the pictures inside the book elicited memories of that apocalyptic cityscape of horror. The photographs showed sorrow-marked faces, mostly women and children, peering out between shards of human dwellings. Those faces were naked, stripped of pretense and vanity. War was the great equalizer, and suffering had no borders. There were women carrying bedcovers and pans, buckets and children. Suitcases at their sides fell open to show charred remnants of their lives. Women, standing in the midst of brokenness like columns of strength. Women frozen in terror, as guardians of the wounded or dead . Women, forever nurturing and birthing new children, had to witness how those children died in front of their eyes. Women wearing overcoats, with pajama pants crumbled up around their knees. Women walking barefoot, scarves wound around their scarred faces, eagerly bartering their last belongings, or themselves, for food.

I carried the book back to the table and stepped outside into the soft Scottish rain. My mother, too, was a woman shaped by the war. Her weaknesses, as well as her tremendous strengths, had simmered in that cauldron of history. Coupling and mating with the former enemy provided food for her children, and it also satisfied her yearning for sex and intimacy.

I opened my umbrella and turned onto George Street in Newtown Edinburgh. The wet asphalt mirrored stately houses with red velvet curtains, brass plates with names on them and polished knockers at the doors. As I walked, I recalled a phone conversation with my sister Helga, many years ago. Her usually soft voice sounded piercing and sharp. It was quiet in our house as my three children were in school. My sister's voice cracked.

"What do you think," she groaned, "what do you think our mother did with those Allied soldiers, with Tom and John, in her bedroom? They had sex, and sometimes I slept in the same room with them. I heard everything—the kisses and pushing and moaning. I thought of our father and hated her for what she did. I hated her then and I still can't forgive her today! You seem to have forgotten!"

"Helga, Helga, I was a child," I choked, "I didn't see the whole picture. I neither understood nor did I want to." Yes, I had skirted around the truth and I only remembered what I could digest. "I thought what happened in our family was normal and usual. I believed that it was all right to have these foreign men in our household. I loved and adored our mother so much, she couldn't do anything wrong in my eyes."

Helga made a wheezing sound, as if her throat was throttled. She expelled short sentences like puffs of smoke. "You always accused our father. He was a Nazi, you said. You always pointed out what's wrong with him. Never her. You were so naïve. And you still are. I couldn't even talk with you about it. When we grew up. For so many years. Just silence. Isn't it strange that you and I never talked about Mother's lovers?" She hung up.

I turned to the large window that opened to our garden. In the distance the mountains were covered with clouds. The children's toys lay strewn in the grass and the wheel of an overturned tricycle rotated in the wind.

A sudden shame clawed inside my stomach like rats trying to bite through the walls. I bent forward and sobbed. My mother had died when I was a child of age nine. I realized that my adoring love for her was frozen in a time capsule of the past. But now and at that moment, she died a second death for me. I lost an illusion that had protected an idealized memory of her, for decades. Finally, I saw her as the woman she was; she emerged out of the thickets of my childish perception into the light of day. And she looked like a real woman. She was like me. She had children and was the age I was now. I could see her not only as a nurturing mother, but also as a woman with lust and desire. I felt helpless, didn't know how to place this new image into the patterns of my orderly life as a young mother myself. My naïve moral system was shaking.

I sat down for long time, without moving. My mother had never hidden anything. She was honest to the bones. It was I, her daughter, who had refused to recognize her as the human being she was.

I called my sister back and said, "You know, Helga, I have lived with this denial for more than twenty years, and now I have discovered that I do not love our mother less after facing her truth. I hope that one day I will say the same thing about our father."

The afternoon light threw long shadows from our fireplace onto the red tile floor. The house was silent, but the wind shook the window frames and knocked branches against the glass.

232

Edinburgh Castle. Photograph by Shanti Elke Roessner.

I took a turn towards the Edinburgh Castle and a left onto Rose Street. Inside the old Abbotsford Pub I ordered a pint of Guinness. It was dark and smoky here, the bottles on the shelf glinted. Placing my hot hands flat on the moist copper counter of the bar cooled my palms. I lifted the glass and let the heavy black drink float down my throat. It calmed my senses with its bitter taste and sticky texture. I yearned for my mother to sit beside me at this moment. All those memories of the past made me aware how little I knew about her. She would be an old woman now, as I was approaching sixty-six myself. How much I missed growing up and growing old in her company. If she were here, we would drink and tell stories. We would laugh and cry and whisper, as we looked back at past times, like women do, when they gossip and share intimately about the big and small events of their rich and colorful lives.

Oh, if she were here, we would talk women-talk and sex-talk. We would open up to share our view about our strong and tender female bodies, and we would discuss woman's way to feel the power of our sex — how it warms inside like a fire in a cave, and how this fiery glow kindles our love for life. Woman's sexuality is a lively burning flame, and it's her own substance that fuels it. Yes, the man lights this fire, but he is just a visitor in her cave. Woman's sexuality is life itself. It is a force, larger than the woman's physical body. It's a creative power that reaches deep into the moist earth where seeds wait to sprout, and it extends upwards, toward the space where stars and comets roam.

I would talk to her about the arousal of laughter during orgasm, when everything pummels inside the belly and explodes into joy and into running-away-laughter that seems to bubble out of fingertips and toes and stretches beyond the room. It sifts into rivers and forests this flung-out-about-across-the-world orgasmic laughter. I think only women get taken over by laughter during orgasm and get caught in its web. Has she experienced it? I would ask. And did she dare to laugh and moan when she mated in a house full of people with open ears and children who wondered? How was it, I would ask her, to be deprived of sex when your husband was absent for years, but you were a young woman full of frenzy and heat in your groin and of electricity in the palms of your hands, eager to touch a man's skin?

I would tell her about my occasional affairs and how, surprisingly, they bonded me closer to my husband, yes, the one I wanted to be married and mated to for all my life. Yes, I would say, I desired him and loved him with gratitude, because we knowingly gave each other the freedom to live our sexuality liberally. I would tell her how I discovered that marriage and affairs were such different territories. Marriage was togetherness with one beloved partner, including all the colorful and sorrowful ways of relating and managing daily life as a team. It was built on the solid ground of a warm familiarity upon which I would trust and be trusted unconditionally. In contrast, affairs were fleeting, hot, strange, exciting or utterly disappointing. Marital love was composed of the steady weaving of past, present and future, but affairs were fleeting encounters of two individuals. No affair estranged me from my commitment to my partner for life. Not once did I desire to be married to another man. But I desired to have sex with other men. I existed — in a sense — in two bodies. The one, which carried me out into the world; it was privately owned by me. The other was fully available for my family, embracing motherhood and wife-hood. And I would tell her how I fell in love, once, with another woman. I was surprised and so smitten by this encounter that I lost my mind and was awkward, shy and anxious, like a teenager. I would also tell her how I giggled with my best friend, who is a lesbian, when we were on a professional trip to Ireland, and we shared a bed in the hotel. In the evening she dressed in her red and baggy winter flannel pajamas, because I was so scared about what might happen in that bed.

I would sit beside my beloved mother and put my arm around her aging shoulders. I would tell her that I believed, a woman needed to know different men, and from this knowing, woman would stand by the side of her husband, as I had done, with wisdom and choice and not because of moral restrictions. My husband and I had agreed to guard our marriage inside a space of freedom — and we were watchful to protect it from damage and lies. The freedom we allowed in our marriage anchored our bond into authenticity. Yes, we were authentic by speaking and living our personal truth.

Yes, mother, I would say, I understand you. I treasured the liberty to experience another man's body, smells and skin. Those encounters tied me closer to my husband, than rules and regulations ever did. I brought the fire of those encounters home to him, and it fueled our intimacy and the fire of sex. I have lived enough life to observe, at my age, how sex in marriage is generally given too much serious weight. It is puffed up in its importance, dwarfing the other wonderful traits and activities that kindle love and kindness between partners. Yes, sex is sacred, but it is ordinary, too, and its body-bound earthyness makes it part of mundane life, like breathing and singing and eating and gardening and caring for each other with our hands and hearts.

Sex is part of nature; it's not elevated or taboo. Rather it's the secrecy and lies between couples that heat it up into such a burning topic that so many people cannot be honest about their cravings, fantasies and personal preferences. I believed, I would say, that those secrets and lies tend to overshadow sexual practices. It's those lies that undermine the trust between partners. But if I am allowed to be honest and frank about my desires, I can negotiate them with my husband. And that's what we did. We lived without those lies, and we loved each other with great commitment. And, yes, I would admit, that's possibly not the common way to be married, but it worked well for my husband and me and I still love him dearly.

Finally, I would take my mother's face between both of my hands and tell her, "I admire your strength and willingness to be truthful to yourself against the rules of society. Yours was a society of war," I would say, "a war that had broken all the important rules about human rights and about respect for other people, as most wars do. I love you, because you opened a fiercely honest view for me into the mystery of womanhood. You challenged me through your wrong-doings and your right-doings, and I cannot judge you for them. Your example encouraged me to move beyond general beliefs and find my personal sexual truth and practice. I embrace life because you taught me to be sternly devoted to it; and, maybe, you even sacrificed your own existence to this devotion. And that's possibly a worthwhile price in view of the devastating war that surrounded us all."

I would hold her old hands in mine and rub my cheeks against them. I would kiss her fingers and cup mine around her wrinkled and beloved face, which was, in reality, never allowed to age.

Loving my mother was not just rooted in my adoration for her, but in the substance that she was made of. She carried the natural essence of womanhood, just as it lives in the strength of trees and the yielding of rivers, in the alertness of tigers and the calmness of seagulls riding the wind. The presence of war made her ruthless in her dedication to life in any form that was offered to her. She was fierce to defend and protect it, sucking the marrow out of its bones. The relentlessly shaping pressure of war forged my mother's character. As this pressure lay heavily around her, she stretched upwards beyond her size and simultaneously downwards, where she grew roots towards the dark middle of the earth. She carried, with assured recklessness, her light into the darkness and her darkness into the light.

Maybe her early death forced me already at a young age to trust my own discoveries and to untangle my heartstrings from hers. She opened a space in which I had to seek and find my own Unicorn in the mysterious territory of my womanhood. Even as she broke and fell, she provided nurturing decay for the life of her daughters, like the redwood trees in ancient forests have been providing for thousands of years. After they collapse to the ground and decompose, new shoots grow out of their bodies. The young ones eat the old mother trees as they pierce their roots through the rotting, wooden flesh into the fertile ground created from decay.

I paid for my Guinness and walked out into the steady Scottish rain that soaked the perfect lawns and the roses in the Princess Street Gardens around the Castle, stopping for a while outside the large open tent from where traditional Scottish music spilled across the park. Animated people danced inside the tent with soft, flat shoes. They hopped up and down like gazelles, placing their arms close to their body or like an arc above their heads, as is customary in Scottish dance.

Little old ladies swung their legs to the right and to the left, their gray hair unraveling in the heat of rhythmic movements, triggered by drums, fiddles and bagpipes. The music flapped its wings and flung itself across the grass and above visitors towards the ancient rock of the Castle. Sitting down on one of the wet benches, cozily nestling under my umbrella, I felt a warm surge of joy rolling through my body. It was the joy of growing older and knowing some surprising things about life, things, which were very personal—and very common, too.

The Rose Gardens, Edinburgh. Photograph by Shanti Elke Bannwart.

The afternoon knows,
what the morning never suspected.

—Swedish proverb

    The first purple light of morning colored the clouds in the east of Scotland when I left the ferry from the small island of Iona to drive across the Isle of Mull and reach the mainland. The air was saturated with silence of an early winter day. I was alone, no other car visible on this single-track road. Gently undulating hills spread on both sides as far as the eyes could reach. A few lazy sheep and cows grazed across the meadows. The land had the character of an old woman storyteller sitting at the fire. Her stories were written in the sturdy grass and murmured into the wind that blew and danced ceaselessly, leaving the taste of salt on my lips.

I had time in abundance to reach the next ferry that would take me to Oban where I traveled once a week to buy food. I drove slowly, leaned my head back and let my gaze caress land and sky. The light changed constantly. Rays pointed to hilltops or valleys, suddenly revealing a hidden fold in the land where birch trees beckoned in the morning breeze. Waterfalls tumbled over rocks and curled playfully through the rough countryside. Gold, brown and dark-red fields surrounded lusciously green meadows. *Scotland is woman,* I thought; *this is female land; moist and nurturing, it embraces like a womb.*

I had spent several months now on the Isle of Iona, a place of pilgrimage. Lore tells that more than forty Scottish kings were buried in the ancient cemetery beside the majestic Iona Abbey; some say even Macbeth and Duncan's tombs are hidden in the ground. St. Columba, the Irish monk, landed here in 536 and built the first simple hut. He attracted pilgrims and this tiny island in the Scottish Hebrides became the cradle of Christianity for northern Europe. The spark spread from here and became a fire.

The moment I stepped off the ferry and set my foot on the land of Iona, four months ago, it wrapped me in its fierce magic. I rented a small house on the only paved road near the ferry landing place and settled down to hibernate. I ached for stillness and contemplation. Iona became my place for inner journey. Settling here through the rough winter months, I had grown into loving it with a fierce and dark passion.

The road curved around a hill and suddenly I was confronted with Big Brother Rain, the giant with huge feet! He stalked across the meadows like a fearsome monster, splashing his mighty toes in the mud, eager to frighten and impress with his wild appearance and dreadful majesty. Pounding his big chest and roaring "me! — me! ho ho ho!" he pulled the gray longhaired furs of his watery coat across the land like a huge broom to cleanse and rearrange earth and sky. I slowed down and stopped the car, paying reverence — and he passed in minutes. The sky was blue again, adorned by a double rainbow spanning the whole island.

But there is much beauty here,
because there is much beauty everywhere.

—Rainer Maria Rilke

My life on Iona was frugal. The only fireplace in the living room exuded meager warmth when I lit it in the evening. There was no wood available on this island; a few lonesome trees provided some protection from the Atlantic winds. One had to start the black coal with firelighters, an arduous task. Like the monks in cold monasteries, I took a hot bath to heat my body before I climbed into the damp bed. The traditional Scottish stone house was often more chilly inside than the air outside. Every day I walked for hours, crossing swampy meadows and climbing rocks; and I strolled along the shore in the moonlight, when it sprinkled silver pallets on the surface of the black Atlantic Ocean.

Never before had I committed myself to a solitary quest of similar intensity, not for such a length of four months and not to such a lonesome place. No one knew me here or cared. When I stretched my arms there was nobody to touch with my hands, no skin to stroke or smell. This winter of seclusion penetrated my bones and made me humble and naked. Solitude is like a stern storm that rips away shielding clothes of social roles and assumptions. My soul was unprotected; my body longed for companionship and ached for skin-to-skin contact.

One morning, I walked along a field where a white horse grazed, tail and mane flapping in the wind. She lifted her head when I stopped to call her.

"Come here, come here, you beauty, you big warm body, come here and let me touch you, let me stroke your wet fur and scratch your nose."

She stepped slowly towards me. Her eyes become dark caves with a light shining inside. This light sparked a scorching hunger for belonging in my belly.

"I crave to touch a warm and living body," I whispered, tears rolling down my cheeks. I mumbled gentle names and stood motionless, until she moved her bony head close to mine. Her soft wet lips and nostrils explored my hands intimately, she sniffled and puffed warm air in my face.

"Are you lonesome, too," I ask, leaning my forehead against her silky brow and inhaling her warm creature scent. Two living, warm-blooded beings, aware of each other's presence, we were *Two solitudes protect and touch and greet each other*, I remembered Rilke's poem.

My life had become a dream. This land had swallowed me and digested me into its body. I was one with this breathing horse creature, with the hard grass beneath my boots and the wild geese screeching overhead. I had forgotten if I was wind or willow, sail or song.

Many times I rested at the western shore, mesmerized by the thundering waves as they rolled in from the Atlantic like fluid hills, crashing with great force against the rocks. Iona is part of the Outer Hebrides and floats like a slim boat along the Western shore of Scotland, receiving the full brunt of wind and water's might. Each approaching wave thrust itself, foam-crested, into the wide coves before it recedes and soaks into the smallest cracks. This fight between yielding water and stubborn rock had been performed endlessly over millions of years. It smoothed the rock and polished it into soft curves like those of a living creature, revealing intricate layers of red, green and orange minerals and crystals. When the tides were low, I would rest in the smooth rocks along the shore, as if melting into a lover's embrace, and lick salt off the water-polished, silky flanks. My body, hungry for touch, received exquisite pleasure from this intimate contact with the body of the earth; the whole being of this island had become my mythic lover. It was drenched with the energy of Eros, the God celebrating sensual pleasure. He was elusive, appeared unexpectedly, surprised me. When walking across the pathless pastures, I would suddenly reach moist patches of black earth, yielding to the weight of my boots. I sank, and the odor of sweet decay and the fear of being lost in the bog gave me a sense of panic as well as ecstasy. Once, I almost fell into a deep well in the middle of a meadow, a spring for nymphs to drink and play. Long grasses hung like disheveled hair into the bottomless hole and the sound of dripping water echoed upward through the opening. A young tree at the edge of the spring made me aware that Daphne was present here.

Ocean-polished Rocks on the Isle of Iona. Photograph by Shanti Elke Bannwart.

Without the web of a social structure and work my life on this island was not supported by the scaffold of ordinary duties and tasks. My connection with the world far from this place dangled on a thin thread that could simply wear itself out and tear. I didn't know if it was me who hovered in a dream or the world beyond this island was dreaming itself. The sounds and smells of that world did not reach to Iona's shores. This amorphous way of existence was full of a tart sweetness that saturated my flesh and imagination. Not adhering to the manmade frames of time, I was cycling in its natural rhythms of ebb and flow, sun and moon, inhaling and exhaling. In a fluid dialogue with the land, my senses were vigilant and awake as if I were a human animal; the wind blew through me, the grass sang underneath my feet, the great ocean's movements penetrated my skin and reshaped the cells of my body.

12

FACE OF THE FAMILIAR

The foam on top of the *Spaten Bräu* beer in front of me moves upward pushed by its own bubbling aliveness. It hovers on top of the golden fluid and sticks to my nose when I take the first long, deep sip. Ahhh, Hamburger Beer, sweet and bitter! From my chair, under the arcades of the *Rathaus Keller*, I observe the marvelous facade of the historic Hamburg City Hall. It is a pompous building, reemerging after the war like a giant ship that popped through rubble and trash towards the surface. And, now and again, it stands as a symbol for the wealth and ingenuity of the Free Hanseatic Town of Hamburg. Its merchants have been trading goods with countries worldwide for more than a thousand years.

The water of the *Binnen-Alster* Lake and canal laps and gurgles close to my feet, pushing the moss and slimy water plants on the stonewall into rhythmic motion as if the

We shall not cease from exploration
And the end of all our exploring
Will be to arrive where we started
And know the place for the first time.
    —T.S. Eliot, *Little Gidding*

"Hamburg!"
Laughed the man of the night,
"then nothing else matters.
You always have to go back there,
always have to go back, if you've come from there.
You have to go back."
    —Wolfgang Borchert,
    The City
    Rowohlt Verlag GMBH

city has a beating heart. A flotilla of swans sails eagerly toward an old woman on the other side of the canal, leaving criss-crossing wakes on the surface behind them. She holds a blue fabric bag in her hand and feeds them bread cubes. The woman is older than I; some strands of white hair hang over her ears and the collar of her woolen jacket. I think *she, too, has seen this town bombed down to the ground, aching with death piled high, and she, too, carries its demise in her memory.*

Ships in Hamburg Harbor. Photograph by Shanti Elke Bannwart.

I look at people in Hamburg with this question in mind, *Did they see what I saw? Did they witness the inferno? Do they carry the memory and weight of sorrow, still, in their limbs and eyes and feet?* Where hundreds of thousands of inhabitants died in one night, *did their spirits disperse and clear the space during the days to follow, or did they hang around, like fog between branches of trees, abandoned to their own destiny?* In this city, history has crested and fallen into two parts: before and after the firestorms.

The swans reach across each other's backs and pick bread from their neighbor's wings. They bob about like dense feather pillows. The old woman leans over the wall, "Come biggy biggy birdies, come here you beauties, and here and here," she mumbles and smacks her lips. Behind her, I see the greenish copper roof of the City Hall reflecting the sunlight. Red geraniums grow along the windowsills, and in front of it, an old woman feeds swans. She calls them endearing names and showers them with laughter and giggles. And I meet myself in her. I find in her the gestures of ordinary, day-to-day life and how they gently cover past horrors like leaves in fall, those gestures cover the corpses and charred bodies buried under her feet. This woman revived again the will to live, to feed swans with dry bread and to build bridges across the abyss between life and death. She offers these small gestures, in spite of the past, out of rebellion or habit or just simply because she loves life and this tiny piece of it, hers, in this town. That's so simple, so ordinary and also exquisitely extraordinary.

The waitress serves me a plate with herring in cream sauce and white potatoes, garnished with raw onion rings, fresh dill and chives. I want to tell her, 'I have come back after sixty years, I love this town, it's alive again, I can't stop crying', but I just smile. Childhood nostalgia is intimate and I feel shy. Being so close to my origins stirs joy and sadness. I find myself mirrored in this town; I discover roots and forgotten dreams. Even the meal with its uniquely sweet-sour taste triggers a flood of memories. As I sit at the small table in the heart of this city, I admire how Hamburg has reemerged to former grace and to newly designed beauty. Metal and glass cased hotel and office buildings circle the *Binnen-Alster*. Modern architecture merges artfully with historic styles.

This town, a living and forever changing being, is it here to contain and harbor my childhood memories, or am I sitting in its lap to hold its life to be remembered and continued for generations to come? Do we call 'home' what contains us or what we contain, or do we belong to each other? My mother once told me, that she lived in Hanover when she was pregnant with me, but before my birth she traveled back to Hamburg, 'so, you my daughter, would be born here in the town I love and where we belong.' Hamburg and its sturdy and down-to-earth people have shaped my character and outlook on life. Hamburg has a living history, like we people have ours, and in many ways they cross over and shape each other.

For centuries, this town has been baptized by water and fire. It was burned to ashes and rubble for the first time in the year 845, when a fleet of six-hundred Vikings destroyed the new settlement. In 1030, the Polish King, Mieszko, burned the re-established fortifications to cinders. And there were great fires in 1284, and another one in 1842 that turned one third of the city into smoke and ashes. It took more than forty years to rebuild and heal the damage. But the worst was the destruction through air raids in 1943-44. Who knows how many victims have become part of the foundation upon which this modern town is built. Those corpses are integrated into the next layer of history in the same way as the citizens before them, their dead bodies and bones supporting homes for the next generations to come. I am aware, here, that I am walking across cadavers, layered into twelve hundred years of urban life.

But Hamburg is a phoenix born from ashes. When a phoenix bird dies in the fire, all the animals in the forest grieve and fall into deep silence; so goes the myth. But then it is being reborn and the whole forest celebrates, the birds sing, the crickets chirp, the owls hoot, and ecstatic butterflies tumble around flowers and blooming bushes. And finally, with the music of the forest in its heart, the mighty bird spreads its wings and takes off to live for another hundred years, or maybe, for a thousand.

Phönix Rising from the Ashes. Photograph by Shanti Elke Bannwart.

Penetrating the familiar is by no means a given.
On the contrary, it is hard, hard work.
— Vivian Gornick, *The Situation and the Story*
Farrar, Straus and Giroux, NewYork

The paint beside the door handle is scuffed, and the brass of the mailbox cover polished by the hands of the people who lived here for generations. I stand in front of that door, aware of the rustling and grinding of time. This house is like an oversized box, harboring the memories of the first nine years of my life. I stroke the dark red bricks around the doorframe and follow with my fingers the shapes of six small windows set into the wood. *Yes, my childhood really happened here in this place, in the shelter of this northern brick house confirming that my recollections are not a dream.* It is the year 2006, and I have finally come back to visit the familiar places from the past. For the first time in my adult life I had longed to be here again and to remember, to love again, what I left behind, almost sixty years ago.

The old-fashioned white letters on the blue enamel street sign are fixed to the corner of the house: *Volksdorferdamm* #154. Young pine bushes, once planted by my father, have grown so high that they cover the terrace and the windows like green lace curtains. The building stands rooted and straight, embracing its history with dignity. Located at the outskirts of Hamburg, the fire waves of death had stretched towards it, but never reached its walls. It was spared in the bomb attacks, and so were we.

It is Saturday afternoon and people are inside their homes. Weekends in Germany are family time. I tiptoe around the house and garden like a ghost from the past, hoping that nobody will ask any questions because I am afraid to burst into tears. The window frames are freshly painted, but they show their age, one can see the streaks of the paintbrush. Grass and dandelions grow between the cracks of the same old cement tiles that pave the path towards the entrance door. Box tree hedges, cut in orderly angles, still leave an opening into the neighbor's garden, where the *Pförtner-von-der-Hölle* family once lived. Generations of kids used it as a short cut, so did Helga and I. This habit was continued after we left, and so it will be in the years to come.

I walk around to the back and find our old garden bursting into summer colors. The apple tree has grown to maturity. The wooden gate is closed. Hollyhock stands high beside the peas that climb the trellises. Nearby grow carrots arranged in neat rows, like school children after the break. Petunias dangle into each other's space and burgundy-colored lupines stretch toward the sun.

Elke's Childhood Home. Photograph by Shanti Elke Bannwart.

The garage door underneath the bedroom window is closed, and all the four small glass inserts are intact. When we lived here, my father had removed one of them, allowing the swallows to fly in and out and feed their babies inside the nest built on top of the water pipe. But swallows don't gather here anymore. The blinds in the second floor, where Frau Gnade and her son, Jürgen lived, are closed. The small window in the kitchen is tilted outwards to let air in and keep the rain out. A white lace curtain moves in the draft. Above the entrance door is still a number 4 stamped into one of the bricks, it's the date of my birthday and I never forgot that it was there, who knows why? Every small mark and movement holds memories and stored emotions, deeper and longer lasting than I ever imagined. Childhood home, a place unique in the world, built from a group of walls shaping and surrounding a space where people love and hurt each other around kitchen fires and tables, in beds with soft covers and at desks with papers and colored markers.

I stand in the open place between the garden and house; our playground, where we girls would hold hands and, dancing in a circle, we sang old rhymes like *Der Koenig in Thule* or *Es tanzt ein Bi-Ba-Buzemann in unserm Haus herum, fidibum.* Squatting against a garage building are the brittle wooden enclosures for our rabbits, now used as a shed for garden tools, shovels, rakes and measuring tapes.

I lean against the house and feel the roughness of mortar between the bricks. Whispering endearing names my hands caress the house, I am so familiar with its texture, color and shape. Sweetness flows through my limbs and my belly as I feel how the house is alive and how it responds back to me. As a child, I had taken this home for granted. It lived naturally around me, like a skin. In those years during the war, the house was shelter and protection, but it could have been broken, it could have covered us like a grave. When alarm sirens announced the approach of enemy bombers, the house sat like a molehill on top of the families that huddled together in the bomb shelter. Familiar with the alarms, I was only concerned about the house, never expecting that anyone in our family would be killed. I believed that death would not happen as long as we were together. My trust was built on three reliable grown-ups, my grandmother, my mother and aunt Gretel, they would know how to use magic or love or just their powerful womanhood, their arms and bellies and hips, to protect us children. When I left at age nine, I didn't know it would be 'the last time,' didn't know what 'time' and "last time" really meant and that this thing called 'time' would change my whole life, and me, too.

252

And now I walk around to the front of the house, where our former children's room opens with big windows to the beech and birch trees dividing the footpath from the road. It begins to rain. Small drops land on my skin, growing into heavier ones that drum their weight onto the leaves. *"Blingg! Blingg!"* My shoes get wet, and I remember how I loved to take them off as a child and walk through squishy grass and dirt and so to feel how the earth plugged the sensuous spaces between my toes.

Opening my umbrella, I stroll quietly down the path and turn right towards the neighbor's house where my friend, Dieter, lived. Mother Beech stands like a giant guardian at the end of the path. Placing both hands and my forehead against her trunk, I whisper, "thank you, my dear, dear friend. You taught me about the life of trees and the whispers of their language. You held me in your arms and allowed me to dream. From your branches I saw the fires above Hamburg. Because of you I knew, later, how to be saved by trees when I was a motherless child. You showed me how to be filled with light and to reflect it outwards."

I seek in the bushes underneath, but the dragon doesn't live here anymore. Or does he manifest in that cold moist touch that nuzzles my hand as I walk away?

A man on bicycle stops just behind me. He puts one foot down for balance and shakes his cap so that the raindrops fly. The stranger has a friendly face and looks at me quietly, waiting to be of help. Northern folks are not people of many words.

"I grew up here, sixty years ago." I say, and tears are mixing with the rain on my cheeks. "I came all the way from America to find my old home again and to prove to myself that my memories are real." He nods slowly, three or four times, his wet hair sticks to his forehead.

"Today might be the last time that I visit this dear and familiar place. I know them all, the trees, the bushes and the garden. Up there, from that beach tree, I saw Hamburg in flames. The sky red, the cloud above the heat like a giant hat." He nods again. "And here I stand today, it's all like a dream, and it's also far more real than yesterday's memories."

"Do you want to come in for a moment," he asks. "Visit your former home?" He stretches his arm with inviting gesture, pointing towards the door.

I stare at him, shocked by the possibility. I imagine the rooms now being occupied with new furniture, the whispers and stories of their new inhabitants filling the space. Our family's history, our conversations and dreams had long ago settled behind the wallpaper and paint. I shake my head, meaning No. "I want to keep the memory of home as I had seen it last, when I was a child."

He nods again and we shake hands for a moment. If there is a physical place where past and future meet, this stranger and I were standing in that spot for the length of the stillness between two breaths.

Following the path along the edge of the wheat fields, I remember the *Ode to An Abandoned House* by Pablo Neruda:

> *Good-bye for now,*
> *house!*
> *I can't say when*
> *we'll be back:*
> *tomorrow or another day,*
> *later or perhaps much later.*
> *I must*
> *tell you*
> *how much*
> *we've loved*
> *your heart of stone:*
> *how generous you are*
> *with the warmth*
> *of your kitchen fire,*
> *your roof*
> *where*
> *raindrops*
> *fall like tiny grapes,*
> *the slippery music*
> *of the sky!*

I cross the *Grenzweg*. Siglinde and I played hide-and-seek here in the blackberry and hazelnut bushes. Summer larks sing in the sky so high that one can only hear, but not see them. Walking towards the old cemetery in *Bergstedt*, I am anxious to visit the gravesite where my grandparents and aunt and uncle are buried. My mother's ashes rest in the lowest layer of the grave, because she was the first one to take her place in the ground. Along this road, my sister and I survived the attack by two low-flying warplanes. On my way I enter a flower and grocery store, wanting to bring gifts for my loved-ones.

I am treading ancient ground. People have buried their dead in this cemetery for hundreds of years. The trees are as old as the skeletons in the ground. Oily leaves of rhododendron bushes reflect the gray light when it breaks through clouds. Late lilac blossoms fill the spaces between them with white and purple bursts of color. Giant beech and oak trees reach beyond those colored patches, and weeping willows whip their long branches in the wind, resembling green waterfalls as they tremble down the flanks of the trunk.

The typical German box tree hedges form straight patterns that represent a world of order and control, camouflaging the reality of decaying corpses underground, eaten by darkness and small creatures. Those hedges hold the trails together on both sides and lead from the wrought iron entrance gate to a circle where four paths meet. I recognize the shape as reminiscent of the Native American medicine wheel. And with this thought comes a flash of memory, bridging this old cemetery where my ancestors rest, with my new home in the American Southwest, where I have been settled now for more than twenty years. Wild geese fly overhead, calling each other into formation, and I think of Mary Oliver's poem.

Standing quietly in the middle of the circle, I look in every direction while anxiously trying to orient myself. I don't know exactly where the gravesite of my ancestors is located. What if I'm unable to find it? It's Saturday and the offices are closed. I feel urgent, have traveled half way around the globe driven by the longing to visit my loved-ones and to connect with my past.

To my left sits one of the big wooden boxes where visitors dispose of wilted flowers after they clean the gravesites. Bundles of daffodils and tulips lay shriveled and tired across brown evergreen branches that rattle in the wind, *"Crackle, crackle."* Moldy scent of cemetery hovers around the trash. Ravens poke into the debris, searching for edibles. Rotten bundles of roses, tied together by ribbons that carry names and messages printed across in golden or black letters. *'Here sleeps Heribert Weisshausen. God Bless Him!'* and *'For our beloved Sister, Susanne Ehrenreich. We will never forget.'* I remember seeing similar ribbons trickling down from the lid of my mother's coffin just before her body was rolled into the fire.

The cemetery is, as many in Europe, an inviting park, cared for and sprinkled with vibrant blossoms, punctured by stone and wrought iron sculptures. I turn to the right and follow my instinct, which leads me around the hedge and through an opening into a space like a green chamber surrounded by trees. As I walk towards the farthest corner in the back, I find myself in front of the marker where the names of my family are carved into the soft white sandstone. The first one is my mother's: Isolde Roessner-Henschke, born August 1915, she died February 24, 1948. Moss covers the raised letters, soft and warm to the touch, like human skin. I kneel, my fingers slowly follow the name Isolde, and then the name of Margarete, her sister, my grandfather, Otto Henschke, and then my grandmother's name, Luise Henschke; it represents her memory here, but her ashes have settled on the bottom of the Baltic Sea. She died the year after my visit with her.

The Ancestral Grave. Photograph by Shanti Elke Bannwart.

Sitting in the grass, I open the ground with my bare hands to set the roots of purple asters and white baby-breath into the black moist earth. And then I arrange the red, red, red tomatoes with silken skin, and I spread handfuls of cherries bursting with juice, cherries adorning the head stone and circling around the edges of the gravesite. The tomatoes whisper and shiver, reflecting the sunlight, their fiery color dribbles and trickles red rivulets through small cracks into the earth. The lively, quivering red wakes the sleeping corpses and spirits. My grandmother shakes off the dust and emerges first from the ground, swaying her big hips, chuckling and swaggering around me. Have you eaten well today, *min Deern*, she asks, and was there gute butter on your bread, your bread, your blessed bread, she grins with toothless mouth... Grandmother aggravates the order of things...the order of my people down in the earth...the others are curious, they want to rejoice, too. Mother emerges, dancing and humming with delight. Oh! those tomatoes and how their red red-red sparkles in the sun...they bring fire into my cold ashes. I'm heartbroken, she whispers to me, heartbroken that I left you so young and before you grew into womanhood; I wanted to grow old with you, my dear, but now I watch out for you from the other side of life, and I bless you...Mother is only dust and ashes, but her shape rolls around and I enter into it and dance inside the hollows, the hollow shape, the hollow shape of mother, the hollow shape of ashes, as in my dream of childhood...Grandpa swishes the dirt from his lapels and pokes his wooden walking stick into the air and shouts Oh! Oh! how blue is the sky, and I have never seen it like this, maybe I don't remember and...maybe I never really looked up to see it, I was too busy with chickens...and eggs and the stock market, I missed out on beauty, what a loss, he sighs...Gentle Aunt Margarete is soft and limp like leaves on birch trees in fall when they sail towards the wet ground and get stuck on the moist and smelly earth...Uncle Albin laughs and stuffs cherries into his bony throat. We stomp and dance and whack each other's thighs, and the ground trembles where my feet and their dry bones *clomp* and *bump*...We fight for a seat on the stone bench that my grandmother had installed beside the grave, it is overgrown by the branches of a lilac tree spanning it like a dome…Where will I be buried, I wonder, one day in the future, will my name be chiseled into a rough rock in the beloved desert of New Mexico, where I have my home now and where I might also die…From my sandy grave between cottonwood and pine trees I would look through the cracks in the dry earth and up towards the splendid night sky into the arching Milky Way. I would hear from my grave the howling of coyotes while they answer each other from mountain ridge to mountain ridge until the silence of the night is consumed and shattered by their eerie laughter…My decaying body would feed cactus and cedars and crooked pine trees bent like my grandfather's leg. I sing to my ancestors about my home in the High Desert and I tell them how the sound of the crickets stitches into the night, raspy and in rhythm like the turtle-shell rattles of the Santo Domingo turtle dancers. *Rattle, rrrrsh, rattle rrrssh, rattle rrrrsh…* in the rhythm of the drums, the drums, the drums. *Ooogh* and *Ouuugh,* my German ancestors sigh, you have traveled far and we miss you here, here and here in our soil, we want to come and rattle our bones, *rrrrsh* and *rrrrsh* in the desert and with the crickets and the howling coyotes and stars above…The other corpses in the cemetery wake up and shake themselves so hard that their bones clatter. They grope out of the ground to join us, listening to our stories and songs as they scrape the sand off their teeth. They cackle and shoo away with bony fingers the raunchy ravens feasting on worms and white maggots that grew fat eating my grandmother's kneecaps and the tough heels of her ashen feet. We dance and *plunk* and *plonk* and my mother and grandmother groan out of their bony throats… the skeletons moan when a hand breaks off or an eye is lost in the turmoil… and my grandfather's bony leg sticks out to the west, *hi-ho!* and *hi-ho…* and other ghosts unite with our mad dance and join the burly, brawny celebration of family and of love between people, a celebration of life and death dancing together on one foot, and we *clonk* and *clunk* on one foot or the other until the moon rises behind the willow tree laughing *hi–ho, hi-ho* and so,

and so, and so….

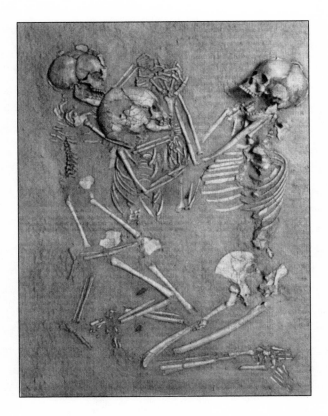

Celebration of Life and Death. Photographer unknown.

13

SONG AND SILENCE

WAR REVISITED

A purple evening sun sinks behind the sharp edges of the *Montagne Noire*. Spring winds shake apple and lilac blossoms from the branches. I am resting on a bench in the rambling gardens of *La Muse Inn*, a retreat house in Southern France, listening to the song of a lovesick golden oriole. It's the year 2007 and the house lodges guests from England, Hungary, Canada and the United States. We cook together and gather in front of the giant fireplace, sharing the delicious local wine and meals spiced with oregano, thyme and garlic. We tell our stories, discuss the arts and read to each other from our works. On Saturdays, we drive half an hour to the medieval town of *Carcassonne* and visit the farmers' market, filling our bags with scrumptious cheeses, fresh bread, olives and all the colorful produce of this fertile land that borders on Spain and the Pyrenees.

Destiny itself is like a
wonderful wide tapestry
in which every thread is
guided by an unspeakable
tender hand,
placed beside another thread
and held and carried
by a hundred others.
— Rainer Maria Rilke

Everything terrible
is something that
needs our love.
—Rainer Maria Rilke

The Red Gate from 1650 at La Muse Inn. Photograph by Shanti Elke Bannwart.

The house is full of spirits; for hundreds of years, nuns lived, worked and died in this building. And then, during the last century, the rambling stone mansion turned into an inn and shelter for the travelers who crossed these wild forests. They were eager to reach the fruitful plains of the *Languedoc*, chock-full of vine and olive trees. Now, the house serves as an abode for artists. I am one of them. My stay is nearing its end and I already feel a subtle homesickness for the place. I treasure this house, filled with the whispers of wind and ghosts and the smell of *coq-au-vin* and *pomme gratin*. The stone tiles of the hallways are softened and indented by the grinding of travelers' boots; straight corners are rounded by age. The heavy door to my room moans when opened and closed.

Oh, how I delight in the luxury of having time in abundance; it allows me undisturbed space to linger in reflection and memory. As I age, I enjoy a slower pace, like my grandmother, I dance through life on one foot, as she suggested, "One foot is on the ground and the other is up in the air. You hobble and jump and the dance jiggles your belly. But there is music inside you, humming and singing, always."

A month ago I was on my way to this place. I had driven from Italy to France along the coastal highway called *Corniche*. The shoreline was rocky and steep. A major part of the road, cut into the mountain, allowed only interrupted and sporadic glimpses of the Mediterranean. A lively spring wind made the surface of the water tremble, showering me with light each time the car emerged from a dark tunnel. I was headed for the *Languedoc* in Southern France.

Several signs along the Italian highway announced the French border, and I groped nervously for my passport inside the bag. But when arriving at French Customs, I encountered neither a border patrol nor police or soldiers to stop me. Instead, a simple sign said, *"Bienvenue en France!"* welcoming the traveler to the country that began right at the point where my car had stopped. I realized that the European Union had softened the boundaries and connected these territories where people had fought each other and had killed their neighbors ferociously until recent history. Former enemies can now freely roam in each other's homelands. *Europe had always been in the making,* I thought, *it has been an emerging vision for millennia. Europe told itself that its birth was a divine plan. Single cultures longed to build this family of diverse philosophies and customs.* After a century of the most horrendous destruction, I found myself in the United States of Europe, on a continent that had grown beyond hostility and separation to form an active union of goodwill. I touched the former border planks and sobbed.

Living in *La Muse Inn*, I am falling in love with this place and the surrounding landscape. I walk through these rough hills and see them crowned with remnants of castles and fortifications built for protection, because in the twelfth and thirteenth centuries, pope Innocent persecuted ruthlessly the *Cathars* who settled in this area. They were highly educated and freethinking people, fiercely resisting the forced integration into the Holy See of the Roman Catholic Church. So, the Pope sent his crusaders, intending to crush the *Cathar's* will for independence as well as their religious customs and beliefs. Those being persecuted retreated into these mountains and built sturdy forts on top of steep rock bluffs. Much blood was spilled and, in one of the worst episodes of the war, almost the entire population of Toulouse, both *Cathar* and Catholic, was massacred. But the free spirit of these strong folks survived and still lives in their descendants. This land sings the songs of the earth and its sturdy people; it is rich with traces of the past. But here, as everywhere, history has been wrought for centuries, or even millennia, with the 'tools' of bloodshed, wars and battles.

The evening sun warms the cracked stonewall in front of me where busy lizards play. I observe their running and resting and they watch me in return, stopping and cocking their heads at an angle. We are both amused. Suddenly, one of them lurches forward and strikes another with his jaws on the throat. He spins him brutally and turns him around so that his white belly flashes in the sun and his legs grope helplessly in the air. When the victim goes limp, the attacker releases his throat to let him hobble away on broken legs as fast as his wounded body allows. The aggressor poses, performs some push-ups and looks around with pride. He has made his point: 'This is my territory. This is my woman. Stay away!'

Strife and threat is everywhere—underneath the dark green ivy leaves and inside the waves of fragrance from the lilac bush saturated with the hum of bees. Fighting is intrinsic to nature, it provides the boundaries that keep animal and plant creatures in their assigned structures and borders. The absurdity of the sudden attack between two lizards makes it painfully obvious how the suffering that creatures and people inflict on each other is ever-present. It can spring up in the most innocent, quiet moments, like this one.

Fortresses of the *Cathars*, **France. Photograph by Shanti Elke Bannwart.**

Nature has always been a powerful teacher for me, it demonstrates the laws that rule this universe. When I lived on the Isle of Iona in Scotland, I observed how the fierce interaction between rocks and the Atlantic Ocean shaped and transformed the shoreline. The insistent grinding of the water and sand on the face of the rocks changed that rock, and it also exposed an elaborate beauty that was hidden inside the rough stone and would now appear on the surface, unveiled by the constant confrontation and ferocious battle between the elements of water and rock. Watching its interplay, I was aroused by the complex mixture of combat on the one hand, and intimate encounter on the other. The ruthless attack was clad in heart-wrenching beauty.

Maybe it is war's purpose to serve as a shaping force that brings to surface the characters of those who are exposed to its violence. We humans are consistently affected by war and destruction. We are required to engage, we are called to resist or to yield, to speak up or be quiet. And, like this magnificent rock, we will be transformed in the process. I know, through my work as a counselor, that conflict and loss are most powerful change agents. Trauma can be the catalyst for profound growth, for individual people as well as whole cultures. Grief may strike like an ax that splits us open. Chaos and pain may peel off the protective layers that veil our deepest self and give birth to our strength and beauty — or darkness.

In contrast to the vigorous challenge of war, the energy of peace has become a lofty vision that is tamed and reduced into poems on Hallmark Cards with pink doves and rainbows as decorations. Peace appears to be something for sissies, placed aside from ordinary daily life and called upon during special occasions adorned by billowing flags. Peace is not attractive and effective this way. It needs to be alive and vibrant; it needs to carry the energy of authentic dialogue; it needs to stir controversial emotions to attract and engage young people, like the topic and practice of war. A pounding and electrifying dance of peace needs to be played by drums, trumpets and rock-bands, not by harps. We need excitement, sweat and heart-rousing beats to be engaged for peace; or war with its intoxicating adventure and heroic imagery of fire and explosions will win out. Forever. I want to burn for peace with fervor, I want to shout, not whisper, my yearning for peace.

All my life I have been seeking to stay awake and not ever settle half-heartedly for black-or-white solutions around the deeply painful challenges of war and destruction. War is an archetype, driven by bigger forces than the passions of single cultures and countries, passions that cause humans to fight and kill other humans whom they don't even know and have never encountered. Archetypes are a-moral like the forces of nature, like tsunamis, avalanches or earthquakes. My attempt to understand war might seem akin to acceptance. But blindly condemning war would hinder understanding and lock me into a righteous war against war. The opposition between war and peace needs discourse and engagement, not separation. As my hunt for truth continues, I feel raw and vulnerable, and so, after years of ruminations, I have finally accepted that there will be no satisfying answers to my questions and no peace of mind. Maybe, like love or birth or beauty, war is a great enigma, calling us to rub our hearts and minds bloody.

Our universe is composed out of two-thirds of 'dark energy' and about one-third of 'dark matter' and we have no idea concerning the meaning and substance of both. We abhor darkness, because we don't understand it and we tend to reject the idea of a dark side of God. We know so little, we have just a glimpse of the small part that is our world, that is visible and includes us humans, all else continues to be hidden. At the end, the mystery of darkness and war might refuse to be pierced by our limited human perspective. If there are answers, they are concealed inside that mystery. But we can be sure that darkness contains meaning and purpose and it cannot be eliminated on this cosmic plane where we exist.

And still, we long for something that transcends our dwindling but never-ending hope for peace. We carry that hope in our hearts and bones. Without hope we could not grow new visions for the future, or give birth to our children, or rebuild our cities after their destruction. We haven't found out, yet, how to create and sustain peace, but we are called upon to involve ourselves in this creative work of not-knowing.

And as part of this creative work we will continue forever to tell our stories, in the attempt to find answers for obsessive questions that haunt and hurt us and keep us vulnerable.

For many years I was not aware how war had broken me. It had not damaged me, but it broke me open, and it left me naked in a world of suffering. Maybe we cannot be fully human without this broken-open-ness. It creates a pain inside me that is pulsating and stinging, moving through me like a river that slowly eroded the dreamlike beliefs of childhood and youth.

The Sufis say: "God reaches inside you through the gap in your broken heart."

I take long walks during this retreat, in the light of the day or under the glimmer of the moon and stars, following the trails of the *Montagne Noire*. They trace old pilgrims routes, leading from France through the Pyrenees to Spain. As I touch the earth with the soles of my feet, I connect and I seed dreams and images into the ground, from where they germinate. They shoot from the soil and provide me with new and surprising revelations. The land here is so ancient and rich with history that my personal memory weaves effortlessly into the web of time. Stories from the past spark inspirations for the present time. This land holds both, the darkness and the light, the pain and ecstatic joy of life in its lap. Like a mother, it quietly listens, embraces and nurtures. One night, when walking in the moonlight, I remember an old tale:

> *Once upon a time there lived a Japanese wise man who went to the market, and on his way back his neighbors came running towards him, screaming, "Master, Master, your house burned down, your house burned all the way to the ground." The wise man stood for some time in deep silence, and then he lifted his arms and his gaze upwards towards the moon that was just flinging herself over the hills to start her journey across the night sky. He leaned his head backwards and said, "Now, without the roof over my head, I will have a better view of the moon as it hangs in my blooming apple tree."*

When I lost my mother at age nine, my emotional house burned down to the ground. The loss of one beloved person mirrored the whole country and continent's suffering. My personal and close-up anguish rattled me deeper than anything I had experienced before. The small, familiar circle of my life was broken, and that gave me the first deep encounter with suffering. It was this experience of my individual loss that awakened me to the larger afflictions of my human brothers and sisters. It took me at least twenty years before I was able to find a gift in the early loss of my mother. Today I know, that her death was – for me - an initiation into compassion.

I am hesitant to utter the truth that is emerging as I age, but there is something brutally freeing in the experience of loss. The most precious things and beings that seem to establish our happiness, security and comfort are also a barrier to the naked encounter with truth. What we desire and protect anxiously brings fulfillment, but it also imprisons us in traps of immobility and habit. Peace, too, has a shadow: it can make us numb, complacent and superficial.

The truth is that, too often, our houses have to be burned down before we would awaken to the beauty that reveals itself in ordinary and familiar things, like the changing shape of the moon. A man who was born blind does not know what darkness is, because he has no comparison. A person who has not experienced war and bloody conflict usually fails to appreciate the fragile presence of peace. I wonder today, if my deep joy of being alive developed in contrast to the dark background that surrounded my childhood.

After more than seventy years of life, I have arrived at a place of integration. I fiercely despise war and aggression, and I am actively involved in healing its wounds, but I have come to understand war as a darkly meaningful part of the human condition. Maybe we already carry the answers inside us, carry them like an unborn child, as we are waiting for the gestation and birth of understanding. Maybe we ARE the answer. We have to grow into it, and maybe we will need many more thousands of years for this process to unfold, but it is happening, right now.

I believe that light and darkness, peace and war, are not enemies, but they are holding hands behind the curtains of history, like twin brother and sister. Peace and war are companions, they keep each other alive; they mirror and challenge each other, they push and pull, beckon and throttle. They interact with each other constantly inside our minds and hearts and bodies. One cannot exist without the other's lure or threat.

Cherry blossoms in *Languedoc*. **Photograph by Shanti Elke Bannwart.**

War is the disease of humankind. Like physical illness, we may prevent and heal it, but we will never eliminate illness or war as part of our humanity. Yes, even stars are born with violence and the birth of a baby tears the mother's body open. Maybe destructive acts are purposefully woven into the process of creation. If we are made in the image of God, our failures make sense as catalysts for learning and transformation, for the gods as well as us humans. Maybe the tears that we are crying in our lonesome chambers express not only personal grief but also the grief of the whole universe. Yes, we are the stuff that dreams are made on, but we are also the stuff of nightmares.

Billowing gray clouds move in from the east above the *Montagne Noire* and shroud its peaks and sharp corners. They carry rain and soft, humid air. Droplets settle on my skin. The birds weave their songs like colorful ribbons through the landscape, and an impatient wind rakes handfuls of wild cherry blossoms from the trees. It whirls them across the valley into a frenzied chase like a snowstorm. But the persistent cuckoo's call from the nearby forest leaves no doubt that spring has arrived.

Give your own story to the earth as an offering,
full of meaning, full of possibilities and full of the song of the soul.
…Just find the seed of your own story; open it with love and place
it in the heart of the world, where it will keep alive the fire that burns there,
that is your offering.

—Llewellyn Vaughan-Lee

MOTHER REVISITED

 I awaken in the quiet retreat house during the dark of the night, wrapped in the intricate web of a nightingale's song. He is rehearsing for the approaching spring that lures crocuses, daffodils and dandelions out of the rocky earth. It is late April and the nightingale's song sounds still a bit awkward and hesitant, but, since three nights ago, when I heard him the first time, he has learned to add more strength and some trills and twiddles to his melody. Deep silence lingers between the sequences of tunes, allowing time to weave their echo inside my heart. The edges of the song are fringed by a velvety stillness that makes you hold your breath.

View from the Old Window. Photograph by Shanti Elke Bannwart.

The old room is lit by a faint and powdery glint of the waning moon. A small desk leans with its shaky legs against the windowsill, holding my laptop, the green light on, indicating that it is charging for the day to come. Behind it stands a row of pictures that I know by memory, but cannot make out in the dark. A dense calmness fills this ancient house. "1650" is chiseled into the stone above the wide red door, opening to a sloping garden that rolls and rumbles through blackberry bushes and grape vines all the way down to the river in a deep valley. The two windows in my room are tall and slim. I imagine past times, when hooded nuns stood here, dreaming about God or of a life outside the nunnery.

I sit upright as the nightingale begins his weeping call again. The song of the bird waxes and wanes like the pulsating, slow heartbeat of the night. The melody lingers and floats like a silken veil in the shadows, it fills my body with joy and longing. Nobody should live or die without having heard this bird's intricate weaving of tunes in the night.

Even when listening
to the nightingale's song
I yearn for
the nightingale.

I swing around, put my feet on the cold tile floor and walk towards the window. The valley is narrow and black. It does not invite the moonlight to penetrate its secrets. I pick up the photograph of my mother and trace her face with my fingers. Her forehead is high and open as though a light filters from the inside out. She looks, and is, young enough to be my daughter.

She was MOTHER, carved into my life with capital letters. Our last encounter, before her death, is locked into my memory. I idealized my mother and kept her image alive as seen from a child's perspective. And now, after years of reflections, I have untangled myself from my fateful attachment to her. My letting go indicates a "betrayal of love" or change of our original contract, and that allows the becoming of Self. I am no longer

273

in the shelter of our relationship, but in fierce conversation with my own life. I feel a sense of exhaustion and exuberance, similar to the moment when I gave birth to my first child. The intensity and danger of labor was followed by ecstasy and deep satisfaction. Birth and death are siblings or lovers.

I am leaning out of the window, one of the many women who looked from here downwards to the bottom of the valley and up towards the weight of the stars above. During all the centuries of this house's existence, the nightingale wove his tunes into the dark between the whispering voices of trees.

Then, in a spontaneous decision, I place the photograph of my mother in the breast pocket of my coat, slip into pants and a sweater, tie my boots and leave the room on tiptoes. The heavy iron handle on the wooden gate screeches. I walk slowly, like a cat in the night, through the sleeping village towards the trail that leads down the hill. The sign with the complicated name of this place stands on my right, *Labastide Esparbairenque*. The road meanders to the river and crosses it where the rocks are covered with a heavy carpet of moss. Motionless trees reach with long arms across my path, leaning into the song. The earth exhales a musty smell of rotten leaves.

I feel the emergence of freedom from the past. Flooded with an indescribable lightness of joy, I grow wings and my heart flutters swiftly as the swallows in my early childhood. Joy trembles inside me, inviting me all over again into my original love affair with life.

I sit down beside the river where the moss provides a pillow, take the photograph of Isolde out of the frame, and hold it in my open hands. She smiles as she listens to the sounds that interlace in the dark — the song of the bird, the murmurs of water and a faint rustle of young spring leaves. And there is another sound, emerging from inside me, the sound of a bell that slows down its swinging movement and, finally, comes to rest in the center where it is balanced and still. I whisper toward mother's face in my hands: "You walked gracefully through your short life with radiance and fierce aliveness. You carried me in your body and gave birth to me. You shared in your beauty and in your darkness. It was you who taught me these ways of loving that hurt and that heal."

Then I lean forward and let the picture of my mother Isolde float away. The water grabs her and twirls her around, and then it carries her smile across the smooth rocks and towards the meadows and the wide, open plains where wine and olives grow.

Listening to the Nightingale. Unknown artist.

Dancing on One Foot. Photograph courtesy of Jenny Hunter Groat.

And those who were seen dancing were thought to be
insane by those who could not hear the music.

—Nietzsche

CPSIA information can be obtained
at www.ICGtesting.com
Printed in the USA
FFOW03n1423140716
25888FF